MATTERING PRESS

Mattering Press is an academic-led Open Access publisher that operates on a not-for-profit basis as a UK registered charity. It is committed to developing new publishing models that can widen the constituency of academic knowledge and provide authors with significant levels of support and feedback. All books are available to download for free or to purchase as hard copies. More at matteringpress.org.

The work of the Press has been supported by: Centre for Invention and Social Process (Goldsmiths, University of London), European Association for the Study of Science and Technology (EASST), Hybrid Publishing Lab, infostreams, Institute for Social Futures (Lancaster University), OpenAIRE, Open Humanities Press, and Tetragon.

MAKING THIS BOOK

Mattering Press is keen to render more visible the unseen processes that go into the production of books. We would like to thank Michaela Spencer, who acted as the Press' coordinating editor for this book, the two reviewers Marianne Lien and Mads Daugbjerg, Steven Lovett, for the copy editing, Erin Taylor for the proof reading, Tetragon for the typesetting, and Will Roscoe, Ed Akerboom, and infostreams for formatting the html versions of this book.

COVER

Cover art by Julien McHardy.
Photo by the author.

AN ANTHROPOLOGY OF COMMON GROUND

*Awkward Encounters
in Heritage Work*

NATHALIA BRICHET

 MATTERING PRESS

First edition published by Mattering Press, Manchester.

Copyright © Nathalia Brichet, 2018.
Cover art © Julien McHardy, 2018.

Freely available online at matteringpress.org/books/an-anthropology-of-common-ground

This is an open access book, with the text and cover art licensed under Creative Commons By Attribution Non-Commercial Share Alike license. Under this license, authors allow anyone to download, reuse, reprint, modify, distribute, and/or copy their work so long as the material is not used for commercial purposes and the authors and source are cited and resulting derivative works are licensed under the same or similar license. No permission is required from the authors or the publisher. Statutory fair use and other rights are in no way affected by the above.

Read more about the license at creativecommons.org/licenses/by-nc-sa/4.0/

ISBN: 978-0-9955277-9-9 (pbk)
ISBN: 978-1-912729-00-5 (ebk)

Mattering Press has made every effort to contact copyright holders and will be glad to rectify, in future editions, any errors or omissions brought to our notice.

CONTENTS

List of Figures   7

Acknowledgements   9

Preface   13

Introduction: Collaboration and the Fruits of Awkward Relations   19

1. Crafting the Field of Common Heritage   43
2. Sharing Heritage Through Friction   63
3. Altering Heritage Through Mimesis   113
4. Valuing Heritage Through the Fetish   153
5. Qualifying Heritage Through Postcolonial Moments   213

Notes   261

References   275

LIST OF FIGURES

FIG. 0.0 Humid wall in Elmina Castle, 2006, Elmina, Ghana.   18

FIG. 0.1 A copy of the invitation to the inauguration of the Common Heritage Site (front page), 2007.   22

FIG. 0.2 The inauguration site from the Frederiksgave building, 2007, Sesemi, Ghana.   22

FIG. 0.3 The Danish Minister handing over the key to the Ghanaian Vice-Chancellor, 2007, Sesemi, Ghana.   25

FIG. 1.0 Detail from a map carefully studied by people involved in the Common Heritage Project (titled 'Map of Danish possessions in Guinea' (1839)). Courtesy of the Royal Danish Library. Available at: http://www.kb.dk/maps/kortsa/2012/jul/kortatlas/object65540/da/ [accessed 16 July 2018].   42

FIG. 1.1 The covered ruin in 2004, Sesemi, Ghana. Courtesy of Jørgen Frandsen and the National Museum of Denmark.   57

FIG. 1.2 A fig tree entangled with the Frederiksgave ruin in 2005, Sesemi, Ghana. Courtesy of Jørgen Frandsen and the National Museum of Denmark.   57

FIG. 1.3 A photograph of the only known map of the Frederiksgave Plantation, Copenhagen, Denmark. Courtesy of the National Museum of Denmark and the Danish National Archives.   59

FIG. 2.0 Old construction secured with concrete bricks, 2008, Osu, Ghana.   62

FIG. 2.1 Fort Prindsensten from the seaside, 2008, Keta, Ghana.   69

FIG. 2.2 Map drawn for an article about the Frederiksgave project published by, and courtesy of, the National Museum of Denmark.   86

FIG. 2.3 An old well at a family house, 2008, Osu, Ghana. — 100

FIG. 3.0 Paving in an old family house, 2009, Osu, Ghana. — 112

FIG. 3.1 The front of the Frederiksgave building from the symmetrical axis, 2008, Sesemi, Ghana. — 134

FIG. 3.2 Symmetry inside the Frederiksgave building, 2007, Sesemi, Ghana. — 134

FIG. 3.3 The Frederiksgave building with the Chief's house in the foreground, 2007, Sesemi, Ghana. Courtesy of Daniel Nii Amarh Ashikwei. — 135

FIG. 3.4 Locally produced postcard sold at the Common Heritage Site, 2009, Sesemi, Ghana. Courtesy of Stanley Akoto Sasu. — 135

FIGS 3.5 and 3.6 Photos of the recovered wall where the two fig trees have protected the building from collapsing, 2008, Sesemi, Ghana. — 146

FIG. 4.0 Layered wall at Frederiksgave, 2006, Sesemi, Ghana. — 152

FIG. 4.1 The veranda with rough brownish wall, 2008, Sesemi, Ghana. — 164

FIG. 4.2 Sequence of four unfinished squares at the back of the main building, 2006, Sesemi, Ghana. — 164

FIG. 4.3 Aquarelle made by a French prince visiting Christiansborg, used in the exhibition at Frederiksgave. Courtesy of the M/S Maritime Museum of Denmark. — 189

FIG. 5.0 View of the Frederiksgave building from the Chief of the village's garden, 2009, Sesemi, Ghana. — 212

FIG. 5.1 Part of the exhibition in the main building, 2007, Sesemi, Ghana. — 218

ACKNOWLEDGEMENTS

I would like to warmly thank the many people who have helped me write this book, either directly or indirectly. Above all, I am grateful to all the persons involved in the Frederiksgave Plantation and Common Heritage Project, who gave their time to engage with me by opening the doors to their offices, to their meetings, to their houses and to the reconstruction ground in Sesemi, and allowing me to follow the process of reconstructing the Frederiksgave site. I also wish to express my gratitude to all the people who, in various ways, were involved in the National Museum's Danish Traces project, as well as to the team of archaeologists and students who excavated part of a former Danish fort in Ghana, and with whom I later enjoyed producing an exhibition on the excavations in both Ghana and Denmark.

I am also very grateful to all my colleagues at the Department of Anthropology at the University of Copenhagen for making my day-to-day work both fun and interesting. A range of people have provided me with fruitful ideas, valuable advice and help: I sincerely thank Astrid Nonbo Andersen, Mikkel Bille, Lotte Buch, Sidsel Busch, Signe Cain, Jesper Enemark, Beate K. Federspiel, Thomas Fibiger, Per Gideon Frisk, Mille Gabriel, Anne Folke Henningsen, Pernille Ipsen, Joakim Halse, Kirsten Hastrup, Maja Hojer, Tine Sønderholm Jensen, Helle Jørgensen, Steffen Jöhncke, Trine Søgaard Parmo Krog, Stine Krøijer, Anja Kublitz, Katja Kvaale, Cecilie Lanken, Akusoa Perbi, Morten Axel Pedersen, Anthony Annan Prah, Marie Riegels Melchior, Irene Odotei, Katja Rosenstock, Gunvor Simonsen, Silje M. E. Sollien, Sara Lei Sparre, Dick ter Steege, Lise Sørensen, Tim Flohr Sørensen, George Tsakle, Anna Tsing, Sebastien Tutenges, Helen Verran, Nii Wellington, Brit Winthereik, Sue Wright and Jakob Ørberg.

The great idea of having an open review process at Mattering Press – thereby encouraging an open, respectful dialogue – gave me the invaluable opportunity to think with and learn from Mads Daugbjerg and Marianne Lien. Thank you also to Uli Beisel, Joe Deville and Natalie Gill, who critically examined the text, and last but absolutely not least, to Michaela Spencer, for her generosity and patience during the making of this book; I am very grateful for our conversations over the years.

I also wish to thank The Danish Research Council for the Humanities for providing the grant that made this research possible, and to Dan and Lillian Fink's Foundation, which generously financed its publication.

Warm thanks also go to all my very good friends and family, particularly my father, Jean Brichet, who with his explorative mind has taught me to meet the world with an open spirit, and Nete Helene Enggaard for her highly sophisticated thoughts on various matters, and indeed, for being in my world. I owe my deepest gratitude to Frida Hastrup who, through a continuous dialogue, several bicycle tours and much laughter, contributed greatly to my crafting of this book and to raising my spirits. Finally, I owe thanks to Gritt Nielsen who, with her wonderful critical eye and curious mind, pushed me to explore worlds of another order – a fortunate privilege for which I am so very grateful.

I dedicate this book to Adrian and Manuel Brichet, who continuously nurture my curiosity and share the small wonders of the world.

FORMALIA

All translations from Danish to English are by the author.
Unless otherwise indicated, the photographs used in this book are taken by the author.

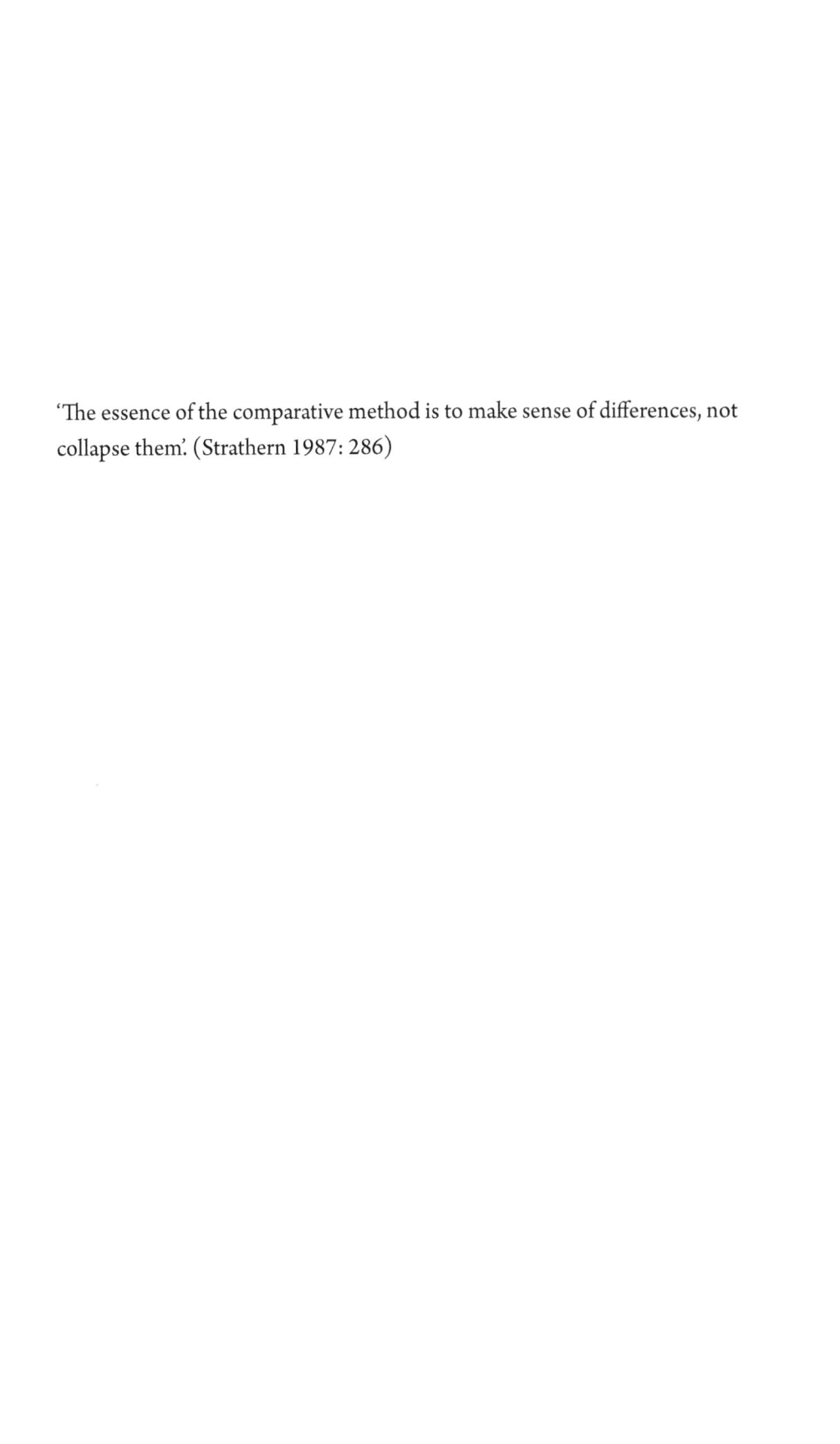

'The essence of the comparative method is to make sense of differences, not collapse them'. (Strathern 1987: 286)

PREFACE

'I STRUGGLE TO KEEP THE TENSION', WRITES PHILOSOPHER OF SCIENCE HELEN Verran in relation to her ethnography of numerical practices in Nigeria.[1] This book takes up a similar challenge in analysing a collaborative reconstruction of a former Danish plantation in Ghana. The reconstruction project explicitly addressed what was termed 'our common past', and my ambition is to explore what happens when differences in such collaborative heritage work meet and awkwardly interact, without glossing over the tensions involved.

Focusing on the reconstruction of a particular plantation named Frederiksgave, this book argues for the need to nurture a common ground, by which I mean a carefully cultivated here-and-now where difference is practised in encounters and engaged with in collective action.[2] Engaging a common ground in no way implies agreement or harmony, but only the insistence that heritage is continuously and collectively made. In paying close attention to the diverse efforts invested in the complex creation of what came together as 'The Common Heritage Project', I want to show what heritage can *also* be, how it challenges perceived orthodoxies, reconfigures power relations and brings about collectives, and how postcolonial heritage work might actively make use of such ambiguities. If there is a conclusion to the book, then it is to stress – and indeed nurture – the inconclusive quality of Frederiksgave.

A common ground, then, entails a new possibility for critique, in that it implies a shared engagement across difference where nobody yet knows the outcomes. In consequence, the purpose of critique is not only to stimulate like-minded academics, but also to potentially open up the field of analysis to all engaged parties committed to working together on some project or other. In such work around a common concern, tearing apart, rejecting or sorting out will not do. Instead, a generative critique – as Verran calls it – offers something new: a moment of hope and the glimpse of a promise that the future could be different from the past. I cannot think of a more appropriate inspiration for my ethnography of a collaborative heritage project addressing the former Danish involvement in slavery and resource exploitation in Ghana. To me, such a project is simply an opportunity for answering in the positive to the question: Can we imagine futures different from the past? Engaging in heritage work on the colonial era must not solely be about replication. Donna Haraway, quoting Jacques Derrida, has beautifully addressed the issue as follows: 'Inheritance is never a given, it is always a task, it remains before us'.[3]

This change in focus from givenness to task captures my overall approach to the reconstruction of the plantation. Seeing inheritance as something that remains before us points to what I most wanted to do when conducting my fieldwork, engaging the material and writing up this book. I wanted to take the unsettled character of encounters and collaborative practices as the relevant unit of analysis, and let emergency and contingency play their part, in an attempt to keep the tensions implied by Haraway's words: 'staying with the trouble' (2009, 2016).

I first heard of the Common Heritage Project in 2006. It was officially presented as a collaboration between the Danish National Museum, the University of Ghana, Ghana Museum and Monuments Board and the people of Sesemi, the small village bordering the former Danish plantation. In the course of the project, the partners involved had started to worry about the future sustainability of the site, and therefore needed someone who could come up with suggestions to make the site economically sustainable when the private grant funding the project ran out. For a short while, that 'someone' was me. I was fascinated by the idea of different institutions and possibly different interests joining their efforts to reconstruct a former Danish plantation in Ghana and turn it into a museum, and the site itself seemed to offer many exciting opportunities for a fieldwork-based analysis of heritage work. The question of how 'we' in common could turn such a site into an attraction simply intrigued me. Encouraged by people from the National Museum, I pursued the issue in doctoral research on how the former plantation came into being, and how its commonness was enacted. How was the reconstruction made at the physical site, and which stories and materials contended to be included in our 'common past' on the posters, in the buildings, and on the guided tours? Further, how to develop forms of relational Science and Technology Studies (STS) and anthropological inquiry that explores knowledge production and histories in the making?

In order to address these questions, I have engaged with a conceptual apparatus that may not be common in heritage studies, but that I find speaks to my concern with emergent common worlds, and thus to my ethnographic interest and experiences. Studying the emergent and unsettled nature of collaboration *and* a violent and traumatic past is a risky endeavour. Awkwardness, disagreement and neglect are shadows that accompany the fine words about the merit of collaboration across difference *and* 'the necessity and importance of knowing one's history' – as it was often framed by people involved in the reconstruction project. On such difficult ground, inviting or allowing an anthropologist into one's circle is a generous move. There is no guarantee that one will feel comfortable with the end result of the work. Furthermore, people might not recognise themselves, and might not recognise the project or the themes discussed. However, and crucially, I have no ambition to *represent* the people involved in the creation of my object of study; I do not believe in any such privileged access to the field. I see my research as the product of my engagement with an emerging field, an engagement that at times felt awkward, but that I nevertheless aspired to carry out in a fruitful way.

This book, in consequence, is fundamentally *not* about the particular people involved in the Frederiksgave project. They are not my object of study. Instead, my object is the Frederiksgave project itself, as it was continuously qualified and made to appear in different ways by a collective of participants throughout my fieldwork. The reconstruction project is thus a site of encounters in which many divergent histories come together without weaving themselves into a single thread. This irreducible multiplicity of sameness and difference, I argue, is paradoxically what constitutes a common ground – to be nurtured or ignored. Collaboration, accordingly, can be seen as accomplished through the awkwardness of things and ideas not quite fitting together, rather than through agreement.

I label the attention to these emerging awkward encounters an anthropology of common ground. There is also a methodological point to this, namely that there is no way of looking upon the world from the outside, as a distant observer harvesting bits of empirical stuff to think about elsewhere. We, too, must keep the tension, share the ground and take responsibility for co-creating our objects of interest. Distinctions between data and theory are too blurred for anthropologists to withdraw from the world we study. Throughout my work I have taken great pleasure in exploring how, when analysing, we continuously create our objects as we find them, and how analysis always entails a moment of finding as well as of creation; this double movement does not challenge our authority as anthropologists or experts, but rather makes us aware of our own metaphysics.

The book is full of detailed stories. In this sense I follow a long fieldwork-based knowledge tradition, where attention to particularities and relations of all kinds dominate. In addition to being integral to my disciplinary training, I see focusing on the wealth of details as a political choice, in that details interrupt assumptions about autonomous entities. They disturb categories, because the relations they enfold continuously expand, transform, neglect and point in different directions. The many details about particular 'small' situations, objects and encounters present in the book are not so much a matter of gathering 'enough' ethnographic material for an argument to hold, but more a matter of providing ample images, stories, conversations and details for people to think through, thereby destabilising both heritage work and collaboration, and arguing that these activities are made up of just such seemingly insignificant episodes. This is another way of describing the common ground I want to engage. Part of my argument is thus enfolded in the style of writing – staying with the troublesome minutiae that continuously generated the Common Heritage Project in ways that go well beyond any project plans or distinct mission statements. In this vein, let me quote Anna Tsing: 'To listen to and tell a rush of stories is a *method*. And why not make the strong claim and call it a science, an addition to knowledge? Its research object is contaminated diversity; its unit of analysis is the indeterminate encounter.'[4] In this book, I engage this method in an attempt to craft an anthropology of common ground.

INTRODUCTION

COLLABORATION AND THE FRUITS OF AWKWARD RELATIONS

FINALLY, THE DAY HAD COME WHEN THE 'FREDERIKSGAVE PLANTATION AND Common Heritage Site' could officially be inaugurated. Dozens of four-wheel drives were parked along the narrow dusty road that ended at the heritage site in the village of Sesemi, 30 km north of downtown Accra, Ghana. Out of the swirling dust, more and more cars and pedestrians continued to appear. It was a sensuous display of people and dresses: chiefs and their followers in traditional clothes; ministers and officials in suits and ties; queen mothers and women in multicoloured robes; men in ironed shirts; and police officers in dark blue uniforms brought in as security guards for the inaugural day. The usual crowing of the village cock was lost in the noise from the engines of cars trying to squeeze themselves into every possible parking spot, mixed with noises from the testing of the sound system, and laughter and greetings between the recently arrived visitors. The inauguration was the culmination of four years of collaboration, financed by a private Danish fund, between people from the National Museum of Denmark, the University of Ghana, the Ghana Museum and Monuments Board, and the people of Sesemi village. Together, they had excavated and recreated the ruin of a 163-acre former Danish farming plantation, originally constructed around 1831.[1] By 2007, a heritage site commemorating what was most often referred to as Ghana and Denmark's common past was ready to be opened to the public.

The focus of this book is the collaborative project of creating this particular site: the Frederiksgave Plantation and Common Heritage Site, as it was undertaken by the project planners. These comprised a group of people consisting of, among others, two archaeologists (one of them also the Ghanaian coordinator), four architects, one historian, one director, and four more or less involved coordinators from both Denmark and Ghana. I myself was part of the project both as a short-term paid consultant, employed by the National Museum of Denmark mainly to assist in making the exhibition at the site, and as an anthropologist doing doctoral research. Presenting an ethnography of common heritage work, I here explore the processes and practices of collaboration between Ghanaian and Danish institutions, heritage professionals and laymen, and focus on how all these people, in a variety of ways, engaged with each other, with lime, stones, climate, rulers, exhibition posters, trees, archives, storage rooms, emails and official documents to reconstruct the Frederiksgave plantation. The idea of commonness was articulated in the project's key writings as the overarching motivation for the reconstruction project,[2] but even as the project reached its conclusion, what 'commonness' was, and how it was to be achieved and performed, still seemed rather undecided.

At the Frederiksgave site, the reconstructed plantation mansion now houses an exhibition. It consists of a small booklet and several professionally designed and pre-printed posters, all made in Denmark, which together with excavated objects and copies of various items from the period unfold and explain the two countries' common past as a result of a Danish attempt to establish a plantation in order to grow crops in Africa using enslaved people as the local work-force. Based on meticulous studies of the State Archives in Denmark, the informational material at the Frederiksgave exhibition communicates a story that has its point of departure in the Danish presence and involvement in the transatlantic slave trade on the West African coast, beginning in the second half of the seventeenth century. The written material informs visitors of the Danish ban on the transatlantic slave trade in 1803 that put an end to the transportation of enslaved humans from Africa to the Danish West Indies, today the Virgin Islands, and other Caribbean islands. From the information at the Frederiksgave site, we learn that even though the transportation of enslaved people across the Atlantic was thus banned, it was still legal to keep slaves on the West African coast until the mid-nineteenth century. Accordingly, the Frederiksgave exhibition tells us that instead of withdrawing completely from the region as a result of the ban, people under the Danish flag[3] settled on the West African coast itself in order to profit from the tropical climate and access to local enslaved workers. Indeed, dreams continued to flourish of exporting exotic goods to the European population increasingly addicted to the sweetness of sugar and the stimulations offered by coffee and other luxury products of the tropics. However, as visitors to the exhibition can also read on the posters in the mansion and in the booklet, even with thirty-two slaves working on the site, Frederiksgave never really succeeded as a plantation.[4] Instead, its location at the foot of the Akuapem Mountains attracted expatriate Danes – mainly based in the Danish headquarters on the coast, Christiansborg Castle – to visit the rather small but majestically built house, sponsored by the Danish King Frederik VI, for other reasons. Only a day's walk from Christiansborg Castle, Frederiksgave offered Danes struggling with tropical diseases a place to recuperate on the plantation veranda, where they could profit from the refreshing breeze, the silence, and the clean water from the nearby spring, and take a break from the busy, humid, and noisy coastal city, today known as Accra.

All of which brings me back to the 2007 inauguration. On this day, all routine seemed reversed in the village of Sesemi. I had the chance to participate in the inauguration and, in addition to doing my fieldwork, I had agreed with the National Museum of Denmark that I would take photos and look after the board members from the Danish foundation that had financed the reconstruction of Frederiksgave. On the opening day, the 200 or so people living in Sesemi took a break from their farms surrounding the village, and from their domestic duties, to take part in the inauguration. Judging by their engagement in the festivities, it seemed as if they enjoyed the fact that the village was exceptionally crowded, noisy, and a far cry from the usual small outpost at the end of a dusty road. The guests invited from outside had been carefully chosen by the Ghanaian and Danish coordinators of the Frederiksgave project and the Chief of Sesemi, and the square stage set up for the inauguration was meticulously organised.

There was no doubt that the heritage project planners intended this to be a prestigious event. A list of prominent guests had been invited. Both the Ghanaian Minister for Culture and Chieftaincy and the Minister for Tourism and Diasporan Relations were there. The Danish Minister for Culture made his first

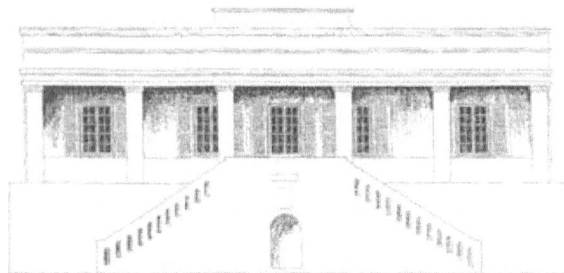

FIG. 0.1 A copy of the invitation to the inauguration of the Common Heritage Site (front page), 2007.

FIG. 0.2 The inauguration site from the Frederiksgave building, 2007, Sesemi, Ghana.

trip to Africa to participate in the inauguration, and the Danish Crown Prince Frederik was also invited, although he could not attend. As mentioned above, members of the board from the private Danish fund financing the project were also present, and chiefs and officials from the surrounding area flocked to the site. Even the highest-ranking king of the area, the Ga king, came, albeit later than the other guests and with his own entourage. The high-profile celebration of the opening of Frederiksgave showed that lots of energy, prestige and money were invested in the Common Heritage Project. Even so, the inauguration events demonstrated that achieving commonness is not always a smooth operation. Three situations at the inauguration addressed and complicated commonness in various ways, namely through speeches, the transfer of a particular key, and through food at the site. I describe these situations in the following.

EPISODE ONE: COMMONNESS THROUGH INCANTATIONS

At the foot of the newly constructed buildings, four huge pavilions, each housing approximately 100 guests on plastic chairs, formed a square, leaving a large central space that would soon be taken over by the many hyperactive photographers – myself included. The first pavilion was mainly populated by chiefs and elders from the area, nicely ranked on rows of chairs. The second pavilion turned the backs of those seated there on the reconstructed main building; this pavilion held many of the Danish guests and other 'white' visitors, as the Caucasian race is often called in Ghana. The third pavilion, behind the rostrum, consisted of a red-carpeted stage levelled a step above the other three pavilions; this housed the most prominent Danish and Ghanaian guests. Finally, the fourth pavilion was full of officials and other people from Ghana somehow related to the Frederiksgave project. In addition, the approximately thirty young men who had worked as masons, carpenters and painters at the site were all gathered next to the fourth pavilion.

On reaching his pavilion, the Ga king stepped out of the crowd of photographers, protectors and drummers. He sat down comfortably on the only empty chair left, spreading his legs and solidly planting his royal sandals on the ground as prescribed by tradition, meticulously folding his elegant clothing. Next to him was the Danish Minister for Culture, in a dark suit and closed shoes; from the crossing of his legs one could glimpse what seemed to be elegant silk socks, but he was evidently unaware of the Ghanaian custom of showing respect by resting both feet on the ground. Besides these two, VIPs from far and wide had made it to the village that day.

During the many opening speeches, we heard words such as 'our common past', 'graced occasion', 'historical landmark', 'thank God', 'overlord of the Ga state', 'Danish ambassador to Ghana', 'nii me, naa me' (greeting of traditional heads in the Ga area), 'museum piece', 'Frederiksgave means Frederik's gift in Danish', 'generous funding', 'almost *exact* replica', 'technical assistance', 'dark chapter in our common history', 'fruitful collaboration', 'common vision', 'African slaves', 'European nations', 'tourists', 'a great moment', 'partners in our two countries', 'future activities' and 'our globalised world'. And, with minor variations, mainly over the point at which to mention the Ga king, the introductory spell was repeated over and over again:

> Honoured Minister, Mr Vice-Chancellor; Members of the Board of the Augustinus Foundation; Members of the Ghana Museums and Monuments Board; distinguished members of the Board of the Frederiksgave Plantation and Common Heritage Site; academics, workers and craftsmen who have excavated and rebuilt Frederiksgave with its exhibition; staff from the University of Ghana and from the National Museum of Denmark; Chief and people of the village of Sesemi; ladies and gentlemen.[5]

This litany of words talked the Common Heritage Site and its participants into being in the hope that in the future the site would attract visitors across differences, matching the attendance and importance given to the site that day.

EPISODE TWO: COMMON HERITAGE IN A NEW KEY

After almost two hours, the speeches gave way to a small but distinct ceremony. People from the Danish National Museum had come up with the idea of having a gigantic key made according to the old *cire perdu* technique famous among

COLLABORATION AND THE FRUITS OF AWKWARD RELATIONS

the Ashanti, an ethnic group from the central part of Ghana. On the handle of the key, an Akan symbol[6] with the so-called Sankofa image was displayed.[7] The Sankofa image on the key showed a bird looking back, which was often explained as meaning 'Return and pick it up' or 'Pick up the gems of the past'[8] implying that it is valuable and important to look into the past, as the Ghanaian coordinator explained to me. From the shade of the carpeted and elevated pavilion, a group of people stepped out into the burning sun. The first in the line, the Director of the National Museum of Denmark, was holding the gigantic key. Instead of the chairman of the Frederiksgave project board – a Ghanaian professor in geography who until this moment had introduced all the speakers – a Dane from the National Museum of Denmark was given the microphone. Without further ado, he asked the Director of the Danish National Museum to hand over the key to the Danish Minister of Culture, who was then solemnly asked to hand over the key to the Vice-Chancellor of the University of Ghana.

FIG. 0.3 The Danish Minister handing over the key to the Ghanaian Vice-Chancellor, 2007, Sesemi, Ghana.

Each handing over of the key was accompanied by a pause for the photographers to take their photos. Finally, with the key in his hand, the Vice-Chancellor of the University of Ghana took the floor and said, 'I now hand over the key to the Chairman of the Board [of the Frederiksgave site]'; another photo session and more applause followed. The chairman responded:

> I realise that I'm given a duty to fulfil, and I assure you that we, the members of the board, are going to work day and night to do all that is within our powers to ensure that the purpose for which this building was restored is achieved. Come over any time and see the progress made and we will not disappoint you.

With his last sentence, the chairman anticipated a growing concern of the Danish partner about how to secure the future of the site. In the moment, the key changing hands was meant to sanction the collaborative process of creating a common past, making visible the idea that the Ghanaians in situ were now expected to take their share of the responsibility for maintaining the two countries' common heritage.

However, the key did not only imply such a smooth authorisation of alliance. One of the Danes involved in the manufacture of the key inadvertently let slip that there had been some discussion about who should be involved in the transfer of the key. Since it was a 'symbol of ownership and responsibility', as he put it, it was very important who actually received and passed on the key during the ceremony. I was told that there were even some worries among the Danes involved in the project as to whether they were in a position to receive and give the key at all. Following the logic of the symbol, holding the key meant that, first, the Danish National Museum and, a moment later, the Danish Ministry for Culture were the *owners* of Frederiksgave. This was not formally allowed by Danish law, which I was told prohibits national public institutions from owning property in other countries. As one Dane involved in the project said with a smile immediately after the ceremony, 'The Director of the National Museum couldn't pass on the key soon enough'. Even though the key caused some legal worries among the Danish partners, though, it was a Dane's idea and not that of the Ghanaian partners to make the wandering key a symbol of shared responsibility for maintaining a common heritage. I learned from the Dane in charge of manufacturing the key that the Ghanaian partners simply approved the idea in advance, but did not express any particular excitement about the symbol. Nevertheless, the next day one of the national newspapers in Ghana devoted a whole page to the inauguration and chose to show a photo of the Vice-Chancellor receiving the key from the Danish Minister of Culture. This little incident points to tricky aspects of funding and making heritage work as a *national* museum outside one's own borders on another nation's soil. This was a complexity that the Danish National Museum, which lacked prior experience of such bilateral work, had to deal with continuously in various ways, as we shall see throughout this book.

EPISODE THREE: CELEBRATING COMMON HERITAGE

After the ceremony with the key, the chairman of the Frederiksgave Board invited people to the exhibition in the main building. The guests who had sat or stood still for hours now crowded into a long line, headed by the people from the carpeted stage. At the entrance to the plantation building, a red and white ribbon had been suspended between two pillars. A young woman presented a pair of scissors on a pillow to the Ghanaian Deputy Minister for Tourism, who cut the ribbon to mark the official opening of the museum. Within a few minutes, the three small exhibition rooms were full of people who stood closely together, shared the available oxygen, and immortalised each other in this particular place with their cameras and mobile phones. The social order and hierarchies established and enacted inside the four pavilions were quickly undone in the crammed museum building.

After some confused running around, inside and outside the main building, we were told that two dishes had been prepared for the guests: 'a locally made dish' and one 'made for the whites'. The invited guests seeped out of the crowded building. Some rushed immediately back to Accra; others, mainly the Danes still present, mopped their brows and gathered under some trees close to the Sesemi Chief's house, where each was provided with a pre-prepared take-away box of chicken and rice. Others, mainly people from the area, gathered in the house of one of the village elders where 'local food' was served. Exhausted and hungry after the inauguration, I moved over to the group of Danes sitting under the trees. I was reassured to see that the group of people I had promised to take care of were all assembled under the trees as well. Within seconds, I was immersed in an exchange of email addresses in order to share photos of the inauguration. After emptying our take-away boxes in the shade, we looked at each other and concluded that the inauguration was over. Later, I learned that there had been a party in one of the elders' houses, a party that would surely have been open to us, the Danes sitting under the trees close to the Chief's house eating food for the whites. However, for some reason, at that particular moment none of us, apart from the Danish architect who had worked at the site for months, even seemed to consider taking part in the local celebrations of the opening of the Frederiksgave Common Heritage Site. Going to the party simply never registered as an option. Instead of moving the fifty metres across the dusty road to the place where the 'local food' was being served, I jumped into one of the Danes' four-wheel drives, where my body was soon cooled down by the car's air conditioning. We drove quickly down the red dust road, and disappeared into the smog and heavy traffic of Accra.

The separation of 'whites' from 'locals', and the uneasy exchange of the key to Frederiksgave, make it crucial to ask in what senses this was a celebration of a common past. Condensed in the event of the inauguration, I saw the formation and emergence of a number of subjects and objects, coming together and relating to one another in a joint, yet awkward creation of commonness through heritage work.

The difficult collaborative process of making this happen is what I engage with in this book by studying the day-to-day practices, challenges, differences and assumptions inherent in the crafting of a heritage project conceived as a matter of commonness and a shared past. Alongside this detailed ethnography of a particular heritage project, I also aim to make a methodological and theoretical claim about ethnographic research, arguing for the value of an acute attention to collaboration across difference, and to the entities that are made to emerge in this process. The book, then, is both a methods story about the relational nature of ethnography, and also a detailed ethnographic account of heritage work. Conditioning and producing one another, these ambitions – studying a common heritage project in a postcolonial society and working 'postcolonially' with ethnography – are central to the book. In short, this is my way of approaching heritage work – and fieldwork – in a postcolonial key.

A COMMON HERITAGE PROJECT EMERGES

The rather detailed inauguration story above sets the frame for some of the overall themes of the book. In the booklet produced to accompany the Frederiksgave plantation site, the aim of the project was described in the following way:

> The intention was to explore the common Ghanaian and Danish cultural heritage and inform the populations of both countries about this chapter of their common history. This would occur through the excavation of and research on Frederiksgave and documenting the history of the plantation.[9]

For the project planners, the heritage project was seen as a last chance to do something about the quickly disappearing traces of the Danish presence in Ghana. As many of the Danes involved in the project stated, in a jointly authored article written for a Danish audience:

> The purpose of the Frederiksgave project was on the one hand to preserve the Danish-Ghanaian cultural heritage, which in Ghana was and is nearly destroyed, and on the other to communicate Ghana's and Denmark's common history in the two countries.[10]

In general, the idea that 'we', as in the Danes, have to act now in order to safeguard the physical remnants of a Danish-Ghanaian cultural heritage that would otherwise disappear, was strongly present in the project design and in comments about it.[11] This 'we' was manifested by the introduction of the so-called Ghana Initiative under the Danish National Museum, acting as a public Danish institution concerned with the preservation of Danish-Ghanaian cultural heritage in Ghana. From one perspective, it did indeed require Danish resources to preserve the heritage, since the relatively poor Ghanaian nation was seen as having other budgetary priorities than renovating its European-built ruins – a lack of finances that was often commented on by people working for the Ghana Museums and Monuments Board (GMMB), the small public institution in charge of Ghanaian heritage and therefore automatically involved in the Frederiksgave project. Neither the importance of the sites – Frederiksgave and other Danish remains on the West African coast – nor the need to preserve them were ever really questioned by the Danish partner, once they had embarked on the projects. The sites were seen as important historical traces, and whenever I visited the dilapidated ruins together with people from the National Museum of Denmark, they lamented that so little had been done to protect the old buildings. Likewise, in a Danish newspaper the Danish coordinator wondered why nothing had been done before.[12] Thus, even if one party to the project of preserving a common past did not for a moment seem to doubt the value of the physical remains, others had different concerns, and not only with ensuring proper funding. Reconstructing the common heritage site was an unpredictable process, fraught with tensions and subtle negotiations of power in spite of being presented by the project-makers as an apolitical issue of salvaging physical remains of a shared and important history. Frederiksgave, then, was much more than a dormant building awaiting excavation and reconstruction; it was an enormous accomplishment to generate the site and make it emerge as a piece of common heritage.

In light of this, the Frederiksgave project invites critical reflection on what it means to 'collaborate' across difference and to characterise an initiative as a 'common,' 'heritage,' 'project'. On the basis of distinct fieldwork episodes, a main aim of this book is to continuously discuss what these four components of the Frederiksgave project might practically entail, and which entities they bring to life. Instead of pursuing phenomena such as, for instance, 'Ghanaian history', 'cultural heritage', 'identity-making in a postcolonial setting', 'colonial legacy' and so on, I explore the project's four explicit keywords: collaboration, common, heritage and project through Helen Verran's ideas of a 'here-and-now' and relational empiricism.[13] As Verran puts it, this approach pays attention to 'vague wholes, specifying the ways [their] parts come to life and perhaps die off, identifying the mediations that are important in the 'doing' of [these] vague whole[s]'[14.] In this case, these wholes might be variously considered a heritage site, a common heritage project or even the work of producing shared pasts. This is not to say, of course, that issues of Ghanaian history or the Danish colonial legacy are unimportant for my work, but I study these by focusing on how they appear in concrete empirical settings.[15] Historical records and geographical setting are not a passive (back)ground on which Frederiksgave is a figure, but emerge and are articulated in particular ways within the vague whole of my fieldwork project and ethnographic account.

My analytic, inspired by Verran, offers a means to engage with commonness in the making. This focus on the here-and-now implies a radically contemporary view of common heritage as arising from encounters, rather than as a natural result of an historical process, possibly topped up with present-day negotiations. These encounters are in no way devoid of history, but in my anthropology of the Frederiksgave project such historical content can only be understood as it is actualised and materialised in collective action in the present. I see no such thing as Frederiksgave or 'common heritage' *a priori* – a primordial material object to which one can add a theoretical layer, to paraphrase anthropologist Martin Holbraad.[16] As Holbraad suggests, things and ideas are conflated, and all one can do is to *think* through things[17] – and, I might add, with a nod to Claude Lévi-Strauss, choose things that are good to think through one's interests with. My point here is that there is no *ding an sich* or given grounds to given figures.[18] The context, whether regional, thematic or theoretical, is in and of itself a perspective and a product of analysis,[19] just as theory as a driver of analyses is not reserved for researchers.[20] For this book, then, 'Ghana', or 'cultural heritage', or 'collaboration projects' would not work as fixed contexts. Instead, in the collective doings of Frederiksgave, common heritage emerges within the practices of the project as and alongside such (also emergent) entities, events and properties as Ghana, Denmark, shared history, slave trade, commonness, collaboration, or what have you, as all of these are practised in funding applications, Danish and Ghanaian newspapers, offices at the National Museum of Denmark and at the University of Ghana, during guided tours at the forts and castles along the

Ghanaian coastline, in construction materials, in histories of slavery, in choices of exhibition materials, in Danish cultural politics and in the village of Sesemi, to mention only some.

This complexity has an important bearing on my field research and ethnographic storytelling. In exploring the heritage project as always emergent, I sought out actors who were most invested in and concerned with creating Frederiksgave through day-to-day project-making. I did not try to look 'behind' these quotidian practices to some imagined field of pre-given national identities or other such entities that could then be represented; instead, I focused on the voices and actions – and, indeed, shared analytical interests – that continuously brought my field to life. Methodologically, my field engagements can be characterised as a sort of dustballing[21] through the making of common heritage, all the while exploring the bumps in its course created by awkward as well as smooth encounters. Jointly, those of us (most) involved in Frederiksgave chose stories and objects that were good to think with, while letting others go. Writing ethnographically about social life in specific settings is thus not a retelling of 'things the way they were'.[22] Indeed, my assembled Frederiksgave was and is generated by all the encounters and activities I participated in and which jointly produced it as a common heritage project.

In light of this, anthropological method to me is a reflection on the creative process of exploring what falls within our definition of our field and what should be left out; it is a matter of paying attention to how we see in order to incorporate this analytical endeavour into a generative methodology. Hence method becomes a matter of making explicit and critically investigating our questions and choices, and their role in creating the analytical object which becomes the field. Method, in this sense, is an adjectival qualification of the object – a process of selection with the aim of exploring rather than describing what I did 'out there'.[23] Even though it might seem trivial to say, I want to stress that anthropological fieldwork is a dialogue, where one must listen carefully and interrupt respectfully. Fieldwork, and the ongoing analyses guiding the work, is a common activity where one is engaged in a constant give and take that shapes the field as we go along, including the conceptual and analytical resources we draw on or create in the process. What we subsequently do and publish is an attempt to answer to this creation. My method, then, is also very much a theoretical stance, implying that anthropological objects of study – such as collaborative common heritage – are figurations emerging in the process of analysis, rather than given data. Instead of concluding what Frederiksgave really is (or is not), this generative approach can say what it *also* is.[24]

My concentrated focus on the Frederiksgave project as it became a heritage site of common interest made some figures more apparent than others during my fieldwork. Such selection is inevitably part of any anthropological project. My narrow focus on the process of collaborative reconstruction has made some of the people involved in the project seem more prominent and dominant than others. The project planners, in particular, appear vital and enthusiastic when talking about turning the ruin into a heritage site of common interest. Other people were involved in the project, but did not engage as much in its explicit goal. I have grappled with this challenge mainly by following the focus and logic of the project and its planners, who differentiated between this main goal and what they termed 'side-effects' of the project. Importantly, this has led me to pay less attention to the project's less dominant voices, although they were a constant presence in the awkward engagements that I analyse throughout the chapters, and are vital clues to the complexity of commonness in collaborative heritage-making that is my overall concern. If Ghanaian workers or villagers seem less outspoken in this book about the project of constructing a common heritage site, this is a reflection of the idea that the object of study is generated along the way, and through the fieldwork experiences of those who take an interest in it. As such, the relative absence of, say, the viewpoints of Ghanaian masons is not a result of 'misrepresentation', lack of access, or national bias, but is in itself an important critical finding, speaking volumes about the politics of common heritage. One of the privileges of anthropology, as I see it, is to explore non-commissioned processes of collaborative and local (can it be otherwise?) theorisation through which subjects and objects emerge via the work of those who care.[25] This localises my analysis just as much as my informants' analyses of their lives and the world, even if we might of course have different genres at our disposal and different aims at heart – say, constructing a building or writing a book. With these considerations in mind, I now turn to discuss what I take the words 'collaboration', 'project', 'common' and 'heritage' (in that order) to imply in the collective ambition of generating Frederiksgave as a site of commonness.

In her book *Friction: An Ethnography of Global Connection* (2005), Anna Tsing suggests that we can undertake an ethnography of global connections by focusing on

> zones of awkward engagement, where words mean something different across a divide even as people agree to speak. These zones of cultural friction are transient; they arise out of encounters and interactions.[26]

Given that the Frederiksgave project in Ghana grew out of spatially widespread collaborations and advances, or even depended upon international relations, I see the Frederiksgave heritage work as global.[27] Thus, the Danish National Museum's recent engagements in 'the hot colonies' – as the former museum director collectively termed Danish interests in India, the US Virgin Islands and Ghana, in order to distinguish them from what he called 'the cold colonies', designating former Danish colonies such as Greenland, Iceland and the Faeroe Islands – were all instances of global connections and collaborations across differences.[28] Importantly, such a focus on the globalised nature of heritage work does not preclude a localised anthropological study of these projects, as also noted above. In Tsing's work, indeed, the global connections *take place*, and friction points to the specificity of these connections.[29] In order to study friction as a productive process, one must therefore 'begin again, and again, in the middle of things'.[30] Taking these cues, my field – the collaborative reconstruction of Frederiksgave as a continuous creation of a common past – can be seen as a zone of awkward engagement, a momentary spot of cultural friction generating new figures, understood as constellations of ideas, nations, persons, tools, artefacts and construction materials.

'Awkwardness' is presented as a productive term for studying the friction implied in collaboration across divides – as a companion to dialogue. In my case, working with awkward engagements allows for what I think of as a generative analysis of the Frederiksgave heritage project. Such an analysis co-creates its object by using differences productively, rather than mapping them as if they were parts of an already given object. I thus explore collaboration as a product of disparity – as a friction that captures relations or connections between things and ideas that do not quite fit. *Collaboration*, then, becomes at once a complex empirical feature (different people joining forces to create Frederiksgave across divides), an analytical key to finding out what the Common Heritage Site was made to be (what they were even building and on what grounds), and a theoretical puzzle in need of investigation (what it means to work together with and through difference).

But what, then, is a project? A project can be defined as ideas and practices that are relatively tightly clustered, appearing as particular historical activities and designed to have a beginning and an end.[31] A project is based on and can be seen through concrete activities. In the case of the Frederiksgave project, these concrete activities were the reconstruction of a ruin and its transformation into a heritage site supposedly of common interest. These activities were undertaken in Ghana and Denmark, in archives, universities and museums, as well as in emails, newspapers, applications for grants, discussions, and so on – a range of 'places' that expands a narrow and physical understanding of location. The Frederiksgave project was initiated in 2004 with a grant from a private Danish fund, and ended in 2007, as projected in the project description and application for the funds.[32] Even after 2007, though, additional grants were allocated for further reconstruction and landscaping of the site, and to help the newly established board with their initial work.[33] With these characteristics, the Frederiksgave project was initially able to appear in reports, plans and applications as a coherent and pre-defined whole. However, projects never fully accomplish what the planners intend in any straightforward way. As Paul Greenough and Anna Tsing remind us, it is in the very unfinished nature of a project that a study of it must begin.[34] The incomplete realisation of projects teaches us about the world.[35] Following this lead, I explore the reconstruction of the Frederiksgave site as a *project* in this specific sense, namely as a concrete, incomplete and unpredictable undertaking – i.e. not as a pre-designed whole which was then merely implemented, but as an object that was created through bumblings, failures and reformulations.[36] A project, in this sense, becomes a valuable prism through which to ethnographically explore the unpredictable process of making common heritage.

This leads me on to look at what 'common' might imply at Frederiksgave, by attending to the manifold practices through which the project came to be characterised as such. As a common heritage project between partners from Danish and Ghanaian institutions, academics and workmen, (both trained and untrained), bureaucrats and trainees, the Frederiksgave project continuously invoked a notion of 'our past' and explicitly aimed to explore the shared Ghanaian-Danish history, as I also described in the story of the inauguration. Soon after I was introduced to the project in the summer of 2006, it became clear that the short but often-repeated word 'common' was causing just as many tensions and challenges as it was providing goodwill, felicitations and celebrations – again, these contradictions are seen in the story of the inaugural ceremony. It became apparent that the word 'common' was not merely a simple adjective added on to the notions of 'heritage' and 'project', even if it was presented that way in funding applications and other documents; instead, it indicated and produced awkward relations.[37] As anthropologist Marilyn Strathern (1987) has argued, greater insight might be gained by maintaining a tension or 'hesitation' between two disciplines – in which each perspective is rendered vulnerable by its susceptibility to being 'mocked' by the other – than by attempting to let one substitute the other, or by choosing between them. The awkwardness generated by such tension, then, is more like a doorstep than a barricade; the genteel dubbing of the project as 'common' is a starting point for my analysis, not a result. The premise for my work, then, is that the *commonness* in the Frederiksgave project is produced as a continuous and unending organisation of, among others, 'Danes' and 'Ghanaians', history and the present, artefacts and words, the local and the global. My concern here is to not readily replicate dualisms of, for example, 'Danes' versus 'Ghanaians', or 'black' versus 'white' – though both these dualisms emerged regularly during my fieldwork in Ghana and Denmark – but rather to explore the hesitations that mock the assumed naturalness of such dualisms. This, in my opinion, is a hallmark of an ethnography of a post-colonial heritage project – a point I will return to in Chapter Five.

The understandings of collaboration, projects and commonness described above have a direct and very important bearing on what I take the notion of 'heritage' – the fourth of the words that I need to discuss in this introduction – to imply in the context of this book. By heritage I simply mean to indicate the ethnographic phenomenon I explored during my fieldwork. Heritage, here, is nothing but its particular instantiations in the Frederiksgave project. These instantiations – the empirical material for this book – are in a sense themselves results of the project planners' analyses, my questions during fieldwork, and all of our activities at the site, and are thereby expressions of theories about heritage.[38] This is to say that as an ethnographic phenomenon, heritage as it was brought to life in the Frederiksgave project was 'theorised' in a number of ways by the project planners and by me.[39] The reason why I engage with common heritage, then, is that it was an important part of the project planners' vocabulary that I encountered and contributed to during fieldwork. As a discipline based on fieldwork, anthropological analysis of heritage has the advantage of taking its point of departure from concrete empirical fields, rather than from pre-given ideas about what heritage is. The latter approach, I think, would unwarrantedly reduce the empirical material to mere 'cases' or 'illustrations' of an already given object. Ethnographies, I believe, can do better than that.

To be sure, pointing to this theoretical element in any ethnographic material is not to imply that the project of the anthropologist is coextensive with that of his or her interlocutors, or that he or she uncritically adopts positions held by his or her ethnographic subjects. But it is meant to complicate neat distinctions between data and analysis – a deliberate complication that is an important premise for this book as a whole, which focuses on the emergence of Frederiksgave through a collaborative process in which project-makers, anthropologists, notions of commonness, historical records, walls and trees took part, among many others.

The notion of heritage was often used by my interlocutors, primarily the people from the National Museum. In qualifying what they meant by the term, they often mentioned the importance of knowing one's history, and referred to various charters and conventions. According to the UNESCO Convention concerning the Protection of the World Cultural and Natural Heritage (1972), which is still in force, heritage is defined as material and tangible monuments, sites and formations worth conserving for the future due to their 'outstanding value' from the perspectives of, among other things, science, art, aesthetics, history, anthropology and conservation.[40] Over the last few decades, scholars have drawn attention to the US-Eurocentric perspective reflected in these universalising formulations.[41] Even though discussions within UNESCO have aimed at broadening the concept of heritage – resulting, for instance, in the Nara Document on Authenticity (1994), and the Convention for Safeguarding of the Intangible Cultural Heritage (2003) – the Frederiksgave project was very much perceived by the project planners as in line with the Venice Charter (1964) and the UNESCO Convention from 1972 in its focus on conserving material constructions of outstanding value, as I will discuss further in Chapter Three. At least, this was the explicit motivation behind the project in the eyes of the planners; the ruin of the former Frederiksgave plantation had enough value to deserve action. Importantly, it was never presented as a community project – a type of project that has been treated relatively extensively in heritage literature.[42] Nor was it a project communicating an oral tradition maintained by generations of villagers living close to the site, or any other such instance of intangible heritage catering to other views of the past than those of the project planners. Being based on a seemingly uncomplicated view of heritage as described in the Venice Charter, the Frederiksgave project did not employ any notion of community to be treated with special care. In this sense, the Common Heritage Project deviated from what seem to be trends in Anglophone heritage work to develop inclusive and alternative practices that recognise subaltern communities or other competing concepts of heritage.[43] In the spirit of the Venice Charter and the 1972 UNESCO Convention, then, the Frederiksgave Common Heritage Project planners understood heritage as something that is already there and has an inherent value – a position that of course gives rise to a series of other difficulties and subtle negotiations of importance, as I will show throughout the book. The point here is to stress that these difficulties were – perhaps curiously – never articulated as having to do with 'community', 'colonialism' or 'subaltern legitimacy', as some newer heritage literature suggests.[44] Rather, to the project planners, all of whom were publicly paid state institutions within the two countries concerned, heritage was understood as something to be excavated, renovated, conserved, collected and researched. And this is perhaps the overall reason why I wanted to explore the project ethnographically in the first place: maybe fieldwork experiences would complicate this potentially naïve approach built into the Frederiksgave project. Maybe seemingly simple concepts of common heritage would turn out in practice to be much less straightforward. Keeping in tension both my fieldwork experiences, and the scholarly literature and debates in which I had been steeped as a researcher and academic, then, the approach I adopted made clear that I could neither see common heritage as already existing, waiting to be unveiled and worshipped for its outstanding value, nor simply as the result of compromises or tensions between distinct communities. Instead, to offer a contribution that draws from, complements and extends the work of the project, I approach heritage, too, as something that people do through various relations with construction materials, ideals, places, archives, standards, policies and each other.

With these qualifications of the words 'collaboration', 'project', 'commonness' and 'heritage' in mind, I think of this book as an ethnographic exploration of the complex ways that the Frederiksgave Common Heritage Project came to life through the difficult collaboration of people, materials, tools, words, documents, scientific practices, valuations, and so on. My overall aim is to contribute to a new generative mode of researching cultural heritage, and, more broadly and perhaps more importantly, to suggest and practise an anthropology of common ground that is appropriate for a postcolonial era.

BOOK OUTLINE

In Chapter One, I offer an account of the making of my object of study. I focus on how the Frederiksgave plantation became a project site and my field site, by describing how I continuously encountered the Common Heritage Project through fieldwork in Ghana, on the basis of documents that described the work, in archival sources, in the texts that I was given, through the Ghanaian location that hosted it, in the National Museum of Denmark that financed it, and in other places besides. As such this chapter is also figured out through fieldwork and does not present a stable background for my ensuing analyses.

In Chapter Two, I shift to an investigation of how people from the Danish National Museum conceptualised, designed and framed the Frederiksgave project from the outset. I critically analyse how they envisioned the Common Heritage Site as a cultural encounter with its roots in cultural relativism. Furthermore, I seek to investigate further the notion of 'our common past' as embedded in an idea of a universal history to be shared equally by the two parties. Although planned and innocently presented as an instance of an encounter between pre-given cultural entities (Denmark and Ghana), and as a simple matter of scientifically informing about and displaying a common (and difficult) history, the main point is to show that in the process of its realisation the Common Heritage Project figured these and other entities in complex ways in moments arising out of friction and contact.

In Chapter Three, I concentrate on the actual material reconstruction process of the heritage site, and on the workings of things. The chapter engages discussions about the authenticity of materials, and my main point here is to investigate the overseeing architect's analysis of the reconstruction site, and explore how his interest in the materials and techniques used in the reconstruction was a vital element in imitating the original Frederiksgave plantation and thus bringing it to life. Rather than finding pure imitation, I emphasise the creative alterations, indeed, the magic elements, of reconstructing a heritage site.

In Chapter Four, I turn to ideas of fetish and powerful materiality in order to understand the constant attention paid to topography and the nature of the materials used in the reconstruction process. The concept of the fetish, originating in a cross-cultural setting of trade in West Africa, is the prism through which I explore the expression and creation of value, which again produced and described the Frederiksgave site as an authentic heritage site that could communicate our common past in truthful ways. The main point is to show that valuing heritage can be seen as complex and mysterious, and that its effect *as heritage* can be shown to rest on different valuations.

In order to qualify heritage work as a generative activity, in Chapter Five – which is also the concluding chapter, reflecting back on the previous ones – I engage the notion of the 'postcolonial moment' to analyse how sameness and difference, rather than being givens, were constantly made during the Frederiksgave project. In order to do so, I purposely stay in the awkward and dissonant situations that kept challenging the difference and sameness anticipated by the project planners. I argue that we should not ignore these difficult moments, but rather use them actively in the further generation of common heritage projects. In other words, there might be a lesson to be learned if we let these moments stay around and do not shy away from the unsettled negotiations and subtle power relations at play in these encounters. Postcolonialism, in this light, becomes an analytical impulse and not a quality of specific regional settings, or a marker of an epochal period. I thus end by suggesting that to pay attention to the details of how subjects and objects emerge in the joints of the concrete is to discover a fresh way of engaging in heritage work for the future – and of conducting postcolonial anthropology on common ground.

KAART
OVER DE DANSKE BESIDDELSER
i
GUINEA

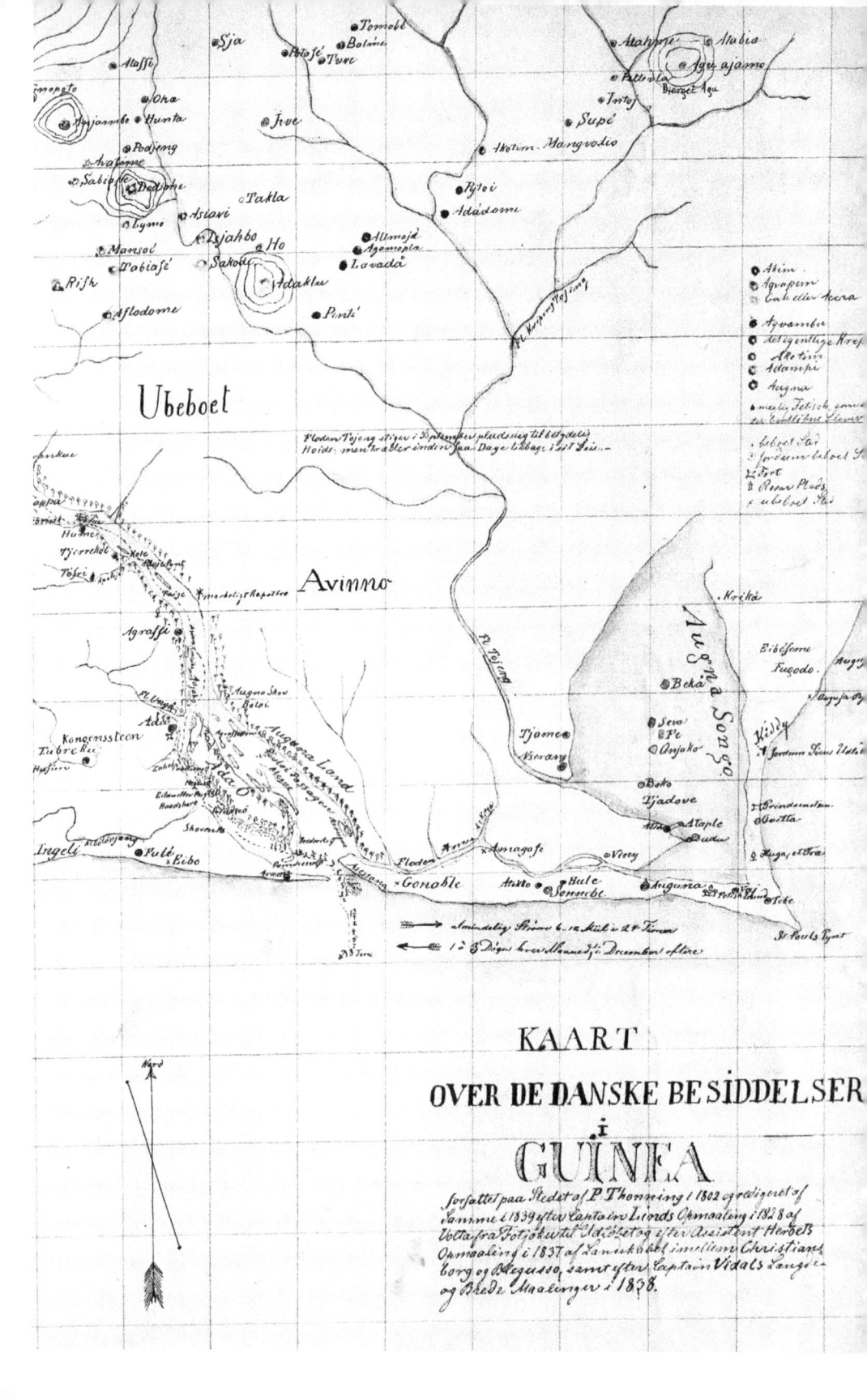

forfattet paa Stedet af P. Thonning i 1802 og revideret af Samme i 1839 efter Capitain Lind's Opmaaling i 1828 af Volta fra Fotjokuetil Udløbet og efter Assistent Herbets Opmaaling i 1837 af Landskabet imellem Christiansborg og Akegusso, samt efter Captain Vidals Længde- og Brede Maalinger i 1838.

1
CRAFTING THE FIELD OF COMMON HERITAGE

WHY AND ON WHAT GROUNDS DID FREDERIKSGAVE EVEN BECOME A HERITage project? What were the project planners' cues for designing a collaborative reconstruction of buildings from a shared past? In this chapter, I turn to some of the relations that explicitly made up and came to shape the background against which the Common Heritage Project emerged. These relations include histories and monuments referencing the transatlantic slave trade, which often featured as part of the background for the project makers. I will also look at the politico-cultural environments in both Denmark and Ghana that paved the way for the project planners' initiation of the project. Embarking on the project of analysing Frederiksgave, it became clear to me that the heritage work invoked a specific context and transnational history, which accordingly became part of my field as I went along, as I discuss in the following.

The process of initiating the Frederiksgave project included several visits by Danish delegates to forts and castles in Ghana, infamous for the role they played in the slave trade. In the literature that the project planners continually referred to,[1] and through their visits to the forts and castles, it was made clear that along the 300 km Ghanaian coastline, more than sixty European-built edifices testify to the major and longstanding presence there of various European nations.[2] In the fifteenth century, Portuguese vessels began heading for the West African coast, soon to be divided and named according to its attractive exotic resources, for example the Pepper Coast, Ivory Coast, Gold Coast and Slave Coast. In the early period of European expansion, Portuguese merchants traded with a variety of West African kingdoms along the coast. Among other things, the Portuguese acted as middlemen by shipping prisoners of war from the present-day Benin region to the local kings ruling coastal states in present-day Ghana.[3] These prisoners of war, or enslaved people as they are also called, worked in mines extracting gold, which was sold to the Portuguese traders in exchange for beads, brassware and textiles.[4] A century later Dutch, British, French, Danish and German traders, to mention but the most active, chased the Portuguese out of the region and took over the trade that soon became supplemented by a large-scale inhumane trade in humans, supplying the Americas and the islands of the Caribbean with African enslaved labour, as requested by the Europeans there.[5] According to documents found in the Danish National Archives by a Danish historian who was consultant to the Frederiksgave project, the Danes were deeply involved in this trade, exchanging beads, brandy, cowries, metal goods, textiles, guns and powder for gold and slaves.[6]

Taking a cue from the project planners, I read that the ban on the transatlantic slave trade gave rise to the construction of plantations 'on location' in the coastal area of present-day Ghana. In his introduction to a book on the files of the last Danish Governor on the African coast, historian Per Hernæs, who occasionally gave advice to the Frederiksgave project, writes that the Danish efforts to establish plantations on the coast never really came to much, since this required a stability, authority, peace and control that the Danes lacked.[7] As an explanation for the fairly unsuccessful attempt to manage plantations in West Africa, the Danish historian hired as a consultant for the Frederiksgave project told me that the Danes did not invest in the manpower and economy that it took to manage plantations in the region. In these historical interpretations, Denmark appears as a failing small-scale coloniser – often as explicitly opposed to the British colonisers who assembled, controlled and exploited African natural as well as human resources through racial laws, violence and displacements throughout the late 1800s and the first part of the 1900s. This contrast between the British and Danish presence was also aired by an official in hypothesising why the British could never embark on a project similar to the Danish Frederiksgave project. After 1850, when the Danes sold their buildings to the British – who by the 1880s had colonised what they termed the Gold Coast – the Danes' plantations were no longer maintained. Consequently, the Frederiksgave plantation soon became dilapidated, and was overrun by trees, flowers, insects and, particularly, dangerous snakes, as the people living close to the site would tell me during my fieldwork in Ghana – thereby positing Frederiksgave as perhaps more than an overgrown ruin between the village and its agricultural fields, and instead as a haunted and dangerous place.

As I talked about my fieldwork to friends, family and colleagues in Denmark, I learned that many were unaware that Denmark had officially taken part in the slave trade, or that the Danes had established plantations in Ghana. Before the Director of the National Museum of Denmark visited some of the former Danish forts and plantations in Ghana in 2003, only a few Danes had come to the sites since the Danes officially left the coast in 1850. This limited knowledge about the Danish engagement in the transatlantic slave trade and use of enslaved people as a workforce on the West African coast was very common in Denmark, according to the project planners, and yet another reason to embark on the project.[8] In light of this, the relatively small amount of literature on the subject was meticulously read and commented on; some publications were rejected for being nationalistic and unscientific, while others were continually referred to in conversations and meetings about the project. In this sense, the literature and historical records certainly created a background against which the project planners envisioned (and edited) the common heritage site, and this material fuelled an explicit and growing dream of 'updating' the knowledge, as it was formulated by some of the project planners. In 1917, the very same year as the Danish state sold its possessions in the Caribbean to the US – today's US Virgin Islands – two books were prepared for publication. Based on written sources hitherto largely unknown to the Danish public, they both related to the former Danish presence on the West African Coast. One book was a compilation of a diary and letters written between 1836 and 1842 by Joseph Wulff, an official working for the Danish state, published after Wulff's death under the title *When Guinea was Danish* (1917). As we will see later, the house Wulff constructed came to figure as a material heritage indicating a 'Danish trace' in Ghana. The other book, *The Danes in Guinea* (1918) by lay historian Kay Larsen, was based on original source material. Published right after the sale of the Caribbean possessions, it was obviously much inspired by this event – too much so for the Danish historian involved in the Frederiksgave project, who thought that the history presented was distorted by being interpreted through this event taking place in a different part of the world. Some decades later, after her voyages to India, Ghana and the Virgin Islands during the 1930s, geographer Sophie Petersen wrote in the preface to her book *Denmark's Old Tropical Colonies*, published during World War II, 'What a great solace in these times of darkness with their bitter solemnity to be able to gather around and explore a subject from Denmark's past, a subject reviving memories of experiences in tropical regions that once were Danish.'[9] The former Danish presence in the tropics was, in Petersen's framing, an occasion to bring the nation together in difficult times.[10] The Danish project planners and the Director of the National Museum were very much aware and critical of this kind of tropical nostalgia, and refused to play along these nationalistic lines. Seventy years on, exactly the same tropical regions that Petersen had travelled to were visited by the Director of the National Museum, in order to assess the potential for heritage reconstruction in the Danish traces. However, for decades in between, in the late 1950s, 1960s and 1970s, a period of change and decolonisation in many colonised countries had created a new interest in the Danish involvement in its former colonies. Prominent among the outcomes of this interest was a seven-volume publication named *Our Old Tropical Colonies* (1952) edited by the former Director of the National Museum, Johannes Brøndsted, in which the tropical regions controlled by Denmark are addressed one by one.[11] This huge effort to collect the sum of Danish colonialism in one publication has recently been updated in a new edition, with contributions from a new generation of historians.[12] Also inspired by the decolonisation movements was the Danish historian hired for the project, who focused on life on the coast. In this period, a Danish writer and traveller, Thorkild Hansen, wrote a popular trilogy on Danish participation in the slave trade that relates a story of the past quite different from Petersen's nostalgia. Rather than being something that could bring Danes together around shared memories and experiences of lost possessions, Hansen's trilogy – particularly the first volume, *Coast of Slaves* (1967) – blames and criticises the Danish nation for having officially approved of and participated in the slave trade. Hansen had studied written material found in the National Archives, and his work collects long quotes from letters and official documents and diaries from the period when the Danes were officially present in West Africa, this collection being augmented by his own normative comments. Like Petersen, Hansen visited the ruined Frederiksgave and wrote that the plantations in general were based on slave labour 'to give the Danish piece of Africa some export commodities that were not slaves. Coffee, cotton, and maize for the ships instead of men, women and children'.[13] In Denmark, the trilogy immediately became popular. In the early Frederiksgave project phase the project planners and some of the visiting Danes read Hansen's books with great curiosity, and it was referred to during my fieldwork in Ghana every now and then. But, in spite of their popularity in the 1970s, Hansen's books did not inspire curriculum planners in Denmark to include Danish involvement in the transatlantic slave trade in history classes – an omission that fuelled the Frederiksgave project. In Ghana, the trilogy has recently been translated into English (2005) and, judging from the piles appearing in the university bookstore at the University of Ghana, it is accessible and can contribute perspectives on postcolonial discussions about the former Danish involvement on the West African coast.

Almost simultaneously with Hansen, Danish geographer Henrik Jeppesen surveyed and photographed the former Danish plantations located in the Akuapem Mountains. Forty years later, his work, too, was studied enthusiastically by the Frederiksgave project planners. Shortly after I became acquainted with the project, I was given a copy of Jeppesen's article from 1966 summarising the results of his survey, along with another piece written by one of the Danish coordinators and the Danish archaeologist[14] who was involved in the project during the excavation, as well as copies from a volume on Danish establishments on the West African coast.[15] Furthermore, my attention was drawn to two newly published volumes on Danish written sources from 1657-1754, regarding the area that makes up present-day Ghana.[16] The two volumes were edited by a Danish associate professor in history with expertise in the National Archives' documentation of Danish involvement on the West African coast – an expertise that eventually led him to be employed as a consultant when the exhibition at Frederiksgave was set up. A copy of the Ghanaian coordinator and archaeologist's PhD thesis about the excavations he had conducted in 1992-3 in the slave village close to the Frederiksgave site also became part of our shared library informing the heritage work.[17] In addition to Wulff's diary and letters mentioned above, I was alerted to another old record, namely from the last Danish Governor, Edward Carstensen,[18] which also became part of the project's source base. Through reading these sources, and discussions with the project planners, what I became exposed to in these early stages was particular historical material that others around me also drew on in conceptualising and substantiating the project. What interests me here, in line with my overall ambition to explore collaboration across difference as generative of Frederiksgave, is that crafting a background for the project was a very specific activity. This compilation of background literature created a particular context within which the Common Heritage Project was figured, even as it was naturalised as description and historical knowledge.

Early on in my fieldwork, I learned that shortly before the Common Heritage Project was initiated, a group of archaeologists and geographers from Denmark and Ghana co-authored an article on the agricultural experiments at the Frederiksgave plantation.[19] In addition to the Ghanaian archaeologist mentioned above, one of the other authors of this article was a Danish professor in geography with research interests in Ghana. Importantly, this professor was also in contact with the Director of the National Museum, with whom he shared an interest in Danish history. Together, the Ghanaian archaeologist and the Danish geographer invited the Director of the Danish National Museum to visit the former Danish sites. I was later told that the visitors' enthusiasm about the sites fostered the idea of seeking grants with which to reconstruct the Frederiksgave plantation and turn it into a place for commemorating 'our common past', as it was repeatedly framed.

In sum, a whole battery of reading materials testifying in various ways to the Danish presence in West Africa over the years was circulated among the Danes about to embark on the reconstruction project at Frederiksgave. All of these writings, it seemed, were part of the heritage, and were seen as equipping the people involved in the reconstruction process. During my fieldwork these written documents – which were recommended to me by the project manager in Denmark, and labelled as the source material for the Frederiksgave project – were just as much part of the ethnographic material of the site as were the buildings and construction materials, showing ways in which common heritage appeared in the project design – as a problematic history of slavery, as guilt, as a national bastion in times of war, as archaeological excavations, as archival documents securely stored in Copenhagen, and so on. The texts also make visible how entities such as 'Denmark', 'Ghana', and 'The Gold Coast' are understood and presented, and they thus carry with them their own important context for my work on the Frederiksgave reconstruction project. In this light, the common heritage that the project intended to preserve was not simply a building, but a heavily and variedly theorised object that even contributed to creating how units such as Denmark and West Africa might be understood. This ties in with the particular political climate in Denmark at the time of the project's initiation, which came to be crucial for its realisation.

COMMON HERITAGE AS CULTURAL POLITICS AND ECONOMIC POTENTIAL

Like other public institutions in Denmark, the Danish National Museum had, shortly before the Director's trip to Ghana in 2003, been hit by rather large cuts that had severely affected the Ethnographic Collection at the museum.[20] This was one of the political backdrops against which the Frederiksgave project was initiated. The new liberal-conservative government that came to power in 2001 was pursuing a policy of no tax increases, since, as the slogan went, 'Money is better kept in the pockets of the citizens'. The government's platform stated that the public sector should be reformed in order to 'stimulate private initiative and a culture of independence, generally rewarding people who make an extra effort'.[21] Public resources were not to be simply handed out as before, but should increasingly be won through competition by those who deserved it. The new Minister for Culture from the Conservative Party encouraged public institutions to seek grants from private funds in order to mitigate the cuts and, in general, he encouraged greater collaboration between public institutions and the private sector.[22]

In this period of transformation in Danish politics, a small group of Danes took the initiative to whitewash a former Danish fort on the Southeast coast of

India for free, as stated in a Danish newspaper.[23] The fort was located in one of the places that Petersen had visited in the 1930s, and for the last twenty years plans to renovate it had been discussed in Denmark, although nothing had been done. Now, action had to be taken since the fort was in 'a sorry state', as one of the initiators from the small private group put it.[24] A few months after taking office, the Danish Minister for Culture was quoted in the same newspaper as saying that the idea of whitewashing the fort in India was 'A grand initiative, and I would like to recommend the project'.[25] In support of the project, the Minister gave the fiery Danish souls engaged in the project a letter of recommendation to use in India.[26] After all, this was an example of private initiative, just as requested in the government's platform. At the same time, the newly appointed Director of the Danish National Museum had to implement staff cuts at the museum and, simultaneously, seek grants for new projects. After his visit to Ghana, as mentioned above, the Director communicated the idea of engaging in 'the hot colonies' to his staff at the museum. But people in the Ethnographic Collection at the National Museum, as I have been told by several employees, were not particularly keen on the idea of directing their sparse resources towards these places. It was not expected that collections staff seeking a specialisation should prioritise the study of regions having a former Danish presence. After the cuts in the Ethnographic Collection's staff, it was feared that other parts of the world that had not been visited by the Danes in the past would then be neglected. Furthermore, the position of Inspector-in-charge of the African region had been cut some years before, and there was therefore no permanent staff member available to coordinate and follow up the project in Ghana on a daily basis. As a result, the head of the Ethnographic Collection was, alongside managing the collection in Denmark, engaged in activities in parts of India, Ghana and the Virgin Islands. Eventually, the museum's activities in the Virgin Islands were abolished since a delegation headed by the Director from the National Museum realised that the former Danish structures could be taken care of by the heritage sector in the US if they wanted to. The museum's activities in Ghana and India, however, soon became officially known as 'the Ghana Initiative' and 'the Trankebar Initiative'.[27] An application for the Frederiksgave project under the Ghana Initiative was sent to a Danish fund, and a grant was awarded. At the beginning of the project, there were many ideas of what to do with the Ghana Initiative. For instance, a collection in Ghana and a subsequent children's exhibition were planned in order to communicate a contemporary perspective about life in Ghana.[28] Some items were collected, but apart from that and a proposal for an exhibition, the ideas were gradually dismissed.[29] It turned out that there was plenty of work involved in the reconstruction of the Frederiksgave plantation alone, and furthermore, changes in directors, heads of departments, heads of collections and coordinators in Denmark had challenged the project and threatened its continuity on several occasions.

The project's official partner in Ghana was the University of Ghana. Unlike the many new faces that were introduced into and subsequently left the project from the Danish side, the Ghanaian partner remained very stable. In practice, the University of Ghana was singularised into one man, one of the initiators, a coordinator and archaeologist with a PhD based on an excavation of the Frederiksgave plantation, and later a board member of the site. In addition to him, an accountant, a technician involved in the archaeological excavations, some drivers and a Head of Department who approved the project were also involved from the university. The Ghanaian coordinator facilitated all communication with officials in Ghana, and advised the Danish National Museum about the best people to talk to. Through his job as a lecturer at the University of Ghana, he was the anchor man securing the necessary institutional affiliation for the bilateral project to operate in Ghana. He presented the Danish heritage workers to the Chief in the village of Sesemi, paid the salaries of the local workers, was invited on several trips to Denmark and was, in general, strongly encouraged to participate in all decisions regarding the project. Furthermore, as mentioned, the public institution Ghana Museums and Monuments Board (GMMB) was involved, since the board 'is the legal custodian of Ghana's material cultural heritage (movable and immovable)'.[30] They had to give permission for the reconstruction. An architect from the GMMB was therefore hired by the project to assist the Danish architect in charge of the reconstruction of the ruin. Symptomatically of the increased international interest in the physical heritage of Ghana, the Ghanaian architect had previously been occupied with several other international heritage projects. Before being appointed to the Frederiksgave project, he had accompanied and assisted a group of Dutch heritage workers in renovating an old Dutch cemetery near the famous Elmina Fort. This increasing international interest took up much of the small GMMB staff's time, and according to a Danish professor in archaeology who was not involved in the Common Heritage Project, this interest contributed indirectly to the neglect of other non-European Ghanaian heritage sites.

Several times during my fieldwork in Ghana, various people working in the Ghanaian tourist industry told me that stories about the transatlantic slave trade had until recently been ignored.[31] Some elaborated that UNESCO's inclusion of the Ghanaian forts and castles on the world heritage list in 1979, and the UNESCO Slave Route Project initiated in Benin in 1994 on the transatlantic slave trade,[32] had led to a wave of renovations and also tourists, among them Ghanaians as well as Europeans and people from the African Diaspora.[33] The initiative to place all the European-built forts and castles in Ghana on the UNESCO world heritage list in 1979 did not guarantee the maintenance of the sites, as the Ghanaian architect from GMMB told me. It did indicate, however, their significance as cultural heritage 'of outstanding value'[34] – or as the review sheet from ICOMOS[35] states, 'The Forts in Ghana constitute an early evidence of the joint activity of the Africans and Europeans, and deserve consideration.'[36] The UNESCO Slave Route Project, which explicitly aimed 'to break the silence' around the transatlantic slave trade, generated a growing interest, particularly among the African Diaspora, to visit the forts from which their enslaved ancestors had once been shipped away.[37] Their interest ignited a new tourist industry along the West African coast, one that had the effect of reversing the historical flow of money and resources away from Ghana. As a result many of the remaining forts have, over the last few decades, been turned into historical sites or 'tourist attractions' as they are laconically called by many of the Ghanaians with whom I talked during my fieldwork. But even before these initiatives, many of the forts and castles along the Ghanaian coast were used as prisons, state offices, and even a presidential palace, due to their robustness.[38] Demolition of these infamous historical sites has to my knowledge never been publicly discussed in Ghana; instead, a 'relentless pragmatism'[39] has characterised the uses and purposes of the buildings in an economically hard-pressed country. And yet, in 2007, the then-government initiated the construction of a new presidential palace called the Golden Jubilee House in Accra. Funding came from a fifty billion dollar Indian loan, and in response to the many criticisms of such expenditure in a poor country the initiators argued that the president could not be based in a castle in which slaves had been kept.[40] Indeed, the old palace and its relations to slavery were increasingly foregrounded. The growing interest in Ghana in and from the African Diaspora was also reflected when the Ministry of Tourism, established in 1993, changed its name in 2006 by adding 'Diasporan Relations'.[41] This addition was discussed in Ghana and, according to an article published on one of the most popular Ghanaian online news sites, 'Modern Ghana', a critical commentator in Ghana thought that such a diasporan 'concern' should simply have a desk in the Ministry of Foreign Affairs, if indeed it was necessary at all.[42] However, as the commentator also argued, linking up with the African Diaspora is much in line with the thinking of the African Union. It is also an echo, as I understand it, of the ideas of the nation's first president after independence from the British colonial regime, the celebrated and cherished father, Kwame Nkrumah, and his ideas of pan-Africanism.[43] The forts, obviously, were not only an internal affair, but of growing concern for an African Diaspora nurturing a new tourist industry in Ghana.

Commercial interests were not a prime motor for the Danish project planners. For example, in the very first application to the fund that eventually granted money to the project, an economically sustainable plan for the future of the site was not built into the project design. The non-profit character of the site was often stressed by the planners. Again, as we shall explore in the following chapters, the Ghana Initiative was set up to rescue a material history that, if no action were taken, was in great danger of being lost. Nonetheless, in 2003 the Ghanaian coordinator explicitly wrote in a project description to the GMMB: 'The Common Heritage Project: Developing the Danish Plantation Sites along the Foothills of the Akuapem Mountains for Cultural Tourism'. The coordinator linked the project with tourism, and saw the Frederiksgave project as related to the UNESCO Slave Route Project,[44] which indeed has brought thousands of relatively wealthy overseas tourists to Ghana. And in another letter written to the Minister for Tourism the coordinator wrote: 'The Project is a cultural heritage developments initiative',[45] thereby also linking the project to the many so-called 'development projects' in Ghana having the same set-up, with an international donor and a Ghanaian collaborator. In this way, however innocently the Common Heritage Project was drafted, in the actual life of it there was a potential tension: on the one hand it was meant to do nothing but inform about a common past, but on the other hand it dealt with the contentious theme of slavery and was a possible way to make money from tourism for the villagers living close by. Indeed, the project's accomplishments were not pre-empted by its design.[46] In this line, many of the Ghanaians I talked to about the project said, 'it's good, it brings development to the village'. And, similarly, one could say, the project was also creating jobs in the economically challenged National Museum's Ethnographic Collection in Denmark. Nevertheless, these opportunities were seen, at most, as 'side-effects' by most of the Danes involved in the project, who foregrounded the project as a matter of knowledge sharing on the basis of an allegedly impartial science, whereas in Ghana these opportunities were seen as vital parts of the project. This was a difference that at times created tensions and awkward moments, as we shall see, particularly in Chapters Four and Five. As we shall also explore in the following chapters, it would be difficult to make any clear-cut distinctions between (proper uses of) heritage and economical profit in the Common Heritage Project of Frederiksgave.[47]

With the increased interest in promoting the histories of the forts and castles, and particularly the wretched and horrible story of the transatlantic slave trade emanating from these buildings, the managers of the sites were perhaps unwittingly following what various heritage scholars characterise to be a much broader trend. As Logan and Reeves (2009) argue, over the last three decades there has been increased interest in preserving the more unpleasant sides of heritage.[48] This may reflect an incipient curiosity, but as stated above, heritage-making is also an industry that can potentially bring money to the sites through tourism.[49] Over the last two decades this tendency to display unpleasant heritage has attracted an increased number of scholars to investigate these places and the attendant processes of making economic profit through 'dark tourism', 'thanatourism'[50] or 'horror tourism', as it has been conceptualised by Tunbridge and Ashworth.[51] 'Heritage of atrocities',[52] 'negative heritage',[53] "heritage that hurts"[54] and 'difficult heritage'[55] are all concepts and approaches that in different ways investigate 'a conflictual site that becomes the repository of negative memory in the collective imaginary'[56] or, put more simply, 'the ugly side of history'.[57] This 'difficult heritage' is often understood as a necessary counterweight to formerly prevalent uncritical understandings of heritage as a positive resource,[58] and as a matter of protecting the 'great and beautiful creations of the past'.[59] For good reasons, the horrors of the transatlantic slave trade dominate Ghana's 'dark heritage'. However, throughout the project the planners in Denmark stressed that rather than being a story of the transatlantic slave trade on par with that which is communicated at the forts and castles, the Frederiksgave site should tell about enslaved people working on Danish-managed plantations *in* Ghana. As we shall see, even though the Frederiksgave project was thought of as a different story from the transatlantic slave trade, it was continually linked to it. Further to this, by focusing on slavery *in* Ghana the Frederiksgave project came to address what had only recently begun to be discussed publicly in both countries. For the project planners, the chosen strategy to deal with this difficult heritage of masters trading and owning enslaved plantation workers was to resort to seemingly apolitical science, building the reconstruction on facts and accuracy.[60] However, in actual practice the project planners could not, of course, depoliticise their scientific project, nor disregard or control the ways in which Frederiksgave, for all its commonness, came to work. I will return to this more explicitly, particularly in Chapter Two and Chapter Five. I soon learned that it is only in recent decades that the trade in slaves has been publicly discussed in Ghana,[61] and some claim that even today it is a delicate matter to bring up, in particular the indigenous slavery *within* Ghana[62] such as that which the Frederiksgave project addressed. The Ghanaian coordinator was very much aware of this new tendency of more open debate, and told me that in Ghana they were 'ready to heal the wounds', as he framed it. In a Danish newspaper he elaborated the recent shift in sentiments in the Ghanaian public debate, which is now seemingly much more inclined to address the hurtful history of slavery: 'If one does not learn from the past, how can one know which way to go? If we just leave it be, wounds will fester that will only get worse', he explained.[63]

A RUINED PLANTER'S HOUSE

So what was the site of these development-cum-preservation ambitions like? After having read all the literature, and talked to the Danes involved in the project at the National Museum, I went to the site where the reconstruction was taking place in the village of Sesemi. Scattered fields and huge trees and bushes dominated the landscape, making up small patches of tropical rainforest in which various bush animals lived. Carved out of this green landscape, halfway up the hill, I encountered a field with a cluster of ruins in the process of being reconstructed. Further up the hill, spread out in the forest, were the villagers' farmlands and the treasured Source of Hope, or *Sasemi*, as it is called in the Ga language spoken in the area. Out of the Source of Hope springs fresh drinking water that is still used by the people living in the village when they have problems with their rather newly established well. In the 1830s–1840s, the Danish historian once told me, the Source of Hope was treasured by the often sick Danes, and also used to water the small coffee plants.

In 2004, when the Frederiksgave project was launched, the 130 m² main building, or planter's house, as it was also called, was covered with plants from the nearby forest. Two huge fig trees had embraced the south-western end and thereby partly protected the building from collapse, but they had also destroyed it with their roots, which sought nourishment and water in the muddy mortar holding the stone building together.

The roof of the planter's house had collapsed, and this made the building even more vulnerable to the burning sun, heavy rain and expanding plants. A small plant had kept a small part of the original floor intact by protecting it from the sun and rain with its leaves. The Danish architect talked about these plants and roots that had simultaneously protected and destroyed the site with great affection, as we shall see later on. Termites had eaten all the wooden parts of the building, and apart from stones, only old iron parts such as nails, hinges and a few utensils were found during the excavation. Indeed, it took a great effort to disentangle the buildings from the soil, the plants and the debris. Frederiksgave had, quite literally, to be carved out of the landscape in particular ways in order to be shaped as a heritage site of common interest. After the main building had

FIG. 1.1 The covered ruin in 2004, Sesemi, Ghana. Courtesy of Jørgen Frandsen and the National Museum of Denmark.

FIG. 1.2 A fig tree entangled with the Frederiksgave ruin in 2005, Sesemi, Ghana. Courtesy of Jørgen Frandsen and the National Museum of Denmark.

been excavated and the soil had been removed, the ground-plan measured 16 x 9 metres; the Danish historian told me that it had been a small plantation in comparison to the Danish West Indian plantations, with only three rooms and a rather large roofed terrace. At some stage the terrace had been divided into three, creating two small rooms and an entrance, which indicates that the Frederiksgave plantation was well-visited by the expatriate Danes living in the forts along the coast, mainly Christiansborg, located only 30 km away. A few steps from the main building in a north-easterly direction, archaeological excavations revealed a small construction that was soon labelled the bath-house or toilet. Some twenty metres down the slope on which the main building and bath-house were located, the ground-plan of another small building was found. The purpose of this building was unclear, but the heritage professionals told me that it might have been a kitchen and/or stable and sleeping place for the overseer of the site. This last construction was not reconstructed on the ruined ground-plan by the Common Heritage Project, but excavated, secured and kept as an exemplar of what the three ruins disentangled from vegetation life had looked like when the Frederiksgave project was initiated – an exemplar which in 2008, after the inauguration, was apparently again slightly overtaken by the green germinating forces. A few metres further down the hill, an almost similarly sized small house had been erected out of concrete blocks in 2006-7. The main house and the bathroom were reconstructed on top of the ruins. This was a decision that was discussed among the project planners, since it contravened the Venice Charter on reconstruction, as the Danish architect explained to me – a point I will return to later. He also told me that due to the income gained from collecting the stones from the dilapidated buildings and breaking them into smaller pieces for sale, the villagers' collection of stones from the houses was 'a primary destruction factor'[64] – a factor that was brought to a halt in the early 1990s by the Ghanaian archaeologist. In consequence, the main building was supplied with new stones from a quarry nearby for the reconstruction – a continuously expanding low-tech quarry that supplied the growing construction business of the still expanding capital city by its demand for cheap labour.

Since the inauguration of Frederiksgave in 2007, two mud huts have been constructed at the site, this being made possible by supplementary funding

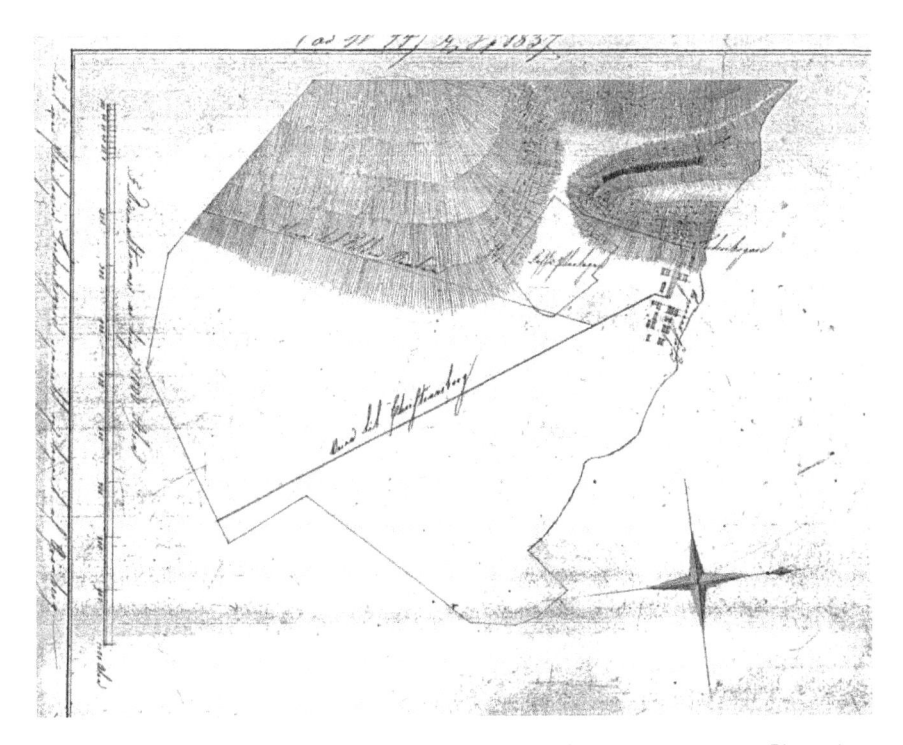

FIG. 1.3 A photograph of the only known map of the Frederiksgave Plantation. Courtesy of the National Museum of Denmark and the Danish National Archives.[65]

from the Danish grant givers. These huts – which were erected after I had concluded my fieldwork at the site – have been erected close to the bath-house and opposite the remaining ruins, and bear a poster informing readers that it was in such huts that the enslaved people used to live. Since there are no remaining traces of the enslaved people's actual houses, which were made of highly perishable material such as clay and wood, the actual size and appearance of the original huts is not known – much to the regret of the project planners. However, an old plan of the Frederiksgave plantation and its land was found in the Danish archives. It indicates some constructions that might have been the enslaved people's houses.

Meticulously, the Danish architect measured the scaled-down drawing, and from his measurements he was able to reconstruct the sizes of what were likely the mud huts. The location of the huts was briefly discussed, since the slaves most probably did not live as close to the main building as the newly constructed mud huts suggest. The old plan, however, suggested a location 500 metres from the main site in the middle of the village, which was also where the Ghanaian archaeologist made his excavations of the enslaved workers' remains. This location, however, was seen by the project planners as too far away from the main heritage site. In addition, reconstructing the huts there was seen as interfering too much with present-day village life. Once again, this was not just an uncovering but a creative carving out that shuffled around particular bits to make up a common heritage.

Indeed, as these early impressions show, the Frederiksgave project presented itself to me as a highly composite and selective background, comprising Danish cultural politics, museum priorities, colonial styles of governance, popular Danish critical literature, school curricula, diaspora tourism, architectural and archaeological expertise, debates in Ghana about enslaved workers, fig trees, and the value of brick stones, among many other things. Agreeing with Sharon Macdonald, I can thus readily state that 'heritage management is fraught with multiple dilemmas'.[66] It is part of the often contested cultural politics of the partners involved, even if they agree to speak and work together on a common project. What is important here is that Frederiksgave was shaped by the provisional, multidirectional and commonly created backgrounds that I have outlined here, and which I will qualify further in the following. Through acutely detailed analyses of particular situations in the course of the heritage work that bring out the sameness and difference of such collaboration, I offer a perspective on commonness in the chapters to come.

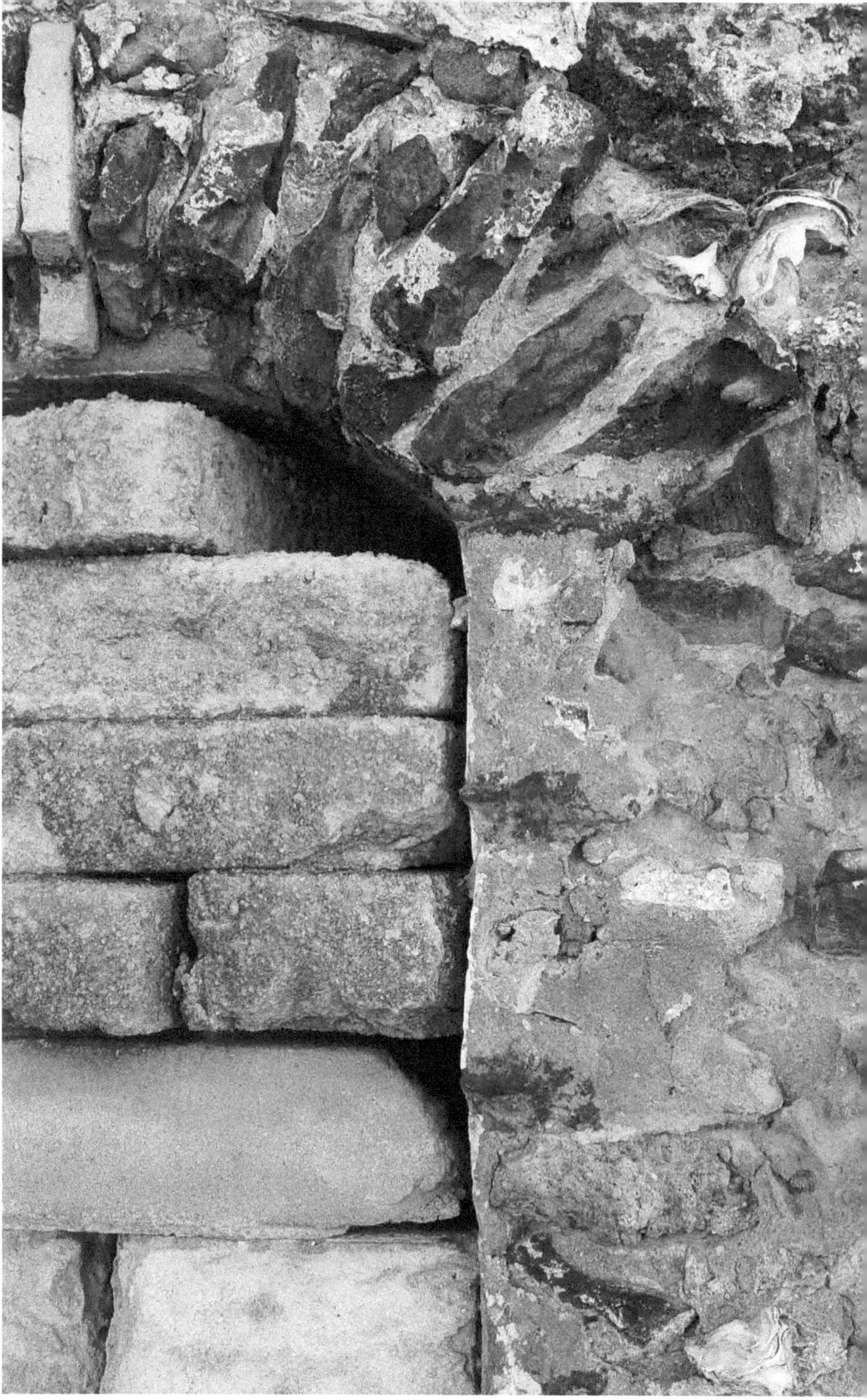

2

SHARING HERITAGE THROUGH FRICTION

CULTURAL ENCOUNTERS IN THE HOT COLONIES

It is important to emphasize that these projects are not undertaken to show how Denmark once acted in the wider world. Neither colonization and foreign politics nor a distant dream of national grandeur are the focus of the projects – the focus is on the cultural encounter.[1]

WITH THESE INTRODUCTORY WORDS, THE TWO COORDINATORS OF THE Trankebar Initiative and the Ghana Initiative explained the National Museum of Denmark's engagements in what the former Director referred to as 'the hot colonies'. More specifically, these engagements translated into initial steps to renovate a former Governor's house in India and reconstruct a former plantation named Frederiksgave in Ghana. If successful, they would later be followed up by further projects in the two countries.[2] By focusing on the so-called 'cultural encounter', the authors were accommodating a criticism that was rarely aired in the museum but which was, every now and then, talked about among the Danes involved in the projects, namely the criticism of creating projects that potentially revived a past in which the Danish nation's grandiose international role was in focus. At one point, this criticism was formulated in a song for an office Christmas party written by a museum employee who was not a part of the initiatives. The song was a rewriting of a well-known children's lullaby which during the 2000s was criticised for being racist because of a line that has a baby elephant using a 'negro boy as a rattle'. The rewritten song had four verses, one introductory and one for each of Denmark's 'hot colonies' (i.e. parts of India, of Ghana and the Virgin Islands). The photocopied song was distributed at the Christmas party, and within minutes we were all standing, slightly intoxicated, with the sheet in our hands, ready to sing.[3] The introduction and verse about Ghana went as follows:

> Now stars are lit in the blue skies
> and in the countries near by Equator,
> And what a thrill to think about
> when Denmark was a coloniser.
> So dream of those days when we were there
> With helmets, forts and frigates.
> But the grandeur of the past is near now,
> And our flag Dannebrog[4] waves again.
>
> Now whites are sent to Ghana's coast,
> Once again to build plantations,
> Where blacks are working like anything
> To create for us affective tableaux.
> And in the midst of the jungle where nothing is up,
> Where there is practically nothing to do,
> Of stones and clay a phoenix bird rises,
> The Danish-most house Frederiksgave

In a bitingly satirical way, the song jokingly pointed to the grandiose nationalistic and neo-colonialist perspective potentially embedded in the museum's hot colonies initiatives. By pointing to a lost Danish past that was now to be revived by the Frederiksgave project and other similar projects, it echoed – humorously – the nationalistic voices also raised in one of the books about the old 'tropical colonies' written during World War Two and referred to in Chapter One. In general, people seemed amused to be singing the song at the Christmas party, but I never heard it mentioned again after the collective singing by all the museum's employees in 2006. If the grandiose nationalistic perspective was discussed by the Frederiksgave project planners, it was from angles other than the satirical. The hot colonies held histories that were delicate and nothing that Denmark could be proud of, as one person from the museum said, but the project planners agreed that these stories of hurt were not to be blamed on present-day Denmark; the Danish involvement on the West African coast certainly presents a difficult heritage, but the project planners did not project this embarrassing legacy onto present-day Danes. This opinion was shared by the people I talked to in Ghana, and a similar statement was made by the Director of the National Museum in an interview with a Danish newspaper.[5] Needless to say, however, such a common understanding of not blaming present-day Danish people for past atrocities complicated considerably the attempts to tell the history of 'our common past' in a straightforward and homogeneous way, as I will explore in the following chapters. The song, and a few critical voices, raised a criticism that the Director of the Museum had already referred to on previous occasions. And with a consequent change of focus, the project coordinators of 'The Trankebar Initiative' and 'The Ghana Initiative' stated that, instead of 'colonisation' or 'foreign politics', the two projects would focus on the key term of 'cultural encounter'. The coordinators further specified that

> The Danish presence in the regions concerned brought about encounters between completely different cultures, and in our times, too, cultural encounters take place, even if on different terms. It is important that the cultural encounters are seen and appraised not only from a Danish point of view, but also from local perspectives. What images of the strangers from the far north do people in these former colonies have, and what were the cultural, economic and social consequences of the Danish presence – then and now?[6]

In this chapter, I will explore how people – primarily from the Danish National Museum – conceptualised, designed and framed the Frederiksgave project and the plans for new projects in Ghana. I will offer a reading of how the Frederiksgave project was visualised and presented as a cultural encounter between equal partners, making it appear to be a heritage project beyond the colonial encounter in a very particular sense. Implied in the project vision, it seems, was an idea that we are all *past* being responsible for or victims of colonial wrongs. In our symmetric present, accordingly, science and history can be cast as neutral and evenly accessible to all, provided we inform people properly about their findings. How did the museum's ideal of a symmetric cultural encounter, in which 'local perspectives' are equally important to Danish perspectives, relate to ideas about a common history also present in the project? In what ways were Denmark and Ghana seen as sharing a past? How was commonness articulated in the design and realisation of the Frederiksgave project, and in what ways were the Ghanaian collaborators expected to be involved? And, more generally, what kind of objects of knowledge does it take to even conceive of the heritage initiative as a cultural encounter? This chapter explores these questions by looking closely at a series of encounters that took place within the Frederiksgave project.

My choice to start this chapter with the above two quotes is, of course, deliberate. Together, the quotes immediately raise the question of what is meant by 'culture' – a highly contested term within anthropology[7]– and also 'encounter'. As I will substantiate throughout the book, the concept of encounter is crucial because it was central to the Frederiksgave project, and also because it structures whichever entities can be foregrounded as things that meet. The quotes give us a hint. 'Denmark' and 'Danish' are both mentioned as being one part of an encounter between 'completely different cultures'. Concerning Danish culture, the authors thereby partly conflate the notions of culture and the nation state, denying space to other cultures qualified as being 'local', that is, in the etymological meaning of being limited to a particular place but not necessarily bound to a nation. Such an understanding of culture might seem straightforward from the perspective of a *national* museum accustomed to classifying and thinking about its purpose according to the Danish nation state.[8] The quotes from the two coordinators of the National Museum's initiatives presented above emphasise the fact that continuous encounters between different cultures need to be seen and evaluated from more than one perspective; in their case, not *only* from a Danish perspective. The other side of the encounter, i.e. how the 'locals' view the Danes, is presented as a necessary part of the equation. The idea of switching between these two cultural perspectives illustrates the presumed existence of a sort of meta-perspective, an abstract neutral space that can collect and structure the information on how different cultures 'see and appraise' the world and each other. In order to study 'what images' we (as in the Danes) have of them (as in the locals) and how they see 'the strangers from the far north' one would thus have to externalise oneself from one's cultural perspective, take the point of view of the other culture's perspective and, finally, abstract oneself from both cultures in question by presenting what is thought to be 'one culture's view of the other' – an abstraction of or meta-perspective on the observations collected. As we shall see, in the design of the Frederiksgave project this abstracted perspective turned out to be a mix of cultural relativism and indisputable and impartial science – which in the actual realisation of the heritage project turned out to be a difficult position to speak from with any clear voice. The two coordinators' statements require a sort of empathetic movement that falls into three steps of, metaphorically speaking, undressing (take off one's own cultural dress), re-dressing (putting on the other culture's dress) and, finally, dressing in an authoritative and supposedly non-distinct white coat in order to speak from a neutral position.[9] Even though most anthropologists have disputed and long dismissed any idea of speaking from a neutral position, there seems to me to be a remnant of this vision in the relativist stance, with its implied external point of view, allegedly enabling a cultural expert to speak and translate on behalf of the (other) culture in question. It should be added that this authority may not be recognised as such, because the notion of cultures here implied is rarely queried in cultural relativism – there is in a sense nothing to exert authority over; rather, cultures appear as universal givens, beyond discussion – an understanding that has been strongly challenged, perhaps most famously in the book 'Writing Culture'.[10] Hence, from a cultural relativist perspective, the (cultural, historical...) scientist seems endowed with a kind of authority without any source, an authority from nowhere or everywhere, which reflects the idea that authority is gained by abstracting the perspective.[11]

In Chapter One, I mentioned the widely held view that no heritage projects are ever devoid of particular perspectives on the past, a view that has given rise to many analyses of the contested nature of heritage and the attendant negotiations of power involved in reconstruction. Here, interestingly, the exertion of authority takes the form of ideally equalising the potentially conflicting points of view by assuming the viewpoint of an allegedly uniform template, geared to accommodate differences of content without the form (Culture or History, as we shall further explore, with capitals) of these being shaken. The relativist idea of cultures as parallels within a given pattern, and as identifiable regardless of perspective, is discernible in the fact that what is constant in the coordinators' statement is the very notion of cultures; what changes is what these cultures consist of. One can see how Danes involved in the project were supposed not only to visualise the encounter from a 'Danish' perspective but also to attempt to extract themselves from their Danishness and enter – or at least look at – the 'completely different culture'. Interestingly, as we shall further explore, this extraction entails a step up to an abstracted sphere provided and guaranteed by the National Museum – which, paradoxically, then figures as a common universal platform rather than a particular national figure. By virtue of its relativist neutral stance, the National Museum supposedly has universality on its side. To create the symmetry and equality needed to imagine the heritage work as an equal cultural encounter between universally given cultures, the Danes involved in the project were supposed to 'see and appraise' how the Ghanaians involved saw not only the cultural encounter itself but also the Danes, described as 'strangers from the far north'. An appraisal of both sides of the equation necessitates abstraction. One might therefore ask whether this externalisation of perspective is a necessary prerequisite for the project-makers in order to reach the desired commonness. And what happens to the encounter if it is only to be reached through a move to an externalised, abstracted and universal space? In this chapter, I will explore these attempted movements to the universal (and thus seemingly anonymous and apolitical) realm to discuss a potential implicit contradiction in the Frederiksgave project design, between the abstracted neutral universality of cultural relativism and the actual encounters of the project work.

PROTECTING REMAINS: 'THE LEAST WE CAN DO'

In Denmark, one of the biggest newspapers wrote in a sub-headline: 'Experts from the National Museum have come to Ghana to save the ruins of Danish colonial times on the former Gold Coast'.[12] Using a well-known rhetorical trick to stress the dynamism of the initiators, the article began by opposing the sub-headline with the following: 'Accompanied by the lazy waves against the Gold Coast, and enveloped by the curiosity of friendly locals, experts from the National Museum are surveying the remnants of...'.[13] Seemingly, nothing would be done in the country, repeatedly being lapped by the lazy waves hitting the coastline, if it were not for the initiators from the Danish National Museum. By countering the invading nature, in what could be termed a *natural* encounter, the initiators of the Frederiksgave project were acting heroically on behalf of history, according to the journalist. Indeed, such natural forces were recognised as acting directly on the former Danish objects, as we shall see.

Fort Prindsensten, the easternmost former Danish fort, painfully reminded the people from the National Museum of this fight against time and the necessity of taking action. The sea had been slowly advancing since the beginning of the twentieth century, and by the 1990s, three-quarters of the fort had been eroded.

Only following the most recent serious flooding in the 1980s had foreign donors sponsored a billion-dollar sea defence to protect the city of Keta. The architect hired to find Danish traces in Ghana was left with only one curtain wall

FIG. 2.1 Fort Prindsensten from the seaside, 2008, Keta, Ghana.

of Prindsensten and a few illustrations of the fort drawn by expatriate Danes in the eighteenth and nineteenth centuries. Tirelessly and with enthusiasm, I helped the Danish architect trace photos of the fort at the public office, at the Chief's office and at various private households in order to supplement our knowledge about the otherwise disappearing fort. People enjoyed showing us their photos of various important moments in their lives. And, indeed, it was exciting to be invited to look at people's photo albums and see all the connections and travels they and their relatives had made. In contrast to the lack of interest in the (histories of the) Prindsensten Fort, the personal histories entailed in the photo albums were clearly of high priority. Having looked at several faded, dusty and treasured photos, we found a handful of old photos depicting various parts of the fort. Bent over the photos, we meticulously studied details and accompanied our discoveries with exclamations of: 'It's fantastic!', 'Wow', 'Oh, look there's also this feature', 'Yeah, you're right, there used to be a door there', 'Oh, it would have been even better if they'd taken a photo from the other side as well', etc. With the aid of a magnifying glass, the photos were compared with the physical remains in minute detail.

Over the last couple of years, I have spent time with several Danish architects in Ghana, learning the importance of one of their basic activities, namely surveying buildings. As an alternative to rescuing the common heritage in time, it was repeatedly suggested that this surveying was 'the least we can do' with regard to the Danish-built forts and buildings along the Ghanaian coast. The Danish architects thus echoed what the museum director had advocated a few years before the Frederiksgave project was launched. In an interview with one of the most popular newspapers in Denmark, the director had been invited to discuss 'general education'.[14] Although he made it clear that *bildung* did not come from the National Museum or other cultural institutions, he was nevertheless scarcely able to imagine what generally educated people would do without the National Museum. Having stressed the importance of the family in creating educated people, he continued:

> that we [the National Museum] have an obligation because general education [bildung] and personal identity simply cannot exist without historical

awareness. This does not necessarily imply that you must know the list of kings. But at least it is important that you have some sense of the sequence of events, and of the frame of reference. Because the reference unites us and provides a shared interpretation and understanding.[15]

Here the director wanted to underscore the importance of an historical awareness among Danes, an awareness that, even minimally defined, could at least frame events and give a sense of sequence. As such, the director argued, historical awareness was vital and a prerequisite to having a personal identity and general education/*bildung*. This is a view that he shared with the Minister of Culture, who, in an interview with another major Danish newspaper, related rootlessness to not knowing one's history.[16] In his critique of the tendency to historicise life and thereby risk mummifying it, Nietzsche suggests that we should 'serve history only so far as it serves life'.[17] The question is, then, which forms of life does the history produced in the Frederiksgave project serve?

Soon after the Frederiksgave project – the museum's first initiative in Ghana – was launched, the director said, 'We approach these foreign sites with a bit of humility. But, after all, we do think that we share a common interest in uncovering the past that we have in common.'[18] Here the director again argues for the importance of an historical awareness and of having a 'common interest' in a shared past, but this time not only to a Danish audience but also, indirectly, to the people with whom we share a past. It is interesting to note the small words 'after all' contrasting the 'bit of humility' with which the Danes should approach these sites. Even though the Danes from the National Museum are humble, 'after all', we need to 'uncover the past we share' and, in the words chosen two years earlier, the need for an 'historical awareness' in order to have a 'personal identity' is expanded to include the Ghanaian population. The unveiling of the shared past was quite simply seen to be of common universal interest. To the Director of the National Museum, a museum has to approach these foreign sites with a little humility but, 'after all', history must be brought to light. And uncovering our common past entails countering the invasion of nature before it is too late; rescuing what remains is 'the least we can do'. In other words, the National Museum here portrayed itself as giving 'a helping hand', as a key person from the museum framed it, to the supposedly innocent activity of preserving a heritage of universal value. Likewise, and in response to the different histories told at the Frederiksgave site, the Danish coordinator expressed this need on several occasions: 'We have to insist on bringing to light the true history – we have to dig our heels in'. In light of the director's statement about the need to know one's past, the coordinator's stake seems obvious; of course 'we have to dig our heels in' – our very identity is at risk. In an interview with a Danish postgraduate student of history in the spring of 2010, the Danish coordinator was confronted with accounts from the 'local guides' that did not coincide with or communicate the story told on official posters at the Frederiksgave site – a 'problem' that was also encountered at the forts and castles. In response, the coordinator explained: 'One cannot blame them [the guides] for telling the story that brings more money, yet this [blame them] is what we must do anyway!'[19] The problem that the coordinator was alluding to was the so-called 'wrong story' that connected the Frederiksgave plantation to the transatlantic slave trade, as told by some of the guides at the Frederiksgave site – an issue I will return to in Chapter Five. The issue here is that the apparent dissonance in the heritage project is seen as having to be resolved. It becomes a matter of trying to make the Ghanaian guides play their part in the common project of informing about the shared history while not blaming (yet in fact, blaming) them for not doing so. It is not that the coordinator does not understand the use of the dramatic – and potentially lucrative – history of transatlantic slave trade; the problem is that the guides somehow betray the project that is regarded as of completely common interest. Collaboration becomes a matter of speaking with one voice, namely that of history. The coordinator was also alluding to some of the stories told by guides at the forts and castles along the coast, who at times portrayed Europeans as unscrupulous robbers who stole Africans and shipped them to a life in slavery. When people from the National Museum and I heard such stories during our visits to the forts and castles, we agreed among ourselves that, true, the Europeans may have been unscrupulous in even thinking about dealing in slaves, but the slaves were *traded* with willing African kingdoms; they were not *stolen*. Importantly, this seemingly vital difference was affirmed by an appeal to indisputable historical records. According to the Danish coordinator, these wrong and hateful narrations that contradicted historical evidence should not be accepted. What is interesting and perhaps paradoxical here is that the reason for this apparent need to set the historical record straight by striving to allow the heritage sites to tell only one story seems to be a 'democratic' notion of equal access to historical knowledge; if we allow more stories to flourish, reconciliation, curiously, is threatened, as expressed by the Danish coordinator:

> From a phenomenological point of view, should we not leave these narratives be? On the other hand this creates reversed racism. Reconciliation is important and we should drag history back into the light. The Ghanaians do not want to talk about personal matters, but are willing to talk about the general history. We cannot create unity by 'hate stories'. This is why we have to dig our heel in.[20]

There seems to be only one story that should be told at the site, namely History (with capital H). It is a history that, just as the director noted, lies slumbering, waiting to be discovered as being of common interest. The commonness of the heritage is therefore found in objective evidence and must result in the *joint* fight against wrong-tellers of hate-histories (and against the expanding invasive nature). In this way, I suggest, history in the singular – as *bildung* extended to all – undermines or pre-empts the practical encounter by attempting to make the 'wrong stories disappear'. Because there is only one history, with its assumed shared importance that is already universal and unquestionable, it becomes the shared and neutral responsibility of all involved in the project to communicate just that. The other stories told by the guides at the sites are false and threaten to erode historical awareness and identity – understood and presented as being uniformly based on and in accordance with archival records, archaeological excavations and architectural examination – and should be eliminated by 'digging one's heels in'. The project self-identified as naturally speaking for a total 'human community', ideally formed by historical *bildung*. It was not a matter of representing different communities' points of view. In a sense, one might say that within the Ghana Initiative's discourse there are no relevant local points of view. For all the praise for cultural encounter, the only encounter which is really allowed to produce changed conditions is the meeting with the expanding and destructive natural world (the rising sea, the growing forest, etc.) or the expanding capital city that threatens to obliterate history. On both accounts, the National Museum is the perfect objective custodian.

In the opening to this chapter, I remarked on how cultural relativism pervaded the ideas of cultural encounters in the Frederiksgave project and demanded a sort of meta-perspective from where one could see and appraise encounters between given cultural entities. Likewise, the quotations above can be seen to communicate an understanding of history that demands a sort of non-situated perspective – a perspective beyond the messiness of everyday life, beyond economic temptations and racial delusions, and beyond hate (which were the concerns of the coordinator). In other words, this perspective stresses a universal history that is, unless the National Museum interferes, under threat from the encroaching natural world, growing urbanisation and cunning wrong-tellers. This universal history should, with the help of the National Museum of Denmark uncovering it, inform about the past independently of economic interests. Moreover, by 'digging one's heels in', this uncovering should bring about reconciliation – which is apparently an automatic result of dragging history into the light – and ensure that no 'hate-histories' are told. The truth demands action, not so much as a human or national 'we', but as a meta-agent talking on behalf of history. This produces a paradoxical figure of an encounter without any encounter, since the truth only has one side. One might say that it is 'the heel' that has to dig in 'the heel'.

To sum up so far, we see the Frederiksgave project design entailing both a symmetrical encounter between different given cultures (no foreign politics or colonial legacy) and a view of a 'now' encountering a common universal history of equal importance to all, which we must protect from erosion whether by nature, modernity or by wrong-telling. What is central here is not just the glossing over of different perspectives by the appeal to a seemingly neutral historical science. Importantly, both of these ideas of encounter also belittle the generative friction out of which *new* entities are produced in a contact zone. Both notions of encounter in the Frederiksgave project (i.e. between equal but different cultures and between 'now' and common history) invoke claims to universal entities, all the while obscuring that these entities are *made* within the very same movement in which they are voiced. Let us take an even closer look at these paradoxical and simultaneously relativising and universalising manoeuvres.

Asking how 'the universality of Nature operates in a world of friction',[21] Tsing examines the development of botany as a universalising science. Such an examination, I argue, could be analogous to an understanding of history as a universalising science, as presented above. I thus ask the same question, exchanging the word History for Nature, to explore the universality of history in a world of friction. But first I must digress into botany as it was developed in Europe in the heyday of the Enlightenment, according to Tsing. Being interested in analysing the movement through which singular observations relate to generalisations, Tsing explores the development of the European botanical tradition. Since the Middle Ages, she argues, this tradition has tried to create singular global systems that make it possible to understand and classify the empirical diversity of the universal Nature.[22] The famous Swedish botanist Carl Linné's celebrated book *Systema Naturae* is, as the title indicates, just such an attempt to create a classificatory system with a global reach; with this book, he wanted to create an overarching system for nature that was useful and applicable anywhere in the world. Tsing argues that the effect of Linné's method is that the *system* becomes the primary object of botanical knowledge, while the multifarious flora that comprise it are reduced to data.[23] Having first discovered such a system, botany then becomes a matter of pure collection, of collecting data that can be put into the system; each plant, or species, to use Linné's vocabulary, has a place and, just as important, rooms are left open for as yet undiscovered species. The species are the parts or entities that are filled into the whole system, which pre-exists its parts. Linné's universal system produces a natural distance between system and singular observations – an external relation between system and data. The development of botany, Tsing argues, can be seen as an index of how analyses use generalisations that aspire to a universal system, as in Linné's case, or are conceptualised along more humble lines, i.e. by providing generalisations that do not aspire to universality. Tsing stresses that making generalisations is something that we all do all the time, and is not normatively bad. Generalisations are a particular way of dealing with difference and similarity and, more particularly, how difference and similarity are set. Making generalisations involves what Tsing analytically calls 'axioms of unity'[24] – an analytical synonym for generalisations. Axioms of unity are, as the name suggests, what unite otherwise dissimilar units and make their unity or relationship appear evident. In order to succeed, the unity must pre-exist the particulars. For instance, as Tsing writes, before uniting apples and pears, one needs the general category of fruit. The difference between apples and pears must recede into the background in order to foreground the relationship of similarity, generalised as fruit. By pre-determining the singular parts, the axiom of unity makes it possible to collect and order different singularities/particulars into generalisations, just as in the case of the apples and pears the generalisation of fruit demands that incompatible singulars be made compatible. Even the smallest conjunction among otherwise incompatible units is promoted to a unification. The abovementioned conjunction between apples and pears creates the generalisation of fruit by backgrounding their differences and foregrounding their similarities – one could say that they need to collaborate on their sameness by backgrounding their differences. There needs to be some shared agreement about the structuring of sameness and difference, and the conjunction legitimates the generalisations it produces. Or in Tsing's words:

> What is most striking to me about these two features of generalization is the way they cover each other up. The specificity of collaborations is erased by pre-established unity; the a priori status of unity is denied by turning to its instantiation in collaborations.[25]

Clearly, the two movements create a circular argument. On the one hand, the generalisations pre-exist the particular instances but, on the other, the particular instances create legitimacy for the generalisations. As a classical circular argument, the two movements need each other while at the same time covering each other up. In order not to naturalise the units and systems that the generalisations operate with, thus letting the circular argument affirm itself endlessly, we need to pay attention to the fact that the axioms of unity (and thereby the particulars and the generalisations) are products of collaborative processes. As such, the axioms are collaboratively accomplished figurations. The system of nature discovered by Linné is, then, a particular figure. If axioms of unity, then, are to be explored as creations, what is the generalising principle and what are its parts, its singular instances? In other words, what makes the axiom of unity work? Or, in relation to the question that has continuously guided me during my fieldwork and in this chapter, where should one position oneself in order to make the generalisation of a universal shared history and common past work in the Frederiksgave project? How is this generalisation accomplished in the project?

Juxtaposing accounts from the project with Tsing's work, my suggestion is that history – as talked about by the project planners from the National Museum – can be seen as sharing features with botany as developed by Linné. Just as the botanical system was seen as external to the data it consists of, the understanding of history, as expressed by the project planners, was likewise seen as if from an external position with regard to the data filled into it. History was seen as progressing along a line (the system), and events such as the transatlantic slave trade (data) had to be duly filled in along that line. Filling the history of the Danish plantation in Africa into the place occupied by the transatlantic slave trade did not work – the Danish plantation belonged to 'another chapter', as the Danish coordinator framed it, a later chapter. The story of the Danish plantation had its own place on the timeline. In order to produce the generalisation of a universal history represented as a timeline, however, one needs singular instances such as the Danish plantations in Africa and the transatlantic slave trade, to mention but two of the events important for the project planners and for telling 'our common past'. These are needed to fill the particulars into the *same* story – a story that by its sameness can ensure *bildung*, reconciliation and indeed unity, as we saw above. And in order to fill the data into the timeline, one needs to focus on a small conjunction between the transatlantic slave trade and a Danish plantation in Africa. These are needed – as different points – to fill the particulars into the *same* story. The small conjunction in this case could be the shared implication of 'whites' making use of African labourers. The conjoined points are both structured according to a course of events; they both have a beginning and an end, which gives them the possibility of covering a period in time, or being a 'chapter' as chapters follow each other and chart progress through a book. Where the comparative feature in the Linnéan system was the reproductive organs of plants, in the case of history in the Frederiksgave project it could be that events related to the European colonisation of Africa are thought of as having a temporal beginning and an end. This makes the events available to progressive sequencing such as can be found in a timeline, where the year 1750 logically comes before 1830. With greater or lesser precision, the events are given a year or a period in time when they occurred. One event succeeds the other, and the fact that the events share the same structure and the possibility of being progressively sequenced unites them in this small conjunction that orders the particular events as different while affirming the system as overarching and general. In order to generalise a universal history (or fruit/Nature) as a system waiting to be filled in with data in the form of particular periods (or apples and pears/species), one needs to structure the singular events according to an external timeline by foregrounding their ability to have a beginning and an end (i.e. their possibility of being designated to an annual period) and backgrounding other potential similarities and differences. The point is that this operation requires effort and collaboration – and if the collaboration is threatened by a mixing up of particulars it is important (for the sake of the system) to dig in one's heel to get history back on track. Heritage scholars Logan and Reeves (2009) have observed that sometimes the local community in which heritage work takes place may refuse to accept national or world interest in their past. The community, they state, might thus have their own 'different yet equally valid interpretations'[26] of heritage sites, particularly if these are sites commemorating or implying 'acute anguish'.[27] The authors go on to state that

> Foreign [heritage] professionals can avoid or at least minimise problems such as these by adopting a sensitive cross-cultural negotiation approach in all stages of the commemoration process, remembering that they are working on someone else's land.[28]

What is interesting here is that to the Frederiksgave project makers this sensitivity to the cross-cultural setting of the project implied in the design of the project as a symmetric cultural encounter is thought to be achieved by an appeal not to local community involvement but to a universal global history as a shared resource for all. In that sense, one might say, the project was not really perceived as being 'on someone else's land'. Instead, the project was designed as if from nowhere in particular – even if informed by bilateral collaboration. The point here, however, is that this is of course in itself a specific perspective, creating progressive world history as the axiom of unity. In other words, history does not pre-exist the singularities, but is made up of multiple instances that may comprise various conjunctions other than a progressive timeline.

Now, to invoke Tsing again, the Common Heritage Project can be explored by asking what happens to the universality of history in a world of friction in which the pre-givens are abandoned and seen – more realistically – as particular contrived figurations of sameness and difference? In a world where universalising ideas are constantly made rather than found? Indeed, the need to ask this question surfaced all the time in my fieldwork material, as we saw above in the case where the universality of history was questioned – and reaffirmed – in the discussions of the guides' 'wrong' stories. The view of collaboration as a way of treating differences and similarities in order to make working generalisations becomes visible in my presentation of encounters as understood in the Frederiksgave project as a relativistic perspective, where one culture meets the other. As we can now see, cultural encounters in a relativistic perspective such as that advocated by the coordinators are, by presupposing that there is a universal form that can be filled out with different particulars, consistent with ideas of a universalism. Both universalisms, seeing history as a given progression of different events and seeing cultures as having the same form but different content, share, as mentioned above, the need for a meta-perspective from where one can see cultures or events from the outside. In terms of the overall discussion of what heritage making involves, the perception of this universal aspiration as a common and neutral system that accords with an external timeline as its ordering principle is crucial, since it allots only one slot for any of the particulars, thereby effectively controlling difference. Except, of course, that difference keeps coming back in to show the contrived nature of such a generalisation. When configured within this particular project imaginary, I suggest that sharing a common past is conditional upon a form of universalising – a common fight *against* nature and wrong-tellers and *for* history. What we share is a universal truth (History consisting of encounters between distinct cultures and/or sequences of events) and where we meet it is in this shared 'landscape' that is threatened by being engulfed by nature and laissez faire. Difference, such as other stories about the Frederiksgave site than the history communicated via posters, is then understood according to the same universal system, and if it does not live up to the criterion of the system it must be forced into sameness; i.e. corrected to confirm the established story. There is thus a self-fulfilling quality to this way of generalising; it is always 'right'.

It was in these universalising senses described above that the initiatives from the National Museum could be understood; they were 'a helping hand' preserving something presumed to be of universal interest and common value, and 'the least we can do' to assist the impoverished Ghanaian nation, as it was often framed by the people involved from the National Museum. In order to fulfil these minimum standards and thereby help the Ghanaian nation to get its fair share of the universal *bildung*, even though it 'lacked money to finance these kind of things,'[29] as explained by the director in a national Danish newspaper, the people from the National Museum wished to survey 'all the Danish traces that were severely threatened by decay', as they repeatedly told me. As a passing remark, the recognition of a natural encounter that acts on and changes the object should once more be noted. In this sense, the museum was not only following its expectations and obligations as the Danish National Museum and the ensuing national legal requirements;[30] it was also following the international charters for the conservation and restoration of monuments and sites – particularly the preamble to the Venice Charter (1964), which was often referred to primarily by the Danish architects involved in the reconstruction project at Frederiksgave. The preamble states the following:

> Imbued with a message from the past, the historic monuments of generations of people remain to the present day as living witnesses of their age-old traditions. People are becoming more and more conscious of the unity of human values and regard ancient monuments as a common heritage. The common

responsibility to safeguard them for future generations is recognised. It is our duty to hand them on in the full richness of their authenticity.[31]

In the Athens Charter, a predecessor to the Venice Charter, the task of maintaining cultural heritage is normatively seen as a task for the 'wardens of civilization' – or, as stated,

> [t]he conference, convinced that the question of the conservation of the artistic and archaeological property of mankind is one that interests the community of the States, which are wardens of civilization.[32]

The salvage operation of surveying the decaying buildings, and the statement mentioned above that surveying all the Danish-built forts and buildings in Ghana is 'the least we can do', could be seen as a continuation of a rhetoric germinating in the 1940s on the West African Coast.[33] At that time, Thurstan Shaw, one of the first curators of collections in the Gold Coast, stated that 'no nation can feel truly self-confident or self-conscious if it is uncertain about its past'.[34] In the same spirit, Julian Huxley, a scientist, was sent by Great Britain to the Gold Coast among other things to research the development of museums, archaeology and ethnology in West Africa. In a report, he wrote that

> knowledge of and interest in the history and cultural achievements of the region will be of great importance in fostering national and regional pride and self-respect, and in providing a common ground on which educated Africans and Europeans can meet and cooperate.[35]

Here Huxley, like his Danish successor sixty years later, expresses the universal and absolute value of knowing one's past. Interestingly, he also understands this particular way of knowing as providing a common ground for cooperation between 'educated Africans and Europeans'. Returning to the ideas expressed by the Director of the National Museum, knowing one's history was understood as a vital part of being an educated human being. Interestingly, upon closer inspection, as we have already seen, this promotion of a universal history requires a concerted effort. It is necessary to dig in one's heels and insist on a proper education that can ensure recognition of the universal history and thereby a common ground where we, the Danes, can meet them, the Ghanaians. 'Education', or 'capacity building' as it was also called by the coordinator, was needed; education and capacity building could provide a similarity that made the idea of a universal history possible and evident, and they both demanded an effort in the form of educational programmes and other forms of promotion since, as Tsing pointed out when identifying the circular argument implied in a generalising logic, this was not something emanating from the universal history itself. Capacity building, then, can be seen as an outcome of the challenge to the universality of history. It has grown as a particular response to an awkward encounter that suggested – for the sake of all – resolving the problem of different ways of understanding how and when the Europeans used the African workforce by erasing the differences and settling the similarities.

Verran discusses what seem to her to be the dangers of such universalising ideas, taking her point of departure in how 'Yoruba numbers' have been repressed by 'universal numbers'. According to Verran, the problem is that the universalist explanation has

> legislated the primitiveness of Africans and established the need for their uplifting through development – modern education. Difference is ruled out in universalism as it legislates a particular and, I would have argued, an abhorrent moral order: "You should give up your nonmodern Yoruba ways to become full knowing subjects in the process of making modernity in Yorubaland!" For a universalist, Western colonizing is an agent of progress in Africa. And any notion of postcolonialism is neo-colonialism – a continuing struggle to roll back the darkness through learning to use the given universal categories singularly embedded in material reality.[36]

As Verran points out, difference, and I would add, truly generative encounters, are ruled out in universalism – there is only one way forward and that is via modern education conveying the only true story and system, to which different events contribute. Together we stand against decay and darkness; so close do we stand, actually, that 'we' turn into 'one'. In the international charters, the Danish Museum Act, and both Huxley's and Shaw's ideas, the rhetoric of the sentence uttered by the Danes at the beginning of the new millennia ('the least we can do'), can thus be seen as a polite continuation or re-enactment of this civilising drive to conserve the artistic and ancient property of humankind – especially when we know that the Ghanaian government lacks the money to take care of these treasures. It was exactly from this normative perspective that the Danish National Museum saw its engagement in Ghana as 'a helping hand' or a contribution to preserving valuable heritage. As noted in an article by some of the people involved in the project, the National Museum's activities in Ghana could 'contribute to giving the heterogeneous population in Ghana a greater understanding of the history of this still young country'.[37] The project, established as a collaboration between trained archaeologists from the University of Ghana and heritage workers from the Danish National Museum, could therefore, as suggested by Huxley in the 1940s, be seen as the academic common ground on which collaboration could commence. Consequently, 'education' or 'training' were therefore also seen as important elements of the project, and included in the budgets accordingly. This was, however, education that flowed in only one direction, namely from from the educated personnel to the local villagers in order to distribute the shared responsibility for our common past. But education and training were found to be more complicated than initially imagined, and therefore gradually faded from view in the development of the Frederiksgave site – perhaps because the universal value of the common heritage was not so straightforwardly universal after all.

An additional grant was, nonetheless, provided for the training of guides, once the National Museum had withdrawn from the project following its inauguration in October 2007. The issue of training, education and capacity building will be further explored in Chapter Five, but for now I will simply point out that it was an aspiration to establish a common ground for the educated, where they could put themselves at the service of history. Training and capacity building thus become yet another way of ruling out difference and potential tension, since education and history are understood as apolitical and acultural. This apparently creates a new platform for an encounter between lay and expert: the project planners saw their task as one of collecting information from near and far and instilling this information into the uneducated guides and visitors to come, thereby making true history: 'The goal was,' as stated on the Ghana Initiative's homepage: 'to shed new light on the common Ghanaian-Danish cultural heritage and inform people in both countries about this historical chapter'.[38] In light of the above, one might ask what, from the perspective of an 'academic communitas', are these cultural encounters in which prevail an understanding of cultural heritage as being of common interest to humankind and an assertion of history as essential to the formation of nations and its individuals.

Cultural encounters, understood as dialogues between two completely different cultures in the geographical sense – in this case, one from 'the far north', the other 'locals' from the West African coast – are displaced into another encounter in which equal academic partners can, through their joint efforts, enlighten the uninformed Ghanaian and Danish populations about 'the history of Frederiksgave', as it was often referred to. The encounter then becomes displaced into one between academics or experts and laymen. This layman/expert encounter, however, was not what the coordinators meant by cultural encounter, and was therefore not talked about in cultural terms. Furthermore, one could say the whole point of the encounter between expert and layman was to turn the latter into the former; the encounter had to be eradicated or made superfluous by enlightening people about the common past, and differences here would hardly fit into the project's ideals.

Through this synthetic reading, I suggest that there seems to be a tension between, on the one hand, working for the expansion of a universal perspective of history and, on the other, taking an interest in culturally specific perspectives. Built into the design of the Frederiksgave project were two types of encounter: the first could be framed as an equal cultural encounter that can supposedly be reached from an abstracted perspective – namely that of the cultural expert who can compare two cultures. The second is a 'now' encountering a past that has to be understood in the right way, and this has to be ensured by capacity building and training which, likewise, can be reached from an abstracted perspective – namely that of a universal history identified with the educated man. Both of these encounters, I suggest, work to preserve rather than generate – more than anything the entities appear as whole given and unquestionable units. By focusing on conservation, the safeguarding of heritage is, as quoted above, 'the least we can do' – preservation of already existing data is key. However, in this ideally encounter-free zone of cultural encounter and universal history, a great many new things and uncontrollable events did happen and emerge. Let us look again, then, at the paradoxical combination of relativising and universalising manoeuvres in the making of the cultural heritage projects initiated by the Danish National Museum.

ON COMMON GROUND

On several occasions, I found myself sitting bent over a table with a group of people at the National Museum. We were all immersed in old maps of the West African coastline which, in addition to their meticulously handcrafted lines, bore old informative inscriptions. These inscriptions indicated that regions were 'uninhabited', that 'In September, the River Volta bursts its banks and floods all nearby areas' and, among the still recognisable names of African villages, Danish buildings were marked out, their names underscored with a red pen on one of the maps. All the maps were highly detailed along the coastline, with all the forts marked with names, at times almost unreadable. The level of detail decreased exponentially the further inland we looked. Staring at these maps, we were reminded of the massive European presence along the West African coast and, at the same time, of the limited European access to the hinterland, mainly due to the diseases that took their toll on foreigners.

When making posters for the exhibition at the Frederiksgave site, it seemed natural to the project planners to use maps as an illustration, since the compass rose is obligatory on all maps. 'Then we know where we are,' we told each other. With this solid ground under our feet we could unfold the history of Frederiksgave. A closer look at the maps indicates where the cultural encounters that motivated the common heritage work are thought to have taken place. A map made by one of the Danes from the National Museum unmistakably shows the Museum's interests.

AN ANTHROPOLOGY OF COMMON GROUND

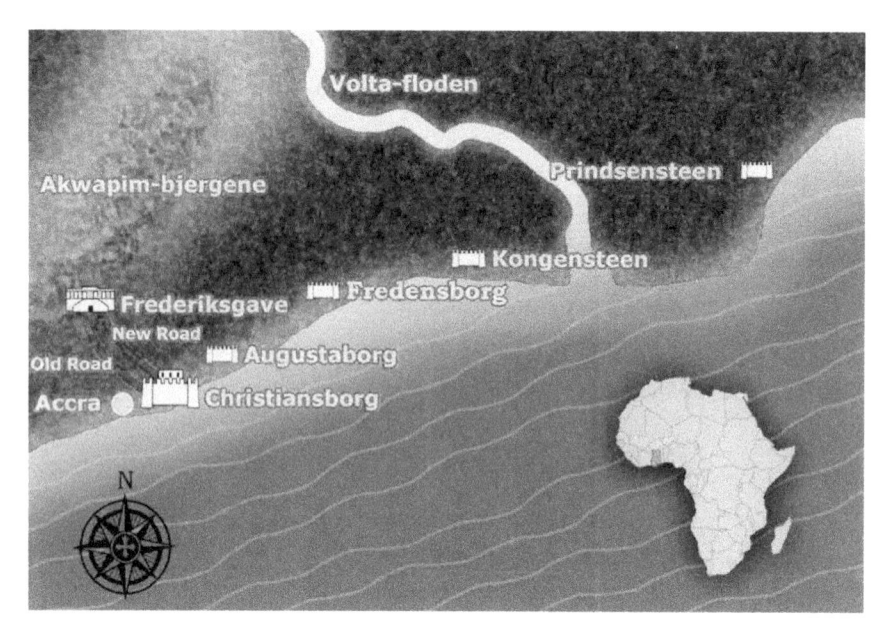

FIG. 2.2 Map drawn for an article about the Frederiksgave project published by, and courtesy of, the National Museum of Denmark.[39]

The map roughly outlines the eastern coast of Ghana, sketched in a few colours and dominated by Danish toponyms. In fact, it is not a map of Ghana but a 'map of the Danish possessions on the Gold Coast' as we are told in the text accompanying the illustration. By using the name Gold Coast, the authors point to a pre-independence time when the coastal region had several names among the Europeans, including the Gold Coast, the most durable name, also used by the British colonisers. Along the coastline, the positions of five former Danish forts are indicated by a cartoon-like icon of a white fort. The newly reconstructed Frederiksgave plantation is indicated by a similar icon. On several occasions during the project I had the opportunity to study maps in Ghanaian schoolbooks, and I was struck by the contrast with the map made by the Dane. Remarkably, the latter turned the present-day maps for juniors[40] inside out by omitting almost all Ghanaian landmarks and instead making the Danish presence stand out. The map therefore illustrates a Danish presence that is emphasised by the absence of Ghanaian names and cities, except for the 'given' physical features such as the river, the mountains and the capital. Considering the minor size of the physical remnants of the Danes' activities, and the limited awareness that these forts and plantations occasion in Ghana (and in Denmark, as discussed in Chapter One), the size and brightness of the white icons almost make a caricature of the Danish presence. If compared to the map showing tourist sites from the Ghanaian school book, the Danish National Museum's interests along the Ghanaian coast appear marginal; they are not even noted on the school map, apart from Christiansborg Castle, where the Ghanaian presidential office is located.[41] Put differently, the absence of Ghanaian names on the map made by one of the Danes, and the relative lay ignorance of the Danish traces, stand in stark contrast to the large fort icons. The sketched map is accompanied by a small geographically accurate drawing of the African continent. In contrast to the roughly outlined map, the thin lines and curves make the small map of Africa look geographically precise, and the thinly outlined nation-states indicate that it is a map of present-day Africa with Ghana highlighted in red. The continental map is conveniently situated in the right corner, floating in the vast blue Atlantic Ocean. The dual map, as I will call the illustration, can immediately be seen as showing where the cultural encounter took and takes place. Here, one could argue, Danish culture, in the shape of small white fort icons with Danish names indicating Danish constructed buildings, meets local culture, by being on the Gold Coast/Ghanaian soil. However, there is more to the dual map than this straightforward representation of the location of the cultural encounter. As I will argue, the map not only describes a site where the encounter was able to take place, but *creates* both the site and the encounter in particular ways. It was produced, like all maps, as a cartographical depiction that conjures up certain features and leaves others out.[42] So apart from illustrating the museum's interest in the former Danish constructions, the dual map is also an image of what the cultural encounter might look like from the perspective of the authors of the article in which the map is used as an illustration. By only sharing with maps printed in school books the features of the characteristic coastline divided by the River Volta, the Akuapem Mountains and the capital of present-day geographical Ghana, the dual map conjures up the nation of Denmark on African soil – in Ghana, an African nation among other African nations, as meticulously demarcated by the red colour on the supplementary free floating geographical map of the continent. Apart from conflating the two geographically far-flung nations or territories into one frame, the illustration also entails other conflations. The idea of referring a particular site to a larger and recognisable region, country or continent is a well-known pedagogical trick used with maps; at best it helps the reader localise the particular site. In this case, the idea is to locate former Danish possessions in present-day Ghana. But whereas thin lines and curves make the Africa map look geographically and nationally accurate in relation to present-day borders, the roughly outlined map of the coastline seems more like a sketch. By using two different types of maps (i.e. a sketch and a geographically accurate outline) the illustration conflates different cartographic genres. Furthermore, the pedagogical trick seems problematic, since there is also a collapse in time on the dual map. The sketched map is, on the one hand, an illustration of the coast at a particular period in time – a time when this region was called the Gold Coast and when Danes built forts. On the other, the geographically accurate map of the present nation state is a contemporary map, featuring national borders that were drawn much later.

So what do these conflations in space, genres and time conjure up? How can we understand a sketched, historical, 'Denmark in Africa' map appearing in close relation to a detailed map of present-day Africa? In what way is the dual map illustrative of an encounter? I would suggest that this particular cartographical depiction is a compact illustration of a specific idea of encounter that runs through the Frederiksgave project design. The several shifts in genre that are enacted in the illustration appear as unproblematised, seemingly neutral translations. This dual map establishes an axiom of unity, as described above, which unites various particulars by focusing on small similarities and ignoring differences. The generalisation is Denmark in Africa (through a so-called common heritage), and the particulars are two different genres of maps, and two different periods, somehow coming together on part of a coastline. As such, the map is literally grounding the cultural encounters that the two coordinators wrote about then and now – what we see is Denmark in Africa in the past and in the present. In a double movement, the map illustrates the physical sites of the constructions once erected by the Danes on the Gold Coast and, at the same time, it shows the present-day interests of the Danish National Museum in Ghana. Via the dual map, the Danish buildings on the Gold Coast/Ghanaian soil are marked out as the historical and present sites of the cultural encounter. The Danish presence is illustrated both as an historical fact (Denmark built forts on the Gold Coast) and as a present-day reality now being located in Ghana as a geographical site. The interesting thing is that these two sites, illustrated by the duality of the places and times of the encounter between Danes and Africans, are depicted as nesting within each other. By focusing on a small similarity – Danish buildings in Africa – the dual map can be said to naturalise the National Museum's projects in Ghana via the geographically accurate map. The dual map becomes illustrative of a natural encounter with history, a common ground and illustration of the times when we shared the territories. If readers look at the geographically accurate map and then zoom in, they will find Denmark in Ghana in the form of Danish forts and plantations. And similarly, if readers look at the sketched map and zoom out, they will see an image of present-day Africa. But such movements demand an effort that is often neglected in its circular argumentation: the map shows where we are in order to show where we were, and vice versa – and it does not therefore matter from a Danish perspective whether it is the Gold Coast or Ghana, as long as the generalisation 'Denmark in Africa' is affirmed. Denmark may meet its history, but only as a strange timeless presence. And Ghana may be in Africa, but only as a host to Danish buildings and as a naturalised space with a river, a mountain and a capital. By collapsing time and space, the map seems out of proportion. The map thus naturalises the Danish presence in present-day Ghana, as if the only difference between the two elements of the dual map rested in zooming in and out. The map shows the 'same' from up close (the rough sketch) and from afar (the outline of Ghana and Africa), respectively. We are thus led to ignore the efforts invested in making such a presence seem natural – that it takes a certain effort to see the Danish forts and plantations in present-day Ghana. One could easily imagine many other things foregrounded – such as, for instance, the sites featured on the Ghanaian school children's map.[43] The result of the unproblematised dual map is that generative aspects of the encounter are ignored; when foregrounded on the geographically accurate map, it is obscured that common heritage, Denmark as former actor on the West African coast, Ghana as a site of plantation exploitation, and so on, all emerge from the making of the Frederiksgave project and from the way it is illustrated by the map. What appears is an obvious coming together of data, just as Linné's species had their natural position in the system of nature and were not seen as a result of classificatory efforts to make small similarities meet and neglect inherent differences. In effect, then, there *is* no encounter; all we have is a naturalised image of Denmark in Africa that we can either see close up or from afar, as if nothing had been foregrounded or backgrounded; the dual map shows only grounded common heritage then and now.

EXAMINING WHAT IS LEFT: 'DANISH TRACES'

In describing the interests of the Danish National Museum, a particular expression, namely that of 'Danish traces', gained a foothold among those involved in the Ghana Initiative. It was repeated over the years of the museum's involvement in Ghana. For example, even in 2006, in an article written by the Danish coordinator and the Danish archaeologist excavating the Frederiksgave site, the expression was used as a sub-headline stating 'Lots of Danish traces'. The sub-headline was followed by a description of several plantations and Danish forts.[44] It also appeared in a slightly different version as an image of 'walking in the Danes' footprints' – in Danish, footprints would be translated as 'foot-traces' – referring to present-day visits as a close re-walking of the former Danish forts and plantation sites.[45] The expression was solidified in a new initiative following the Frederiksgave project but still under the overarching Ghana Initiative, entitled 'Conservation of Danish Traces' – abbreviated in everyday speech to 'Danish Traces'. In line with the cartographic encounter, 'Danish Traces' framed and condensed, I will argue, the National Museum's interests in Ghana, and can be explored to further qualify the ideas of common heritage embedded in the museum's projects. After the completion of the Frederiksgave project, a group of people who had been involved announced that

> the museum looks forward to continuing, together with the Ghanaian partners, to communicate our common history, including to ensure that the physical traces, our common material cultural heritage, are preserved for the future.[46]

The ambition of the preliminary study into 'Danish Traces' was to obtain an overview of the Danish remnants in Ghana in order to support further applications for funds in Denmark. This was attempted through an architectural registration and description of all Danish physical structures in Ghana, concurrent with an historical search in various archives in Europe and Ghana for Danish traces regarding our common Danish-Ghanaian past. These works were accompanied by anthropological fieldwork at the various sites in Ghana in order to explore and collect knowledge from, and ensure the interests of, the people living in or close to the sites. I conducted this third part of the Danish Traces project, seeing it as an opportunity to further study collaboration and interest in common heritage. All three studies were conducted in order to advise people at the National Museum on the possibilities and relevance of renovating other sites, which might thus qualify for further funding. The project echoed an encyclopaedic ambition to trace, survey and collect information on all the physical Danish traces related to Ghana in the period up until the Danes officially left the coast in 1850. And it echoed an idea of specialists being sent out into the world to gather information upon which new actions could then be taken in offices back in Copenhagen. On a small scale, we were re-enacting the totalising knowledge-building ambitions of former European explorative scientists. Whereas the expansionist conquerors' ambition was, as Pratt brilliantly reminds us, to take over huge tracts of land, appropriate and control resources and civilise people, the European travelling scientists claimed no such transformative infringements. By tracking, observing and registering Danish traces through our knowledge-building project's 'descriptive apparatuses of natural history,'[47] we were creating 'a new kind of Euro-centic planetary consciousness'.[48] Pratt refers to this utopian descriptive scientific paradigm, both abstract and benign, as '*anti-conquest*'.[49] Essential to the notion of anti-conquest is the idea that description, often made with the observant eye, does not interfere with the world. Through a variety of techniques and tools, a removed observer carefully comes into being and systematises the world by way of description rather than conquest. I suggest that the National Museum's survey project, referred to as 'the least we can do', can be seen as such an anti-conquest – a benign non-interfering process of description. One might argue that, together with the museum's initiatives in the cold colonies, the mapping of the hot colonies created not a Euro-centric planetary consciousness, let alone a cosmopolitics,[50] but rather a nationally-centred one – a consciousness of all Danish traces spread over the planet. So, rather than teaching the Danish population about 'the cultures of the world, and their interdependence' as the Museum Act (§5) has it, the museum inverted the argument via its focus on the former Danish colonies. By this emphasis, the initiatives actually taught about Denmark in the world. The relation between a national focus and a universal history is seen as just a matter of having a particular starting point – a Danish contribution to history, a case or an event from which to begin filling in data on the given universal storyline. In this way 'nations' become an unquestionable, one might even say innocent, ordering of particular events.

With the Danish Traces project, the National Museum was not engaged in reconstruction work, as was the case with the Frederiksgave project, nor was it interested in taking over land, resources or people. The express idea with 'Danish Traces' was only to make pre-studies that could qualify applications for future initiatives, including reconstruction projects. The intention with 'Danish Traces' was to build knowledge in order to gain a complete idea of what the Danes had left behind. It was primarily a meticulously explorative and descriptive manoeuvre. With this all-encompassing ambition, the project went far beyond the small white icons on the map entitled 'Danish possessions', as indicated above. Several severely dilapidated former Danish plantations were traced, many only with a few stones remaining that could indicate a ground-plan. Merchant houses built by Danes in the neighbourhood close to the main Danish fort of Christiansborg in Accra were 'discovered', 'investigated', 'registered' and added to maps and lists. Archives in Ghana, Denmark, Germany and the UK were visited, and additional information and photos unearthed and, likewise, added to the expanding knowledge bank. These physical Danish traces on Ghanaian soil, partly illustrated on the map discussed above, were the *raison d'être* for the Danish National Museum's presence in Ghana. Or, to put it more precisely, the museum was present in Ghana in order to take care of (i.e. to collect, register, preserve, research and communicate – see the Museum Act §2) these Danish traces, since the Ghanaian nation lacked the money to do so. As 'wardens of civilization' (Athens Charter), or rather as 'wardens of the Danish nation', the museum followed the old international charters, taking on the task of caring for a 'common cultural heritage' for the future. By engaging in such a knowledge-building project, just like the former explorative scientists, the museum created a national consciousness (to be extended to the Ghanaians by way of capacity building, as we saw above), in this case particularly with regard to the outreach and influence of Danish history and heritage.

If the 'Danish Traces' project focused on surveying and describing what the Danes left behind, in what way did it fall within the overall ideology of cultural encounter? I will look closely at the specific making of these sites, and explore how they were turned into stories of 'our common past'. Following on from this, I shall explore some encounters at these particular sites – in these contact zones – and see how the encounters and the entities that take part in them are constituted.

A NON-ENCOUNTER IN THE MEETING ROOM

In an article written by most of the Danes involved in the Frederiksgave project, the sites of the cultural encounter and the consequences of the Danish influence were described in the following way:

> In addition to Danish toponyms and a long list of descendants with Danish family names, the Danes left six Danish forts, a long list of plantations and merchants' houses behind.[51]

Following on from this interest in the Danish influence and what the Danes left behind (which became the physical manifestations of the cultural encounter), I have met a good many people who have old Danish/German names such as Wulffs, Svanekiers, Lutterodts, Engmanns and Richters to name but a few, precisely because they are the descendants of former expatriate officials sent out by the Danish State. These descendants live in and/or own parts of family houses built by these expatriated ancestors who centuries ago established a family on the coast. Present-day Ghanaians with Danish/German names could literally be seen as the children of cultural encounters, understood in terms of nations. As such, they attracted a great deal of attention from the National Museum. The museum's attention was all the greater because these families owned the old houses that their expatriated forefathers had erected using Danish measurements, architecture and materials, meaning that the houses qualified as Danish traces. In this way, what was known among the Danes from the National Museum as 'Wulff's House' or 'Frederichs Minde',[52] as the founder W. J. Wulff called his house, was an obligatory stop on official visits from Denmark. In the area where the house is located, however, it was not recognised as Wulff's House but went under another family name. Employed by the National Museum to detect these family houses, I came to see how complex and contested they were as manifestations of cultural encounters.[53] Patrilineal inheritance down many generations had led to a proliferation of legal ownership of the houses to such an extent, I was told, that some of the Danish-built houses I visited now had over 200 formal owners, often spread all over the world.

Wulff's House was a special case for the National Museum since, according to the Danish architect, it was 'very authentic and well preserved'. Furthermore, it was situated on the road leading up to the former Danish fort of Christiansborg. Another recommendation of the house was that W. J. Wulff, its founder, had written a diary that was published in Denmark in 1917, and he was therefore well-known and read among interested Danes. The house, to the National Museum, provided a unique opportunity to meet with this semi-famous forefather. Over the years when the National Museum was engaged in the Frederiksgave project, interest in the house increased among people from the museum, culminating in an official visit in the autumn of 2008 by the museum's Head of Ethnographic Collections, the coordinator for the projects under the Ghana Initiative, and myself. Two years previously, I had joined the Director of the National Museum who, together with the Danish and Ghanaian coordinators and the people from the Danish fund granting money to the Frederiksgave project, had also visited the house. In 2008 we therefore knew that the people living in the house were happy to show their house to interested Danes. Their hospitality was always repaid with some money, discreetly passed to the person in charge of the visit. As arranged with the residents, we drove down 'Castle Drive' leading to

Christiansborg Castle, where the Presidential office is located, shortly before 10 a.m. one morning in 2008. In addition to Wulff's House, a number of other big old houses are majestically positioned along the eastern side of this road. They, or their backyards, form the border with the slum area of Osu. On the other side of 'Castle Drive', to the west, a vast green area leading up to 'Independence Square' forms a contrast to the densely populated slum area. Today it is a huge green lawn with an allotted area for small-scale farming – and patrolled by the military that guard the presidential offices in the castle. It was once a part of Osu village, but due to several bombings and fires, the last at the end of the nineteenth century when the British were forcing the inhabitants to pay taxes, the area had been left a wasteland. This sudden laying bare of a vast area generated many fantasies in the minds of archaeologists – maybe this huge area could be excavated, just as archaeologists had excavated a similar ground in Elmina.[54] In addition, a small old Danish cemetery built in connection with Christiansborg Castle takes up a part of the vast area. Together with other curious Danes, I have made several attempts to visit the cemetery. Because of its proximity to the presidential castle, however, it is not easy to gain access without special permission, and on several occasions we were chased away by the military pointing their guns at us.

On this late morning in November, the sun was already strong; the military were patrolling in the shade under the trees along the road. Our driver knew that, being so close to the presidential palace, he should not search too long for a place to park the car. Immediately after passing Wulff's House he therefore turned the four-wheel drive into a small, dusty, dilapidated space. On rubble, open drains and huge furrows in the red soil, he smoothly parked the car. Our small delegation from the Danish National Museum was received by three men. They welcomed us, guiding us into the main room on the first floor, apparently characteristic of Danish-built houses in the region. A fresh breeze constantly aired the room, and we soon cooled down. On several occasions the Danish architect had talked about his fascination with the skilled builders of the past, and the intelligent design built into the houses. With the right materials and construction skills, he explained, they had succeeded in making a house which, in contrast to houses built in Denmark, could resist the strong sun and, at the same time, be as cool as possible. And it certainly felt good to be in this centrally located large ventilated room, with its open windows and fluttering curtains. Indeed, the builders had taken the encounter with nature into consideration. Along the light blue walls covered with old pictures, sofas and big chairs were lined. Our host asked us to sit down, and our eyes immediately began to explore the room. The beamed ceiling, the boarded floor and the old framed photographs of descendants of W. J. Wulff all reminded us of why we were there. A formal presentation of all the people in the room followed, after which we were given a cold soda. A photo was passed around. It was from the 1980s, and revealed that a Danish minister had made it to the house – the photo provoked a smile from the Danes. To me, it was not just any minister but one that immediately took me back to demonstrations in the huge square in front of Christiansborg, the palace housing the Danish parliament in Copenhagen. Together with what seemed like all the Danish students and pupils in the country, I had demonstrated against his reforms and belted out satirical songs. But here in Wulff's House in Accra, close to another Christiansborg, we and the minister suddenly shared the same interest, as became apparent from the photo. Through the minor conjunction of being a Dane visiting descendants and their Danish constructed house in Africa, we created and participated in the same axiom of unity that could be formulated as a Danish interest in Danish physical traces in Ghana/Africa.

During the rather formal conversation, a representative from the Danish National Museum aired the idea of converting the house into a museum. The people receiving us seemed open to this idea. They showed us around the house while we pointed to beams, touched walls, investigated a painted door and window frames and gazed down from the balcony on the densely populated slum area to the east. As on previous visits, we ended in a dark room on the ground floor, in front of W. J. Wulff's grave. Before we had even seen the grave, all of us from the museum knew 'his story': that as a Jew he could not be buried in the Danish cemetery when he died in 1842. Instead, he followed local tradition and was buried in his house, albeit upright as Jewish tradition prescribes. We took pictures of the small quadratic grave, which was accompanied by the small rectangular grave of one of his children. Outside the room again, we mounted the staircase and took some group photos just as our Danish minister had done twenty years earlier. Finally, a person from the museum discreetly handed over some money to one of the Wulff family, upon which we walked off into the dusty road where our car was parked. The visit had seemingly been a success: our new leader from the museum had seen the house and, in a good atmosphere, he had aired the idea of converting the house into a museum. However, as we shall soon see, for the owners this was a 'non-encounter', i.e. a meeting that should not and could not generate anything new – it should simply re-enact a passive Danish interest in a Danish trace. A month later, back in Copenhagen, the Danish coordinator received a letter from a branch of the Wulff family's lawyer, which stated:

> We have been instructed that the purpose of your visit was to indicate your intention to have Frederichminde converted into a museum. It is our instruction to inform you that the […] family […] has at no point in time decided that Frederich Minde which has served as a family house for well over 150 years be converted into a museum. We hope you will be guided accordingly.[55]

Upon receiving this letter, the National Museum immediately dropped all their visions of turning the house into a museum; in Pratt's terminology, the National Museum had to retreat to anti-conquest – that is, from an active interest in the house to a passive registering and observing interest. As a physical manifestation of an encounter both in 2008 and in the past, the family house spurred different interests and complex notions of family ownership, together with ideas of continuity that were not of the same kind and not compatible with ideas of establishing a museum. A change in function from a lively and highly contested family house (due to its many owners) to a museum preserving and commemorating a Danish trace or common heritage, as desired by the Danish National Museum, was clearly not approved of. The owners of the house did not embrace the ideas of the people from the National Museum, a fact that once again shows the effort it takes to make (seemingly self-evident) generalisations about a common notion of the worth of heritage. The present-day cultural encounter between a huge family with Danish ancestry and a National Museum involved incompatible understandings of physicality and ownership. First of all one could say that the fluidity of the object[56] (the house) reached its limits in the encounter; in the eyes of the owners there was a limit to what the house could be – it should remain a family house even during and after profitable visits from Danish delegations. As the letter said, it was 'at no point in time' considered to convert it to something else. Nothing new was to come of the meeting in the eyes of those hosting it, although to the museum people from Denmark the house was potential common heritage and as such not restricted to the exclusive possession of formal owners. In the eyes of the visitors, the house was also owned by history, one might say – being an important trace belonging to a series of events. In the letter from the Wulff family's lawyer that followed the encounter in the house, however, formal ownership was asserted, whereby the Wulff family were reconstituted as united heirs, fully entitled to disregard the importance of the house as a contribution to a museum and/or Danish history. In other words, at this particular time, history could not be manifested as a museological trace through the family house, and the delegates from the National Museum did not have the power to assert the seemingly universal significance of the house. The object had reached its boundary, to paraphrase Griesemer and Star's article on boundary objects,[57] or perhaps different and colliding boundaries emerged in the remaking of a family house.

Furthermore, the encounter marked a legal difference in terms of continuous family ownership that was not easily overcome. One might say that the museum's ideas of commonness, where the house is in a sense history's possession, were incompatible with ideas of ownership. The idea of turning Wulff's House into a museum was based on the assumption that it was universally interesting as a common heritage site, but this time the Wulff family was practising an encounter with only one party, in that they were the owners. Such one-directionality or non-encounter has, as we have seen above, also characterised several of the museum's encounters in its aspirations to conserve our common past. My point here is that the case of Wulff's House points to the zones of awkward engagements in which the museum acted, and to the effort it takes to make and agree on an axiom of unity, which is never simply a given. Here, the small conjunction of being interested in Danish traces was what we from the National Museum and the Wulff family had in common – even if perhaps for different reasons and for a moment only. But other ideas of, for instance, turning the house into a museum of common interest did not work as a generalisation; the particulars of a museum and a family house could apparently not be filled into the same system.

LOOKING FOR HERITAGE: DISCOVERY OF THE ONCE FAMILIAR

As mentioned above, I myself was hired by the 'Danish Traces' project to track down other Danish-built houses in the area. Furthermore, I was to ascertain whether the places I found could potentially be turned into heritage sites, by engaging with the people living close by and listening to their knowledge, ideas and wishes in this regard, in recognition of the fact that heritage work takes place on someone's land.[58] Sometimes, together with a Danish architect (the same person who directed the reconstruction of the Frederiksgave plantation) and two Ghanaian architects, I would walk curiously around Osu, the slum area close to the former Danish main fort of Christiansborg. One of the Ghanaian architects was from the Ghana Museum and Monuments Board – the institution with responsibility for public heritage in Ghana. He had assisted the Danish architect during the Frederiksgave project, and had now been hired again to assist the Danish architect in detecting and investigating Danish traces. At times, he joined our tours around Osu along with the other Ghanaian architect. The other Ghanaian architect was born in the Osu area, and was hired as a consultant because of his expertise in the history of Osu. He was interested in the history of the family houses, and showed us several buildings with Danish traces. These tours of 'discovery' indeed awoke the interest and professional knowledge of the architects. Enthusiastically they shared their knowledge of old techniques, materials and styles, as they identified Danish traces such as paved yards; two-storey buildings; timberwork of German pine; thin, precious Flensborg bricks used to make symmetrical arches; local sandstone whitewashed with thin layers of lime, just as in Denmark at that time; doors, windows and beams erected according to old Danish measurements; dark rooms originally built to store goods but now inhabited by poor members of the families; hinges forged according to Danish tradition; and wells located in the central yard of the house, to mention just a few of the identifiable traces.

FIG. 2.3 An old well at a family house, 2008, Osu, Ghana.

Walking around the area gave me the opportunity to talk to residents, and when I asked about the owners of the houses on the streets, they mentioned names I could recognise in Danish. This information gave me clues as to where, through my techniques of tracing Danish names, I might find physical traces of Danes. In these complementary ways, we tracked down, visited and registered the Danish-built houses in the slum area, and carefully marked their positions on city maps. After the incident at Wulff's House, we were carefully instructed by the Danish coordinator not to visit the house again and, as far as possible, not to air or share any plans or ideas with the people we met in relation to our visits – and, most importantly, never to promise anything to anybody. At this stage, the local people, then, were to work only as repositories of knowledge guiding our non-interfering discoveries. Our work simply consisted of detecting the Danish traces and obtaining as much information about the sites as possible – it was an anti-conquest, and 'consisted of what in European culture counts as a purely passive experience – that of seeing'.[59]

Indeed, our role was in line with that of former European explorers travelling across Africa and reporting back to Europe on all the things they observed. Like our European forefathers, we were also sent out, this time not by kings or royal societies in order to discover the foreign land, but by the National Museum of Denmark to rediscover once familiar but long forgotten land. And, with the help of 'local inhabitants [...] [we] proceeded to discover what they already knew', to paraphrase Pratt's analysis of British explorers' attempts to 'discover' the source of the Nile.[60] This time it was not foreign land that was to be discovered, but sites that were once known and inhabited by our fellow countrymen, and until this moment forgotten by the Danish nation. And our 'local inhabitant' was a Ghanaian professor of architecture who had lived and worked for many years as an architect in Germany – and who was clearly not satisfied with being reduced to what he felt was a mere tourist guide, 'I am *not* a tourist guide,' he repeatedly told me, when I was handing over an agreement on his position in the project, written by people from the National Museum. More specifically, he did not like his knowledge being reduced to mere information for the Danish architect and myself about Danish traces in the Osu area. He stressed that he was a scholar and that he wanted to be an equal partner, and therefore also part of our final report. This demand posed a problem for myself and the other visitors from the National Museum. On the one hand, we really wanted engaged partners to collaborate with, and wanted 'the Ghanaians themselves' to come up with suggestions for future projects (as mentioned above, we had a chance of creating a common ground for the educated). But on the other hand we could not allow this professor into the work in the way he wished because, it was argued, 'it was too early in the process' – after all, we were still only observing, as we had done until recently every now and then in Wulff's House. What is at stake here is important for the general question of what collaboration in common heritage projects can entail; is commonness an add-on and an automatic result of already given entities meeting up to collaborate, once it is established what the shared heritage is and when and where it took place? Or might the very collaboration be allowed to make common heritage emerge along the way? This has a bearing on who the heritage makers are even thought to be, and as we have seen by now, the National Museum somehow cast history and the Danish buildings themselves as the non-interfering creators of common heritage. The encounter with heritage in the shape of Danish traces was thought of as a one-directional Danish meeting, so by referring to the innocent praxis of 'only seeing', the Ghanaian's expertise became reduced to simply being a matter of providing information. The professor, to the contrary, refused to be treated as a tourist guide, and insisted on an encounter whereby he could play a role in the reconstruction of heritage directly, unmediated by us. He ended up not wanting to sign any formal contract, but was instead paid for his 'acts of friendship' as he put it.

This was indeed a postcolonial setting (understood simply as 'after' the colonial period; both as a quality of specific regional settings and a marker of an epochal period), but it was also a setting that echoed how we, like our (pre-)colonial European explorative forefathers before us, were sent out to do preparatory work consisting of detecting, registering, surveying and collecting information by observing, measuring and talking to people in the area. Our work was to result in a professionally based prioritised list of potential projects which could then be used to inform decisions taken in Copenhagen by project managers and grant givers. Again we see the peculiar and paradoxical character of the National Museum's heritage initiatives in their concurrent emphasis on symmetry and universality: Ghanaian partners are sought after as collaborators, just as they are seen as an equal party to the symmetric cultural encounter and the encounter with our shared universal history, which has now taken all of us beyond colonialism. Yet the museum's supposedly neutral and objective design is self-fulfilling to the extent that it apparently comes as a surprise when these encounters are not smooth, as in the case of Wulff's house or in the instance with the Ghanaian professor above.

So, after a long day's work jumping over open drains and walking down narrow alleys in the crowded slum where few white people dared to go, we returned to our hotels where we washed off the dust. In our rooms, we meticulously transferred our measurements, observations and oral information gathered throughout the day onto maps and papers, and, as requested in our job description, ended our mission by writing up reports containing information about the Danish traces in

Ghana and offering ideas for potential future actions, as we saw them. With this information, the museum could qualify applications for new projects in Ghana.[61] Seeing or observing was understood as an innocent accumulation of 'data' that could support an encyclopaedic ambition to trace, survey and finally sum up information about all the physical Danish traces related to Ghana in the period up until the Danes officially left the coast in 1850 – 'a knowledge bank', as it was also called. With regard to the Linnéan botany, Tsing argues, 'The system itself was knowledge, not its component parts'.[62] Having found the universal system of Danes in Ghana once and for all, it was then just a matter of filling or collecting raw data into the system. However, this requires collaboration. The two encounters with the Wulff family, and the professor's refusal to be reduced to a tourist guide, indicate that, at times, 'particulars' refused to be filled into a story.

FREDERIKSGAVE: A CROSSING OF EUROPEAN STYLE AND LOCAL MATERIALS

During the preparations for the reconstruction of the Frederiksgave buildings, the Danish architect in charge was annoyed that even though he had visited several Danish archives, he could neither trace the identity of the original architect nor find any detailed plans of the buildings. Nevertheless, he saw many similarities between Frederiksgave and a number of official buildings of the time in Denmark, designed by the royal architect. With the help of a Danish historian hired as consultant to the Frederiksgave project, journals and letters in the Danish State archives indicated that it might have been a Danish mill-builder by the name of H. Grønberg, from the small Danish island of Bornholm, who was originally in charge of the reconstruction. In the same article that features the dual map, it says of the Frederiksgave main building,

> We do not know Frederiksgave's architect, but he has appreciated how to make use of advantages from two building traditions to create a beautiful crossing, suited to the hot and humid climate (…). The materials were local, but the shaping style was rigid empire just like the contemporary North European architecture.[63]

Just as the family houses and descendants of Danish men were seen as products of cultural encounters, this quotation suggests that the main building was a product of a cultural encounter – a 'beautiful crossing' between local materials and North European form. In the hands of the skilled anonymous architect, local materials were formed to the highest fashion of the time – a fashion which in spite of its out-datedness was still able to impress the authors of the article and – hopefully – future visitors. Rather than being a named person putting his subjective ideas into the building, the architect was more importantly seen as embodying a style also used by royal Danish architects of the time – rigid Northern European Empire – combined with a knowledge of tropical materials.

From this perspective, the Frederiksgave building was a successful encounter, a crossing between the entities of local materials and North European form that, interestingly, also seemed to aspire to universal aesthetics – in the sense of a style (Empire), once the mark of its time, but since then transformed into a style. The crossing is an encounter between these given entities: local materials and North European form; European culture meeting local African nature. The point is again that the African side of the encounter, in this understanding, is reduced to mere data – a particular tropical nature to be given form elsewhere, in the system of European aesthetics, by a skilled Danish architect. The beautiful crossing, as it is termed, becomes an apolitical encounter, out of which nothing new is generated except a replication of an already existing form. It is an encounter between the tropics, the climate and a Danish architect who, with skill and a sense of beauty, gives form (according to a style) to the building.

COMMON WORDS: ENCOUNTERS IN LANGUAGE AND ARCHAEOLOGY

While Frederiksgave was under reconstruction, I was able to participate in several guided tours when Danish delegations found their way to the reconstruction site. At these events, the Ghanaian archaeologist and coordinator, in collaboration with the Danish architect, would present excavated artefacts and explain about the reconstruction work. Both seemed to enjoy telling curious visitors about the site, and the visitors seemed similarly engaged. With potsherds, rusty cutlery and pieces of broken glass in his hands, the archaeologist would tell the visitors that, together with traditional African potsherds, they had found remnants of soup bowls made of porcelain. These European soup bowls were originally used in the main house, but had been found during the excavation of the slave village 400 meters down the road. 'This,' the Ghanaian archaeologist said with a smile to a delegation of Danes, 'indicates that the Africans did not eat European food, since we did not find potsherds of ordinary plates during the excavation of the slave village, only soup bowls'. 'Instead,' he added, still smiling, 'they needed soup plates or even bowls for their fufu and soup'. Having said this, he burst out laughing, and we all joined in. Fufu and soup is a Ghanaian dish invested with great national pride. Furthermore, food is an often-debated issue for many overseas visitors to Ghana. Many struggle with or at least worry about stomach problems, and the pasty lump of ground yams, plantain and/or coco yam that constitute fufu seems rather strange to many foreigners. Ghanaians have often asked me if I like fufu, and my positive answer makes them first of all laugh, then add 'Oh, you're a real Ghanaian, that's good'. They thus reveal some sort of contentment that I have accepted and taken pleasure in their national Ghanaian dish and, through this particular dish, internalised or taken part in a collective Ghanaianness.

In the situation with the potsherds, I suggest that the smile and laughter, together with the archaeologist's words, all point to this division in the understanding of food. This is a cultural encounter as understood by the two Danish coordinators of the hot colony initiatives from whom I quoted at the beginning of the chapter. Within this relativist logic, Ghanaian food is different to European food, although both are foods. The Ghanaian archaeologist's presentation points to a past in which European china could be used by 'the Africans', but only insofar as it fitted local food traditions. Implicit in the archaeologist's smile, words and choice of object is possibly an echo of a traditional postcolonial critique often heard in Ghana, namely that not everything brought by the Europeans was attractive and useful in a Ghanaian context – Ghanaians have their own traditions, not necessarily to be mixed with the ways of the 'strangers from the far north'. This was a criticism I often heard echoed in other contexts; for example, it was reflected in the idea put forward by the former government, 'of wearing traditional Ghanaian clothes every Friday in order to keep our traditions and culture' as a group of students at the university explained to me – a call that created ambiguous feelings among the students, who treasured their jeans and t-shirts. After showing us the broken pieces of the soup bowls, the Ghanaian archaeologist took the rusty cutlery and said that the influence of the Danes was still present since, in the local Ga language spoken in the region, a fork was still known as a *gaffel* – the Danish word for fork. The audience gasped. Then he added, 'and turkey is called *kalkun*' – the Danish word for the bird – and everybody chuckled. It was strange to be so far away from Denmark and hear a non-Dane – an African – pronounce two arbitrary Danish words and tell all of us Danes that these words were now part of an African language; obviously it called for laughter. The Danish words constituted audible proof of an old and until now forgotten encounter between Danes and an African ethnic group – the Ga people – that expatriate Danish officials mentioned in their reports, letters and diaries centuries ago as trading partners and owners of the land on which the main fort of Christiansborg was located. Now, so long afterwards, and having been almost forgotten by both the Danes and the people of the area, this old liaison was re-enacted. The Danish words showed that remnants of this liaison were woven into an African language. And insofar as language is often seen as a marker of a culture,[64] the shared words could be seen as a sign of 'a common past', and of a cultural encounter in which an element of Danish culture had gradually been integrated into the Ga culture. This was 'Denmark' from a local point of view, just as the two coordinators wanted. The shared words provided a kind of information about the consequences of the Danish presence now and before. The words therefore qualified (and legitimised) the museum's presence and project in Sesemi, the small village at the foot of Frederiksgave. The words were in themselves a cultural encounter in a rather tangible form (cutlery, plates and animals) – but seemingly also harmless and apolitical, apart from the slightly comical touch of postcolonial critique that might have been reflected in the archaeologist's smile when talking about the deep plates. I also found these shared words curious, and together with people from the National Museum I enthusiastically told other Danish visitors about these linguistic borrowings. If this was an instance of the wished-for attention to cultural encounters from a local perspective, one might ask whether the Ga people still living in the area knew of this liaison. Did they have any 'images' – to paraphrase the two coordinators – of the Danes who once were there? As far as I could tell from my own questioning of Ga-speaking people, these words did not evoke any 'images of strangers from the far north'. Rather, my claim to linguistic (co-)ownership of these words made the local people look at me quizzically, though they listened politely to my explanation. But my explanation did not create any dialogue; the information simply seemed unimportant to them. Being 'the same' – a *gaffel* is a *gaffel* – no encounter seemed to emerge, and no sense of commonness was produced from these linguistic borrowings. And neither did these particular stories of potential commonness resonate with any historical awareness, that had been stressed by the Danish museum director as decisive in the formation of personal identity. The cutlery, plates and animals were reduced to data that could, provided one wanted to make a working generalisation, be filled into an already given system comprising the symmetrical sets Danish culture/Danish language/European food and Ghanaian culture/Ga language/Ghanaian food. Paraphrasing Tsing, the axiom of unity was made up of a generalised idea of nation states, plus particular things such as cutlery, turkeys and forks. Importantly, it took an interest in the system to connect the data. Danish words in the Ga language did not change any idea of either the Ghanaian/local culture or the Danish nation – they just provided information on one entity being adopted by another culture. Although this was of interest to the National Museum, it was an interest that was not necessarily shared locally, the museum's wish to view the encounter from 'both perspectives' notwithstanding.

Information about Danish ancestors – the 'strangers from the far north', as framed by the two coordinators – was very sparse in Ghana. Instead, other concerns surfaced. Many of the people I talked to when visiting their often dilapidated family houses asked for money to renovate them. In general, the encounter between the people from the National Museum and the people living next door to the Danish traces made us appear as potential sponsors, or as development workers, and them as people with scarce resources. In this light, the Danes involved in the museum's projects became relevant as strangers from the far north, not so much in our capacity to inform about a shared past or as party to a symmetrical encounter, but as potential resources to improve lives, for example through tourism, better houses and jobs. We all had to get used to being seen as 'a pot of money', as the Danish coordinator said. Being objectified in this way felt strange; it was not our intention in being there. It was 'a side-effect' as it was often called by the Danes – a point I will return to particularly in Chapter Five. We saw our mission as first and foremost one of preserving a common cultural heritage, although we were not entirely unaware of the project's economic aspect. As stated by many of the Danes involved in the Frederiksgave project,

> Without being a development project, the collaboration between Sesemi, the University of Ghana and the National Museum in Denmark has lifted the area upwards economically, and it will most likely make Sesemi an obligatory point on the tourist maps produced by the Ghanaian tourist departments in the future.[65]

As we have seen, in the case of the Frederiksgave project the small conjunction necessary to contrive a generalisation was provided by small similarities that could fit into the general idea of a common heritage. As a consequence, other differences were backgrounded. For instance, our different financial situations and different priorities were things that some of the Danes in Ghana found difficult to confront. However, tourism could be seen as providing the foundations of a small conjunction, a space where we could agree to speak across difference; through tourism the villagers could be aided economically and the Danish interest in the common heritage could be maintained. Even though at its inception the Frederiksgave project was not explicitly intended to be of economic benefit to the present-day villagers, Danes and 'locals' could meet in this small conjunction. Tourism, it seemed, could be a place in which to unite otherwise different ideas, possibilities and wishes. Here we can see once again, as I also discussed in Chapter One, that the workings and consequences of a project cannot be exhausted in its design; differences will abound, but small and momentary conjunctions might make the project 'work'.

OBJECTS OF ENCOUNTERS: THE MUSEUM ACTS

Within this reading of heritage work in a relativist mode, the project site is figured as a setting where pre-given cultures meet and relate to each other. This relativistic understanding, I argue, restricts cultural encounters to an issue of folklore, of data that can be filled into predefined systems such as, for instance, Danish culture filled into Ghana, as the dual map illustrates. As I have suggested, this cultural relativism was paradoxically coupled with an appeal to universal history as something that people of all cultures share. In this particular version of heritage-making, a shared history was construed as an innocent instrument of the cultural encounter. The relativistic aspect could be seen in the projects' focus on linguistic borrowings, Danish buildings in Ghana, descendants of Danes, European style and Ghanaian materials. This particular information could be filled into and thereby help confirm the universally given history that was understood by some of the project planners as inherently valuable and necessary for identity making. But the National Museum's projects were not planned as nationalistic attempts to tell of a former Danish grandeur, as the party song mockingly indicates. As I see it, the projects are instead attempts to create a 'national global consciousness' – to inform the world objectively about Denmark, including its dark chapters (as they were often framed), such as Danish participation in the transatlantic slave trade and use of slave labour in plantations on the West African coast as these fitted into the timeline. This universal history was to be communicated in both Denmark and Ghana for the common good. The National Museum's initiative in Ghana was therefore seen as 'a helping hand' for the impoverished country. If nothing else, then a kind anti-conquest, i.e. observing, describing and surveying, was 'the least we can do'.

But a cultural encounter is not just a meeting between two given groups. An encounter implies friction, a contact zone where those involved are redefined and changed through exposure to the 'other'. Think only of how the letter from the Wulffs' lawyer defined the museum delegation as much as the owners of Wulff's House. My fieldwork provided ample opportunity to question the givenness of entities such as history and culture. By highlighting the effort it takes to create such generalisations and make them work, I foreground the very practice of collaboration and explore its role as generative of common heritage. As we have seen, the circular argument that makes axioms of unity appear self-evident was continuously interrupted during my fieldwork and analyses. Focusing attention on particular events and engagements in the here-and-now – such as the visit to Wulff's House, the displays of the dual map, the shared vocabulary and so on – makes it clear that it takes tremendous and often fraught effort to carve out Denmark in Ghana and our common past.

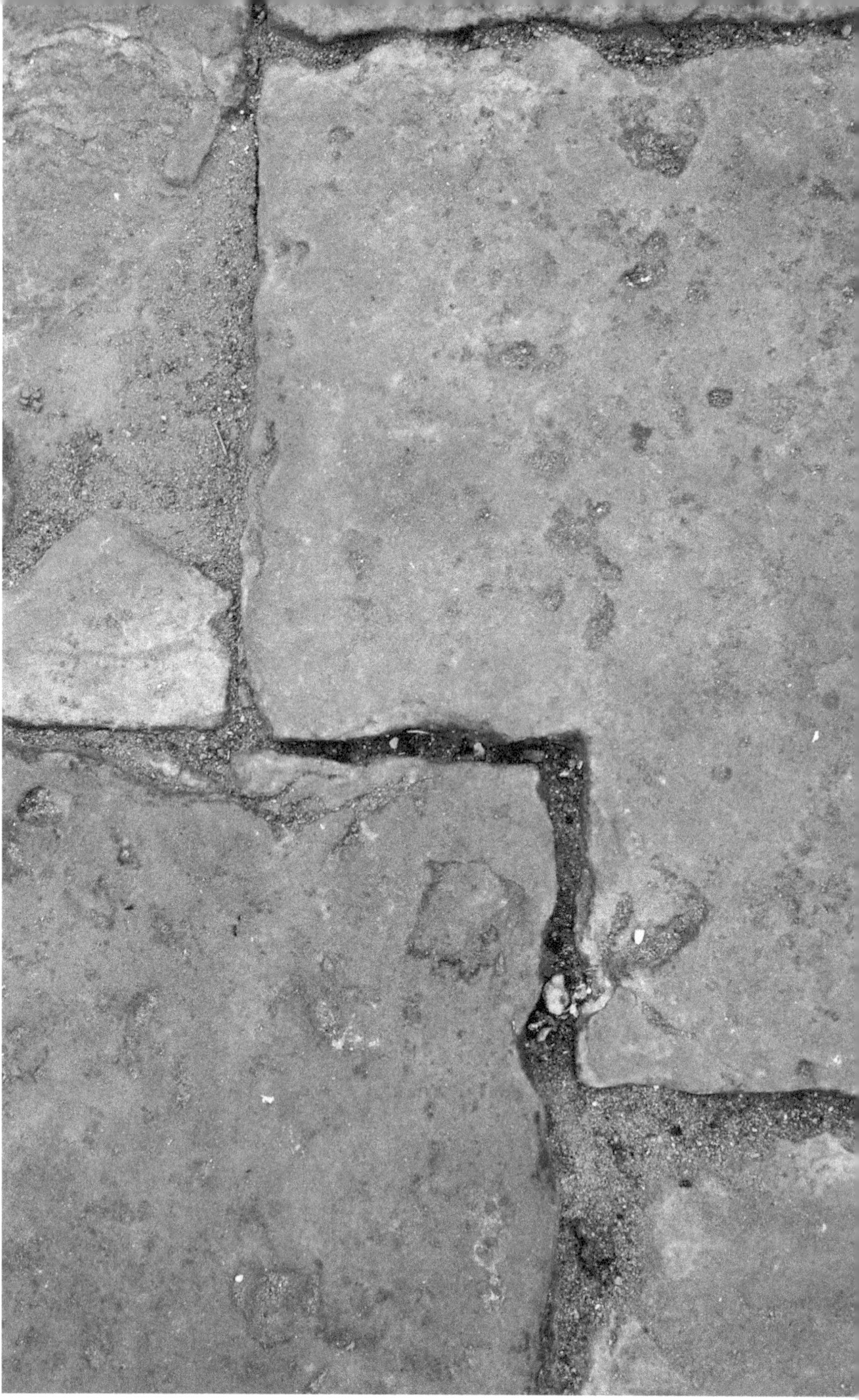

3

ALTERING HERITAGE THROUGH MIMESIS

STANDARDISATION AND ACCURACY

IN PARIS IN 1875, SEVENTEEN COUNTRIES, INCLUDING DENMARK, ACCEDED to the Treaty of the Metre, thereby taking the first steps to 'ensure world-wide unification of physical measurements', so that exactly the same measurements applied in Paris and Copenhagen.[1] More than a century later, the offspring of the Treaty, a foldable wooden ruler, was one of the most treasured tools used by a Danish architect working on the reconstruction of Frederiksgave. With the ruler in his hand the architect figured as a professional who measured, admired, touched and rebuilt the Frederiksgave buildings.

France had led the way in developing metrical standardisation, even holding the template of the metre – made from corrosion-resistant platinum – in its state archives. Like the newly invented stamps developed in Britain in 1840 for standardising the cost of global postage, the metre was a new global standard to aid travel and trade.[2] Key to both standardised stamps and the metric system are convertibility and accuracy. By folding out a ruler along, for instance, clothes, wood or iron, it becomes possible to convert the extension of the material into an accurate, repeatable standardised number, e.g. two metres. And, as Verran has shown in great detail, numbers are particularly well-suited to both producing and transgressing scales.[3] When it is expressed in an accurate and universally recognised number or measurement, a material is easier to sell and trade on a global market, where these standardised transformation systems are welcomed because of the efficiency and transparency that they allow. Measurement, in this mode, works to support and facilitate the trading of value.

To open up these transformation systems I need guides, and here I turn to a great thinker of translations: Bruno Latour. In an article entitled *Circulating Reference* (1999) on scientific knowledge production during a field trip to the Amazon, Latour describes how the so-called Munsell Code, one of the tools of the expedition, was used as a universal standard for arranging 'all the nuances of all the colors of the spectrum by assigning each a number'.[4] The assigned number is then, in turn, rendered understandable and the colour reproducible by all colourists in the world thanks to the Munsell Code. Latour describes one of the French scientists who participated in the field trip, standing there in the Amazon:

> Lost in Roraima, made so tragically local, he is able to become, through the intermediary of his code [the Munsell code], as global as it is possible for a human being to be. The unique color of this particular soil sample becomes a (relatively) universal number [...]. Though seemingly always out of reach, the threshold between local and global can now be crossed instantaneously.[5]

The Munsell Code, a catalogue of rough rigid paper with small holes above each colour and code, is all it takes to make this vertiginous movement between the local and the global, provided people are familiar with the code. Again, numbers are key performers in transgressing scales and localities. For those not initiated into the universe of the Munsell Code, however, the text in the form of black strokes will remain just that: black strokes on a piece of paper, or at best numbers appearing to have been randomly assembled. In other words, the globalisation of this universal colour code can be realised only through the proper use of a particular standard; as a universal, its global outreach lies embedded, its potential waiting to be activated by the knowledgeable user. The distribution and knowledge of this universal standard is therefore vital to its global existence – and thus to its efficiency as a universal standard.

In this chapter, I will explore relations between the present-day builders of the Common Heritage Site, the Frederiksgave building and particular concepts within heritage work as they are developed through the role and function of different tools. I suggest that the abovementioned ruler, alongside other 'scaling technologies' such as architectural models and geographical maps, made the construction of the Common Heritage Project possible in particular ways. Due to their accuracy, standardisation and interchangeability, the ruler, maps and models not only made possible travel from Denmark to Ghana, but also journeys between the past, present and future. In the previous chapter, I explored how the Frederiksgave project design envisioned the heritage site as a cultural encounter of common interest and universal historical value. Here I will investigate another phase of the project, and focus on the gradual physical reconstruction of the site as it materialised during my fieldwork; I thus explore the concrete production process that made the Common Heritage Site emerge. By focusing on how techniques, materials and intuition were enacted, I pay close attention to the physical emergence of 'our common heritage', culminating in the completion of the Frederiksgave Plantation and Common Heritage Site. I am interested in exploring questions such as how the notion of accuracy in reconstruction was related to ideas of authenticity, how ideas of an original or a model are at play in the design, what tools were at the reconstructors' disposal, and how these helped them bridge the gap between then and now, here and there.

AUTHENTICITY AND APPROXIMATION: CHARTING FREDERIKSGAVE BY THE RULER

Discussions about authenticity were central to the reconstruction work at Frederiksgave, as they have been in heritage literature generally.[6] Using accurate standardised measures attained with a ruler, a plan of what the main building at the plantation once looked like could be created, thus giving the reconstruction a certain degree of authenticity as a building as similar to the original as possible. And indeed, a great deal of energy was invested in reconstructing the site to its former design. First, the remains of the buildings were excavated by a small team of Danish and Ghanaian archaeologists. This was followed by detailed surveying and 'construction-archaeological investigations', as the Danish architect-in-charge called it. Fourteen Danish archives were searched, and people who had visited and photographed the site over the years were consulted.[7] For the exhibition that was to be displayed in the main building, a Danish historian from the University of Copenhagen, with expertise in the Danish establishments on the West African coast, was hired as a consultant to ensure that the exhibition remained consistent with the information found in the Danish archives. The National Museum of Denmark went to great lengths to make sure that the reconstruction and exhibition were in accordance with all known historical sources. In so doing, the museum was in concordance with various charters on heritage. The Venice Charter from 1964, in particular, was, as mentioned before, often referred to directly by people from the National Museum. This Charter states that:

> [n]o new construction, demolition or modification which would alter the relations of mass and colour must be allowed. [...]. It [restoration] must stop where conjecture begins, and in this case moreover any extra work which is indispensable must be distinct from the architectural composition and must bear a contemporary stamp. [...]. All reconstruction work should however be ruled out 'a priori'. Only anastylosis, that is to say, the reassembling of existing but dismembered parts can be permitted.[8]

The emphasis in the Charter on material authenticity contained in the idea of anastylosis is clear: no introduction of new materials can be allowed. The materials and the architectural composition together form the nexus around which heritage properly evolves, according to the Charter, and this heritage construction should ideally not alter what is left, at least not without clearly differentiating between what was found and what was subsequently added or altered. All of the charters on cultural heritage (Athens Charter, 1931; Venice Charter, 1964; UNESCO Convention, 1972) mention conservation and preservation as means of safeguarding structures and places of universal value for humankind. However, increased awareness of new and different ways of securing heritage meant that, during the 1980s, a growing critique of the universalising perspective of the Convention and charters led to the formulation of 'The Nara Document on Authenticity'. This document, drafted in 1994, problematises the narrow universalist understanding of authenticity enshrined in the former charters, by stating that it is not possible to base judgements of values and authenticity within fixed criteria. On the contrary, the respect due to all cultures requires that heritage properties must [be] considered and judged within the cultural contexts to which they belong.[9]

The Nara Document allows for a wider understanding of authenticity by stating that, instead of being based on 'fixed criteria', values and authenticity 'may include form and design, materials and substance, use and function, traditions and techniques, location and setting, and spirit and feeling, and other internal and external factors'.[10] With the Nara Document, authenticity is no longer limited to materials and architectural composition, but can equally be based on intangible forms – a principle that was further developed in the Convention for Safeguarding of the Intangible Cultural Heritage (2003). For instance, the Nara Document acknowledges Japanese ideas of authenticity based on ancient techniques handed down, rather than on specific original materials. The Nara Document thus introduces an idea of multiple understandings of authenticity.[11] I never heard the Nara Document mentioned during my fieldwork, where the other international charters focused on guidelines for material reconstruction took precedence. Nonetheless, the heritage workers I engaged with talked about and practised authenticity as a paradoxical figure exploding 'fixed criteria'; rhat is, as something to aspire to but also something unattainable. Searching, exploring, observing, enlarging, reinventing and refining techniques and information to 'get as close as possible to the original', as one person involved in the project put it, was a key theme. In this way, an ideal of authenticity still shaped the project and made the Frederiksgave site appear a genuine and serious heritage work to many of the people involved. Aspirations to authenticity were, in this way, both a premise and an ideal goal for the heritage work at the Frederiksgave site, and as such, it was not a theme I brought to the field. Discussions of authenticity were raised in a complex manner by the project participants, and the ambiguities woven into the very notion of authenticity were continually debated. A 'working notion' of authenticity – as both an aspiration for accuracy between original and reconstruction and as an intensive quality of reconstruction work, as copying and creating anew – emerged in the process of erecting the buildings step by step.

Critiques of authenticity as universal and pre-given have been raised forcefully by Richard Handler and Eric Gable.[12] Much as I appreciate their observation that truth in heritage work is socially produced rather than found, I think there is a need to extend this finding beyond the discursive realm to the materials involved in reconstruction. In the case of Frederiksgave it is not enough to state that the aspiration for authenticity is a social construct – in particular ways at the site, it becomes an interesting material construct too. Jones has called for a view of authenticity in heritage work as a combination of materialist and constructionist approaches,[13] and as we shall see in the following, there is good reason not to consider these approaches separate and discrete: the materials, tools, techniques and practices involved in remaking Frederiksgave resist such dichotomies. The real and constructed character of Frederiksgave is thus a premise for beginning to explore the ways in which the project makers engaged with authenticity, and the means by which authenticity, as a concept, participated in bringing particular enactments of a common heritage to life.

A fatigue with merely stating that life is constructed has long been the concern of many Science and Technology Studies (STS) scholars and anthropologists. Among them is Michael Taussig, whose book *Mimesis and Alterity* (1993) has greatly inspired my exploration of cultural heritage in relation to the Frederiksgave project's aspirations to authenticity. Seeing socio-material reconstruction as an opening rather than a conclusion, Taussig suggests exploring 'the mimetic faculty',[14] i.e. 'the nature that culture uses to create second nature, the faculty to copy, imitate, make models, explore difference, yield into and become Other'.[15] Somewhat counterintuitively, the mimetic faculty is not just a matter of making exact copies – it is also a matter of othering, of exploring difference – 'a compulsion to become the Other'.[16] Inspired by J. G. Frazer's idea of sympathetic magic, where the copy or part draws its power and character from the original or whole[17], Taussig questions the external separation between representations and what is represented, by arguing that there is a sensuous relation between the two. With its sensuousness, mimesis creates and explores difference, but not as an outward relation to the material world, not as something added on to it. Therefore, Taussig suggests, much analytical vitality can be gained from looking into the very act of mimesis:

in imitating we will find distance from the imitated and hence gain some release from the suffocating hold of 'constructionism' no less than the dreadfully passive view of nature it upholds.[18]

Whereas the distance between signifier and signified is an external arbitrary relation, the distance in mimesis is internal, through its sensuousness. In recognising the distance between the thing and the thing imitated as internal sensuousness, we can be released from constructionism and the way that it detaches us from a passive material world. In relation to the Common Heritage Project, instead of merely stating that constructions with aspirations to authenticity are taking place, we might thus ask *how* is it being done? What is involved in this mimetic work where the copy (the reconstruction) relates sensuously to the original? How were imitations or aspirations to authenticity accomplished in the reconstruction work? These sorts of questions also imply the potential for working with and through analysis in imagining new futures[19] or, in Verran's wording, for provoking 'postcolonial moments'.[20] In this vein Taussig impatiently asks, 'Why don't we start inventing?'[21]

Taking this exhortation as my cue, I want to explore some of the tools, such as the ruler, architectural drawings and illustrations, that were involved in the reconstruction of the Frederiksgave site. These tools were more than just instruments applied externally in order to animate a dead original; the tools shaped and were shaped by the world they measured or were related to in various ways. Following Taussig, I do not want to end my analysis by simply stating that the recreation of the Frederiksgave site was actually a creation, and assuming that the materials or tools were given entities external to each other. My ambition here is to leave behind 'a foundationist'[22] way of thinking whereby the world is understood as something 'out there' to be reached by either relative representational signs or by universal given codes (as unpacked at length in the previous chapter). The overall point is to see my analysis as a generative and co-creative engagement with the object, offering new and qualifying perspectives on heritage. I will start this co-invention by returning to the ruler and exploring its role in the project more thoroughly.

PREDICTIONS AND SCALES: EMBODIED MEASUREMENTS

When it was not lying unfolded on irregular rocks or wood, the ruler was always sitting in its own specially designed pocket in the working trousers of the Danish architect at the Frederiksgave reconstruction site. It was his personal possession, never to be borrowed and only to be broken (if at all) by the architect himself, as he once confided to me. As his possession, it was a part of him and his professionalism. As a sort of 'prosthesis' in the sense presented by Strathern, one could say that the ruler was a part of his architectural training, although there was never a complete merging between him and it.[23] Instead, with the ruler in his hand he was transposed into a certain kind of architectural profession – a profession that was both more and less than him, and also the other way round: a man who was both more and less than a profession. The architect's ruler was nailed together ingeniously to allow for the movement of endlessly folding and unfolding the twelve wooden parts that covered two metres when fully extended. The ruler also possessed another rare feature: it had an old Danish standard, Danish inches, inscribed on the one side, and the international metric standard on the other. Old Danish standards, the architect told me, were all based on the proportions of the Danish human body, or on agriculture at a particular point in time. But on this ruler, the old Danish standards were based on a standardised 'Danish body' and had apparently been used by the Danes to built forts and houses on the West African coast. The difference between the two standards – the Danish inches and the metric system – could be seen as one between dimensioning and measuring, according either to the human body or the body of the earth. Briefly described, the metric system grew out of ambitions to replace the relativised bodily measurements that had been regional standards all over Europe since the Middle Ages.[24] Instead of the regional bodily measurements (e.g. an inch, a foot, an ell – which varied from place to place), a universal unit, the metre, based on theoretical mathematics, was developed by French mathematicians in the late eighteenth century. At some point the metre was defined as being based on the

> distance from the North Pole to the Equator, along the meridian of the Earth running near Dunkirk in France and Barcelona, in Spain. Geometrically it was

one ten millionth of a quadrant of the Earth's surface – clearly a theoretical mathematical measure, founded on the physical body Earth.[25]

With further technological developments, this definition of the metre has been replaced by more precise measures, such as wavelengths in a vacuum or the speed of light. Length in the metric system thus no longer refers to a body but to an interval of time.[26] Interestingly, it seems as if standard measurements have followed a path that began with a template – a stable Vitruvian man – but then shifted over to an even more unchangeable and stable earth, and then onto a moving particle – a ray of light. If so, (increased) accuracy does not follow from stability but rather from movement.

Back in the village of Sesemi, with a simple gesture of the ruler in his skilled hands, the Danish architect could swap between these different measures – metres and old Danish standards. Enfolded in the architect's treasured tool were the human body, the body of the earth and the speed of light. In this very concrete way, we might say that 'an other' is always present in the ruler. With regard to its non-absolutist character, the ruler can be seen as a spatial version of the rather culturally relativistic Nara Document. By avoiding any notion of *the* only right way to measure by way of a universal metre, or *the* only way to maintain heritage authentically through fixed criteria, they both entail an idea of movement and of an 'other'. At the reconstruction site, it was obvious that the ruler was vital in the process of reconstruction. The Danish architect told me that by measuring with the ruler he could 'predict' the positions of some of the original walls, corners and steps of the ruin. Prediction might seem a peculiar term to use when it comes to reconstructing something from the past. The question of how one can predict the past points to a central and paradoxical figure in the project. Prediction in a reconstruction heritage project contains an idea of an as-yet-not-existing-former-construction to be actively created by an architect, and which at the same time appears as something that is already there and is now lying passively ready to be decoded and uncovered. In other words, with the aid of the ruler, the architect simultaneously creates the buildings as they once were and imitates them as if they were already there. The surveying done with the ruler, then, is both a matter of creation (of a new building) and imitation (of what was once there). This paradoxical or mimetic figure of both prediction and decoding contained in the ruler was of great importance in the reconstruction work. One could say that in a dual movement the ruler is both carrying a scale to be applied (the metre scale) and scaling *itself*, in that it is a perspective that creates the Frederiksgave site in particular ways that live up to the standards of international heritage. It is both copy and invention.

The stock of buildings that comprised Frederiksgave was designed using the old Danish standards. During the actual reconstruction work, the Danish architect opted to convert the old Danish standards into presumably more universal units, namely centimetres, metres and the UK standard of inches, because, as he later told me, 'that was the only thing that made sense down here'. At one point, while excavating and surveying the buildings of the former plantation, he enthusiastically explained to me the way in which he had found the 'original' thickness of a wall by removing the eroded material:

> It was very exciting, and what made us decide that it actually was the thickness of the foot of the wall, of course because we measured it, right, because that was the most true, the most true surveying one could make down there, that was, it fitted when we measured in centimetres and then turned around the ruler. I'm always carrying a ruler that has centimetres on one side and Danish inches on the other side. Whenever we turned the ruler it clearly fitted the Danish inches, every time, no matter what we measured, lengths of holes for the windows, for the doors, thickness of external and internal walls, the pillars [...]. It clearly fitted inch for inch. It was not like [...] twelve and three quarter inches, it was twelve inches and fourteen inches, perfectly precise. It was a huge joy and such a delight to receive such a message from the people who once built it. Of course they measured in inches, in Danish inches and feet and ell.

Again, mimesis could be seen to be a central feature of the reconstruction work. The architect could, through the use of former Danish measuring standards, imitate the gestures of the original builders, and the 'messages' that the architect talked about ran along these mimetic lines. By imitating the previous builder, probably a Danish miller named H. Grønberg, and his measuring standards, the architect could receive the messages sent to him – just as with the Munsell Code, where users have to know the code in order to use it. Only thus does a code become efficient; only then does it become a tool for mimesis. This ability to receive and understand the dispositions of the past seemed to move the architect emotionally. By imitating past builders, the ruler somehow collapsed the gap in time between then and now, acting as a sort of time machine that, by means of the enumerated inches and yards extended and inscribed on a wooden stick, took the architect back to the 1830s. By bringing a standardised 'Danish body' to Ghana, the ruler also collapsed the gap in space between here and there – between Ghana and Denmark. The 'admission ticket' or requirement for such travel in time and space is precisely this wooden stick, as well as a familiarity with length as one single stretch making up a unity of extension – a familiarity which is not a given, as Verran has shown in her description of different ways of measuring lengths in Yoruba classrooms.[27] In this sense, the ruler as used by the Danish architect was not only an instrument for measuring spatial extension, but also folded up time along an extended timeline, thus connecting him to fellow Danish professionals from an earlier period. The old instrument allowed for pursuing 'moments of bodily and temporal resonance'.[28]

The excitement the architect expressed about precision and regularity was remarkable. He was elated by the fact that, every time, the measurements fitted clearly; they were not random, but exuded accuracy. Interestingly, it seemed that the better the imitation, i.e. the more precise and in agreement the ruler was with old Danish measurements, the shorter the gap in time appeared to be between the original Danish builders and the present-day architect. This accuracy was, on the one hand, a sign of a frictionless and compatible translation between then and now, here and there, made possible by the ruler. As such, it was an aspiration to achieve an exact copy, an imitation without difference. On the other hand, as argued above, the mimetic faculty is never without difference. So while the accuracy implied in the fact that the measurements fitted clearly every time collapses a relation between then and now, here and there – in the act of making an exact copy – the relation also seems to produce differences. An example is the 'messages' from the past that the Danish architect received from the old builders: these were both similar to the knowledge of the Danish architect (they were all professionals using a specific professional tool to construct houses) and different (they were different people living in different times). The ruler, in this sense, embodies and enables travel across differences in time and space. It works like a magic wand.

THE MAGIC OF MIMESIS: ACTS OF DISPLACEMENT

Taussig suggests that *'to give an example, to instantiate, to be concrete,* are all examples of the magic of mimesis' – whereby the copy gains power from the imitated.[29] He asks 'does not the magical power of this embodying inhere in the fact that in reading such examples we are thereby lifted out of ourselves into those images?'[30] To me, there is something very interesting about this 'lifted out' movement, and in the idea that images worked out in examples, instantiations or concretisations have the power to lift out the reader. Let us return to the architect and his beloved instrument, the ruler. By using the old Danish inches, the architect could imitate what the original builder supposedly had in mind. How might this be a case of 'the magic of mimesis'? My point here is to argue that by way of the ruler, the architect was 'lifted' into a professional community of architects, sharing, among other things, precision in construction work according to recognisable standards. Like the Munsell Code, the ruler could be said to function perhaps not so much as a universal code whereby local and global can be transgressed instantaneously, but as a national code that has the ability to 'lift' people with the right skills 'out' of themselves and transgress the past (1830s) and present (2000s), and Denmark and Ghana, instantaneously.

I like to think of the movement of being lifted out of oneself as an act of *displacement*.[31] Displacement, like its synonym, 'transposing', is a term related to 'transformation', which refers to the change and instability of whatever is subject to it: 'things' change during transformation.[32] The architect, or what seems to be the orchestrated assemblage of architectural professionalism and experience, sensitivity, eroded soil, stone, ruler, are momentarily displaced and transformed into an old Danish builder community. By imitating, learning and taking part in their actions and habits, the architect is reconfigured and transformed into something 'other'. Through encounters with former colleagues and environments, the architect emerges anew – as a conservational architect with knowledge of Danish construction work close to the equator in the 1830s. The encounter might thus be seen as an instance of Tsing's awkward engagement; the architects and assemblage of involved things are the same then as now, yet they are also *not* the same, and this makes the encounter something to be worked on in the here-and-now rather than through a meeting of given entities (see Chapter Two). Through mimetic gestures, the architect has participated both in the past – by using old techniques, among other things – and in the present-day reconstruction; he is transformed, and may never look at a Danish or Ghanaian official building from the beginning of the 1800s again without the experience of this particular encounter, one that now structures and transforms his mind, senses and movements. The architect's excited curiosity about the former builder and the original site, I would suggest, can be seen as an instance of the magic of mimesis, a magic that only works when there is an acceptance of a certain way of guaranteeing authenticity – through replication.

CONVERTIBILITY OF STANDARDS: IN AWKWARD HANDS

Delight in the accuracy obtained via the ruler and the drawings it engendered was something I often came across during my fieldwork. During my years of coming to Ghana, I have accompanied several Danish architects, and I soon learned the central importance of the basic activity of measuring. The people from the Danish National Museum wanted to measure all the Danish traces that were severely threatened by decay; that was what seemed to be 'the least we can do' regarding the buildings once constructed by Danes along the former Gold Coast. I shared the architect's fascination with the ruler. Often the architect in charge of the reconstruction project and I could be found folding out the ruler along our bodies, chairs or along buildings we were passing, just to compare whatever was at hand with old Danish measuring standards. Walking around a neighbourhood close to the former Danish Fort of Christiansborg in Accra, we identified old Danish-built houses by stretching out the ruler along the walls.

Most of these houses were originally built using Danish inches, feet and ell. Such 'discoveries' excited us both. More than 150 years ago, builders had brought their treasured instruments, along with a few other personal belongings, on ships from Denmark. Just as we were doing now, they had stretched out their rulers, first to survey the proportions of the houses, and later to build and check if the constructions were in accordance with their measurements. With great enthusiasm, we imitated these gestures by measuring houses according to these old Danish standards. Walking around with the ruler, we found and measured a particular standardised Danish body in Ghana through these old Danish standards. The mimetic gesture confirmed and substantiated our actions and reasons for being exactly where we were – in the former 'Danish village', as Osu, the part of Accra situated next to the former Danish main fort of Christiansborg, was once called. The ruler thus allowed for a bodily retelling, but it was also the pivotal point or the mirror in which mimesis worked. It formed a connection between a national standard of measurement and the time this standard was in use. In other words, it opened up a space for further exploration of differences and similarities – relations in both time and space.

Mimesis can confuse and blur any attempt to identify a primary cause or origin.[33] Did the house imitate the ruler or was the ruler imitating the house? And what precisely were we imitating? At first glance, we were miming measurements: old Danish inches, showing for example, a foot as a foot. But we were also imitating the original builders' gestures of measuring, by interweaving our more or less well-trained hands and eyes with the ruler and with the cues given by parts of present-day houses. Mimesis, then, was our way of understanding the relation between tool (the ruler) and building through measures that showed our heritage to be at once the same as then yet also different. My point here is that if one experiences the magic of mimesis then the ruler and the house are converted into each other through a series of translations; the magic is one of imitating and altering by the same gestures.

The ruler, then, both closed and maintained the gap in time between the 1830s and the 2000s, between the old standards and apparently global metric units. It also both closed and upheld the gap between Ghana and Denmark, by creating Danish-built houses in Ghana, and by taking us back to the original

Danish builders' measuring and building practices. In all senses of the word, we were moved by the ruler. Given this fascinating capacity of the magic wand enfolded in the ruler, one might wonder why the ruler was only found in the hands of the Danish architect. The Danish architect had initially given a ruler to each worker at the site as part of 'a training process'. However, during my fieldwork I did not see one worker using his ruler at the reconstruction site. The only person attached to the tool – as we often jokingly pointed out – was the Danish architect himself. It thus seemed as if the only people who were fascinated by the old measurements and questions of accuracy and regularity, and who joyfully immersed themselves in this kind of mimesis, were the Danish architect and other initiated Danish visitors, myself included. The rulers given to the workers were in metric units, and when I asked why nobody else involved in the project was working in Danish inches the architect replied,

> Architect: No, Danish inches don't make sense.
>
> Nathalia: But they do in relation to the building.
>
> Architect: No, but then I do not have any measuring tools for my people [the Ghanaian workers on the project], unfortunately they are not produced any longer, the rulers with Danish inches [...]. They [the Ghanaian workers on the project] work in English inches, they all do. By the way, they mix up millimetres, feet and inches and yards and meters, and sometimes you really have to pay attention when talking about a certain length. And sometimes it can be a bit thrilling if I have to take a measurement with one of the workers, [...] their hands [start] shaking because they then have to read the ruler, and it takes them a long time and then what they sometimes come up with is really wild. For instance, if it was [...] eighteen meters and ten centimeters, they would say 'one hundred and eighty one meters', and then I would have to figure out what they meant [...]. I also learned a lot from this, in that way I have also learned a lot, you know.
>
> Nathalia: What did you learn?
>
> Architect: A humility that one should not expect too much, but on the other hand, one should make some demands, right, and it's always a balancing

act. By the way, it's the same story in Denmark, but there it goes for other things, because every Danish workman can of course read a ruler or a centimeter ruler, right. But it is not, clearly not, something to be taken for granted down here, not at all, absolutely not at all.

In contrast to the Danish architect, the Ghanaian project workers did not immediately see the point of having been given a ruler. It seemed they lacked the requirements, and possibly the interest, to imitate and make the journey in time by way of the ruler. Furthermore the potential standardisation of measures was not recognised, whereby, of course, it shows itself to be but one standard among many. Like the Munsell Code, the referentiality of the ruler becomes important and obvious when in use; indeed, that is when it becomes clear that it is a self-maintaining 'circulating reference'.[34] Apparently the Ghanaian workers had had no similar experiences of 'thereness' – for example, of experiences with small official buildings in the countryside in Denmark – that might help them travel in space. Altogether, these sorts of mimetic relations simply did not make sense to the Ghanaian workers. Instead, it seemed to make them insecure, causing them to mix up metres with millimetres and inches, feet and yards. One might say that the mimetic gesture obtained via the folding ruler did not work for them – instead it only produced differences. The humility and low expectations that the architect mentioned express the challenge he faced as the architect-in-charge of the reconstruction project in Frederiksgave. Together with a group of predominantly unskilled workers, he had to rebuild a former Danish ruin, following standards that were more or less unfamiliar to his crew of workers. Needless to say, different skills follow from different experiences of measurement. The abovementioned tension between the architect and his men arose, I suggest, when they did not agree on the similarities and differences at play in the reconstruction project. To the Danish architect, similarity was expressed as a matter of neutral translation offered by the ruler. But as the shaking hands expressed, difference was also produced. Translation is not just about a frictionless transformation of one thing into another, and neither it is just about similarities: clearly, it is also about maintaining differences.[35] Pure similarity in translation – or in imitation, I might add – is unattainable. This is why mimesis is the capacity to become other. The shaking hands and jokes with the ruler point to all these differences and ambiguities; but it is also all these differences that make the architect's experience and project different from those of the Ghanaian workers. The humility that the Danish architect spoke of, the nervous shaking of hands and jokes with the ruler seem to me to manifest a set of awkward relations produced by the ruler. For all its precision, standardisation and alleged objectivity, to make use of the ruler required a whole range of mimetic gestures, of magic translations between differences and similarities, of which the actors were aware, and which turned it into a much more ambiguous artefact; the ruler paradoxically produced differences in time and space, created unease and tension, at the same time as it was meant to be producing an accurate and universal common understanding.

MODELS AND DRAWINGS: SCALING UP AND DOWN

During the reconstruction of the Common Heritage Site, the ruler also played roles other than causing hands to shake and spurring humility in a trained architect. Through processes of numerically scaling up and down, the ruler could survey the dilapidated building and transform it into models on pieces of paper. Surveying a building means recording all positions in the built material. Strings are carefully suspended between several points on the building site, making it look like a large-scale graph paper, as the Danish architect explained to me. Through a process of numerically scaling down, the enumerated lengths are then converted into an architectural drawing. The more detailed the survey, the better, the architect said. He added that when building the huge European cathedrals of the Middle Ages, the builders had made 1:1 models of parts of the constructions. At the Frederiksgave site, he had primarily used a 1:50 model, which was a scale he liked to work with when building houses. Whereas a 1:1 model made in a material other than the building materials creates a physical form to be likened to the building, the 1:50 model produces other perspectives. The forms and points of the dilapidated structures at the Frederiksgave site were transformed into scaled down versions on paper: architectural drawings.

These architectural drawings or models on paper were treasured by the architect, who made several drawings of the group of houses at the Frederiksgave site, of each house and of details from each house. His detailed surveying of the ruin was turned into elegant architectural drawings of the main house as it had once looked, while also predicting what it would look like when the reconstruction was finished. The architectural drawings were taken back and forth every day between the site and the house where the Danish architect lived when in Ghana. Upon arrival at the Frederiksgave site in the morning, one of the workers would take three wooden stools out of the tool shed and place them around a table in the open shed. We each had our assigned seat around the working table because, as the Danish architect explained to me, it is important to have routines and rituals at a work site. These rituals seemed more important to the Danish architect than to his Ghanaian colleague and myself, who swapped stools whenever it seemed convenient. From his vantage point in the shed, the Danish architect could see the buildings and the way the reconstruction was developing. The wooden stool on the left side of the table provided him with a stable position from where he could follow the progress of the building and compare changes (differences) between his drawings and the physical building. If making generalisations is a matter of focusing on small conjunctures and ignoring other differences, as discussed in Chapter Two, the architect's assigned seat afforded him a way to momentarily carve out and cut away (all) other perspectives in order to maintain a single one – here, accuracy was certainly located in an exact and stable position. From this position the architect took on the role of creator, but without abandoning his aspiration to make an accurate copy – a reconstruction. The dual position of the architect is apparent: from his fixed point his 'creation' becomes complicated by his aspiration to make an exact copy of what was there. This is a copy with no perspectives, or just the neutral perspective of history. To paraphrase Verran, it is simply telling things the way they are.[36]

Every morning the Danish architect would place his briefcase on the table and, depending on the programme for the day, we would look at plans, maps and sketches. Sitting in the shade with a nice flat table as support, he would unfold the drawings and together we would study the ground-plan of the building, or the façade, or a detail of the building that he had made. The scaled down models on paper of, for example, a ground-plan based on the detailed surveying of the ruined building, gave us an opportunity to view the building from above, a perspective that was quite different from walking in the burning sun on the uneven ground inside or around the ruin. As Lévi-Strauss also notes in a commentary on art *qua* plastic or graphic transformations, all scale models imply that some of the object's dimensions are lost, for example, in paintings the fullness, the smell, the tactile inputs.[37] Humans, Lévi-Strauss argues, are inclined to perceive an object by perceiving parts of it as a way of overcoming the danger that the whole object might impose on us.[38] With scale models it is different. The 'reduction' of sizing down the object in a scaled down model, and the cutting away of some of the dimensions, entails that

> Being smaller, the object as a whole seems less formidable. By being quantitatively diminished, it seems to us qualitatively simplified. More exactly, this quantitative transposition extends and diversifies our power over a homologue of the thing, and by means of it the latter can be grasped, assessed and apprehended at a glance.[39]

Mastering the object comes, according to Lévi-Strauss, from our ability to control its size. When it comes to scale models, he argues, the perception of the total precedes the perception of the parts.[40]

It is interesting to note that the construction drawings for the huge cathedrals of thirteenth- and fourteenth-century Europe did not 'show anything in its totality, providing only partial views or at best particular elevations [i.e. drawings of the façades]'.[41] This lack of totalities in architectural drawings from the Middle Ages might, in Lévi-Strauss' terms, lead us to perceive builders of that time not as artists trying to control what they saw by way of scale models of totalities, but as people trying to control the building via detailed models of parts. This could, of course, partly be due to the time span involved in these constructions, which often took centuries to complete, and therefore involved many generations of professional builders. Each builder was in charge only of what he could build; that is, a particular part of the cathedral. From another perspective, these parts might be wholes; for instance, a whole statue, arch and/ or a whole life's work. Turnbull notes that this kind of architecture did not follow any predetermined course, and that throughout a cathedral's development there was no masterplan, no immanent need; instead, it was an irreversible process that turned accident into necessity.[42] In these construction processes there was no frictionless reversibility between part and whole, and scaling up and down was not a matter of numerical sizing.

The Frederiksgave reconstruction seemed to be characterised by an opposite move: accidents were avoided by plans and images of the whole – a drawn whole that was rather quickly produced after surveying the building. This seemed to follow Lévi-Strauss' argument that the scaled down model was easier to control; the 'whole' could be mastered on paper, and accidents thus avoided. The reconstruction evolved bit by bit over the months, all the time relating to a whole – the buildings in their totality as figured out on paper – as it once had been. Accidents that would interfere with the copying of the whole building from then to now were eliminated as far as possible. Only through necessity and knowledge of its past form can a future form emerge and the buildings qualify as authentic cultural heritage. The complete buildings of the past, as a whole, become the goal of the future to be achieved through a meticulous knowledge of parts and the elimination of accidents in the present. Even accidents, though, had been planned for in the overall project design as contingent expenditure; they had a budget line and in the architect's report they were mentioned as 'delays', covering issues such as 'weather', 'shortage of materials', 'forgetfulness', 'visits' and 'absenteeism'.[43] As described in Chapter One, projects appear as wholes, so by calculating delays, accidents were recorded and could in this way be controlled, making the Frederiksgave project appear as a whole – a whole that even controlled its contingencies, its uncontrollable parts. Like the climate models Tsing writes about, they 'are made more reliable by incorporating uncertainties into the model, that is, by modelling them'[44] – indeed, one can control uncertainties by modelling and writing about them, and paying for them.

The drawings used in the construction of the cathedrals of the Middle Ages seem rather unsystematic to twentieth and twenty-first century professionals.[45]

On the old drawings of architectural details are also drawn images of humans in the process of construction. In a way, their presence on the drawing, working with parts of the cathedral, stresses the performativity of constructing a cathedral – a cathedral-in-the-making. It was quite the reverse with the architectural drawings for the Frederiksgave project: on the invitation to the inauguration described and shown in the Introduction, for example, illustrations of humans are completely absent. The invitation gives a drawing of the façade with no depth, no background and no humans. Humans would disturb the intended copy of the original. The perspective, one might consider, should not be human at all, but instead reflect universal history itself, speaking through codes of pure and rigorous professionalism. Rather than stressing the performativity of reconstruction, the drawings and the sketch on the invitation stress the accuracy of professional work. The ruler was also vital in remaking the completely symmetrical 'Empire' construction that made up the main building at Frederiksgave. Symmetry appeared to be highly treasured by visiting Danes and people from the National Museum. Having visited the site, it seemed that we all departed with at least one picture taken from the symmetrical axis, most often a photo of the whole building, usually without people, or a photo of the entrance doors opening into a back wall where three posters were exhibited according to the symmetrical axis. These posters displayed a list found in the Royal Danish archives naming all the slaves working at the site at a particular time, flanked by two portraits of Danish Governors.

The symmetry was perfected in the illustration on the invitation card for the inauguration, and this illustration was also chosen as the front page of the accompanying booklet that was made especially for the exhibition at the site. Alongside an architectural drawing, the front page showed a two-dimensional façade of the building. No tropical trees, goats, children, workers or visitors disturbed the harmony of the construction; the main building just rose out of the white ground of cardboard. Interestingly, the people who live in the village chose to use a photo of the building from an oblique angle on the postcards that were later produced, something I will return to in Chapter Five. Similarly, a young man from the village who borrowed my camera chose to portray the building from another oblique angle, namely from the Chief's house.

FIG. 3.1 The front of the Frederiksgave building from the symmetrical axis, 2008, Sesemi, Ghana.

FIG. 3.2 Symmetry inside the Frederiksgave building, 2007, Sesemi, Ghana.

FIG. 3.3 The Frederiksgave building with the Chief's house in the foreground, 2007, Sesemi, Ghana. Courtesy of Daniel Nii Amarh Ashikwei.

FIG. 3.4 Locally produced postcard sold at the Common Heritage Site, 2009, Sesemi, Ghana. Courtesy of Stanley Akoto Sasu.

It seemed that many of the Danes photographing the building, myself included, took great pleasure in (maybe even felt seduced by) the possibility of capturing an ordered totality offered by the symmetrical architecture. Just like Verran's description of Althusser's two Frenchmen shaking hands, the building 'interpellated'[46] us to perform a small 'ritual of recognition'[47] by making us take a photo of the front of the building – with its symmetrical shape it almost felt as if we were looking into a face. It was not so much a feeling of overpowering the object by capturing it in a photo, but more the pleasure of being face to face with Danish history in Ghana.

THROUGH THE LOOKING GLASS

One day, I was sitting with the Danish architect around the table at the site. We were looking at a photocopy of the only illustration ever found of the Frederiksgave plantation site, dating back to 1837. The A3 photocopy, which had been found in the Royal Danish archives, illustrated an aerial view of the area, made on the basis of old Danish decimal inches. With a thin detailed ruler in one hand and a magnifying glass in the other, the architect crouched over the paper and measured the tiny buildings illustrated on the map. His forehead was almost touching the paper; the two were only separated by the magnifying glass. Then he raised his head, adjusted his eyes to my scale, and with excitement in his eyes and voice he came up with a number. It was a number regarding the length of the small building on the map. A moment later, it was my turn to look at the drawing through the magnifying glass. I imitated the architect's movement; suddenly the otherwise clearly delimited small square boxes had fuzzy edges, probably due to the draughtsman's ink having been absorbed by sand sprinkled over the paper. In a way, it seemed paradoxical that this scoping in on the object allowed the architect to come up with a distinct number, when the magnifying glass simultaneously made the object much more fuzzy and hard to delimit – or, as Norbert Wise has framed it in his article, 'Making Visible', the telescope and microscope reveal a vast 'optical zoo' of new objects, from galaxies to microbes.[48] Increasing the level of detail by highlighting the resolution does not make the object less complex, as Strathern has noted.[49] It took a trained eye to benefit from the accuracy provided by the magnifying glass. Precision was, quite literally, a matter of viewpoint; the perspective and the thing in view are, as argued throughout this book, created simultaneously.

Writing about the variety of methods that Alexander von Humboldt used on his expedition to South America, Wise notes that precision instruments were a means of

> extending the senses beyond their normal reach [...] not merely in the quantitative sense of smaller or larger but qualitatively, as extending human sensibilities to qualities of nature not previously available even to the most sensitive observer.[50]

As we saw in the previous chapter, then, sensuousness is a vital part of the magic mimetic gesture of reconstructing Frederiksgave. With the magnifying glass, the ruler and the map in my hands, I was equipped with magic tools that suddenly made apparent the sensuous relation involved in map making, in making accurate illustrations and, ultimately, in reconstructing an historic building. The Danish architect explained that he was almost sure that the original draughtsman, supposedly the miller H. Grønberg, had been just as meticulous as he himself was now being with his ruler, and that Grønberg, more than 150 years ago, had scaled the tiny buildings on the drawing in the right proportions according to the vast area also mapped on the illustration. It was a source of great pleasure to the architect that it actually seemed as if the scales and proportions for the main building, with its bipartite staircase and roofed building, were accurate according to the old numbers. Assisted by the magnifying glass, this was as close as we could get to the original Frederiksgave, because we were looking at the only antique drawing of it known to exist – although, as mentioned in Chapter Two, we also experienced intimations of closeness when walking in the ruin or the other Danish traces. Interestingly, this proximity resulted both in an exact number and in fuzzy objects produced by the nature of Mr Grønberg's quill pen. One might say that the accuracy provided by the drawing when seen through the magnifying glass was accompanied by a cotemporal inaccuracy as fuzzy objects came into view. The Frederiksgave building, then, could be displaced both into an exact number produced by intimate relations between the ruler, the magnifying glass and a professional eye, and also into a fuzzy entity produced by the sensuousness of Grønberg's quill, both displacements being effected by magnification. The accurate tools used in the Frederiksgave reconstruction apparently produced a complex kind of precision that went beyond a simple referential decoding of passive matter. Curiously, the other square indications on the old illustration did not concur with the foundations of buildings found in the present-day archaeological excavations of the area. The main building was there, but not the other two buildings that had been excavated. It is possible that the other square indications on the map were some of the easily perishable 'slave huts' that we knew from written sources had been attached to the plantation. This discrepancy again shows that accuracy can be thought of both as absolute and relative at the same time. One could ask in what way the drawing was a model for the present reconstruction project if it displayed elements that were not there today and would not become part of the reconstructed site, and, vice versa, if buildings had been excavated that were not featured on the drawing. The architect chose to focus on and magnify what was intended to be imitated, that is, the main building. His perspective did not 'see' the smaller square indications and the absence of the other two buildings. What this shows is that his actions with the ruler and the magnifying glass were perspectival and creative in themselves, rather than a neutral discerning of a passive material. Neither the newly created architectural drawings nor the antique one provided a frictionless scaling up and down – in other words, zooming in and out *changed* the objects in question. The magnifying glass and the ruler did not so much *apply* externally to the site as internally *create* it in sensuous mimetic ways. Hence the accuracy obtained via the ruler and the magnifying glass is in itself a magic viewpoint, and both of these instruments contain their own scales and perspectives. Accuracy is not something inherent in the world, to be decoded from an external point of view, but something that can only be approximated by freezing the thing and the eye and keeping a chosen perspective constant. Reconstructing the Frederiksgave plantation was neither a matter of the material speaking precision to an audience nor of arbitrary social construction, but of actively working with the magical power of replication.

CHOICES AND REJECTIONS: MAN-MADE MODELS OF RECONSTRUCTION

Reconstruction work implies many choices along the way, choices that cannot at all be predicted in present-day drawings, regardless of whether or not these drawings are made before the building is constructed or derive from a ruin. The totality illustrated in the Frederiksgave drawings therefore had to be continuously redrawn according to the challenges encountered along the way. In the quotation above, Lévi-Strauss discusses how the miniatures are 'man-made', made with the hand, and therefore 'they constitute a real experiment with it [the object]'.[51] The fact that the scale model is a man-made experiment makes it possible to explore the way in which it is fabricated, and to study the choices made in order to resolve certain problems encountered along the way. But as Lévi-Strauss interestingly argues

> The choice of one solution involves a modification of the result to which another solution would have led, and the observer is in effect presented with the general picture of these permutations at the same time as the particular solution offered. He is thereby transformed into an active participant without even being aware of it. Merely by contemplating it he is, as it were, put in possession of other possible forms of the same work; and in a confused way, he feels himself to be their creator with more right than the creator himself because the latter abandoned them in excluding them from his creation. And these forms are so many further perspectives opening out on to the work which has been realized.[52]

According to Lévi-Strauss, this means that all the choices and rejections are embedded in the scale-model, in this case the architectural drawings. If this is so, then the architectural drawings become all kinds of other things in addition to accurate decodings, regardless of the fact that they are based on meticulous surveying. And, just as important, the spectator is turned into an active participant who, in a confused way, becomes the creator of the choices and rejections embedded in the work. On a general level, this confirms a very important insight, namely the intimate and mutually constitutive relation between perspective and object. Perspectives create objects and objects entail the perspectives that they are made up of – and therefore, I might add to Lévi-Strauss' analysis, the objects are never finite totalities – they always point beyond themselves.[53] Instead, a particular perspective makes a totality emerge by removing other perspectives – thus the totality is a generalisation built on a small conjunction of similarities. Architectural drawings, one might say, create an axiom of unity – a common heritage site – a generalisation created and confirmed by focusing on specific particulars, while ignoring others. Another version of the circular argument implied in this theory of generalisation can now be seen: the drawings made by the architect in the present extend into the future by pointing towards what the Frederiksgave site should look like when completed; but this happens on the basis of extension into the past, revealing what the site *used* to look like. With a pencil stroke, the scale models conflate the distant totalities of past, present and future but, at the same time, they also separate them by containing all the choices made at any point in time to make the building look as it did and does.

Let us take a closer look at this temporal collapse. Using the ruler and the scaled down versions of the Frederiksgave buildings on architectural drawings, the architect could measure where the exact symmetrical points in the building would be. He could predict corners and openings to doors and windows, and get an idea of the house yet to be constructed, including its proportions. Measurement and reconstruction fused together in the ruler, and it became an instrument of both copy-making and creation. In one and the same movement, the ruler measured then and now, and in so doing, it showed the choices and rejections of the past and present. Even though it was not materialised, the small building drawn on the scaled down version brought us into futures yet to be realised. And, slowly but surely, the building came to look like the scaled down version we had pored over for months at the site and in offices at the National Museum in Denmark and Ghana. It was a collapse in sequences: a drawing of the house becomes the house. And, finally, in October 2007, with mimetic playfulness, from our stools around the table on the reconstruction site we could alternately look at the drawing of the façade and lift our eyes to look at a copy of the scaled down version in real time and life size.

According to Taussig, as we have seen, the mimetic faculty is not a simple matter of making exact copies; it is also a matter of playfully othering, of exploring difference. With these ideas on mimesis, Taussig jumps right into debates about the status of the sign, of the signifier and signified – which is exactly what is at stake in our discussion of the architectural drawings and the ruler. Neither satisfied with simply reducing the relation between signifier and signified to arbitrariness, as Saussure would have it, nor with the relation being naturalised, Taussig suggests exploring exactly the space in-between – a space that is marked by what he calls 'a certain magic of the signifier'.[54] Following Taussig, I want to explore the sensuous relations present in the Frederiksgave project as a mimetic faculty.

In our above discussion of the Munsell Code, we noted that it works only because people believe that it works, and because they value the particular authenticity it supports and legitimates (if they don't, then the code is just black strokes on rough paper). People must invoke it to decode it, and can do both in the same movement. As we saw above, this was not necessarily the case with the two-sidedness of the ruler: it produced confusion, too. Both the Munsell Code and the ruler, then, are magic as signifiers. The same goes for the architectural drawings: they are not just depictions, but are also time machines collapsing time and space, for those who know how to navigate the space between the signifier and signified.

In a section on the effectiveness of small figurines in curing practices in Panama, Taussig writes:

> Note the replicas. Note the magical, the soulful power that derives from replication. For this is where we must begin; with the magical power of replication, the image affecting what it is an image of, wherein the representation shares in or takes power from the represented.[55]

The replicas, or in the case of Frederiksgave the architectural drawings, are more than just a copy of the represented: the Frederiksgave buildings under reconstruction in Sesemi. As we saw, the architectural drawings did indeed affect the building, there was a dual dependency between them. In fact, the term 'affected' is too unidirectional, leaving 'the other side' passive, a position that constructionism might take in animating a dead nature.[56] In this case, it puts the building in a passive position to be affected by the drawings, as of course it was. But the point is also, I would argue, that the building, in turn, affects (or even effects) the drawings. Thus, the way in which the drawings were used in relation to the reconstructions indicates that the building and the drawings presuppose each other, and that neat sequences in time break down accordingly; indeed, it is difficult to discern copy from original. Then and now become nested into each other, just like part and whole did in relation to the architectural drawing and the building, and as choice and rejection did in the model. When one is seen through the other in this way, it gives rise to a productive meeting that changes both. In this sense, rather than merely affecting each other, my point is that building and drawing produce each other. The drawings wedge themselves in between the ruin and the reconstructed building. They come to occupy the sensuous space in which the building is produced. In this light, the drawings emerged through a sensuous process of seeing, measuring, touching and drawing – and, likewise, the building was built, measured and seen in relation to the drawings. In other words, they conjure each other up with the help of the architect, who becomes both magician and copyist; his work is prediction and decoding in one. The drawings even exuded a sort of magical power bestowed by the represented, and indeed it felt a touch magical to sit there in the open shed, letting the eye alternate between the drawing and the building – to compare differences and similarities. The building, too, exuded a sort of magical power bestowed by the drawings, but only in this relation and from this perspective, only when this particular one was seen through this particular other – what I would call a certain and specific mimetic perspective producing magic. Even though they were also very different, in some ways building and drawing really looked like exact copies of each other or, alternatively, were equally original, the small pencil-drawn building on the two-dimensional paper and the imposing building almost rolling down the hill into my eyes. The nuances in the whitewashed colour of the building, though, depending on the position of the sun, contrasted with the mono-colour of the drawing. And instead of the beads of perspiration and shortage of breath that hit you when walking up to the building, it was possible, comfortably and coolly, from a fixed spot, to point out specificities in the façade by looking at the drawing. The relation between the drawing and the physical building was one of similarity and otherness at the same time, and the drawings were simultaneously more and less than the building. Likewise with the building's relation to the drawings, it was also both more and less than the imitation; they were partially connected without exhausting each other. Accurately mapping building and drawing onto one another entails magic, and enacts the architect as both constructor and imitator.[57] If ideas of accuracy and authenticity as a way to eliminate accidents were dropped, then the creative efforts invested in carving out similarities and differences would no longer be obscured. It would then be obvious – and perhaps celebrated – that it takes more than accuracy to make the construction: it takes magic, enfolded, for example, in the ruler.

THOUGHT AND OBJECT: ROOTS SPEAKING TO OUR SENSES

Imagine the architect's trained and vigilant eyes investigating the specificities of the lime used to paint the house in the nineteenth century as he moves close to the ruined wall, picking with his knife in order to help his eyes shape his thoughts. Are these remnants of sea shells that appear in the surface or something else? Through this sensuous moment (the orchestra of sand, shells, sea, river, eyes, thoughts, lime, knife) he is able to create a rhythm and transform what might have been messy or qualified guesses into pure data, by happily exclaiming to his fellows, 'It's lime made up of seashells'. In his report, written long after this sensuous moment, he can state that 'When the Danes built on the Gold Coast they used sea shells as raw material in the production of lime and mortar'.[58] And, depending on his knowledge of lime, the environment in West Africa and the materials available in the area at the time, coupled with the knowledge gained through a microscope or other scientific investigations conducted at the National Museum in Denmark, the content of the lime can be determined with more or less scientific specificity. There is thus a movement from the sensuous moment at the site to the exclamation: 'It's lime made of seashells'. In a sensuous way, it objectifies the sensuous experience by naming it. And this movement is more than both translation and explanation: in Taussig's words, it is 'the peculiar power of the mimetic faculty'.[59] Through sensuous relations of touching, smelling, seeing and listening, the architect creates an object that gains power from the orchestra of sand, lime, knife and so on, and with these sensuous movements, his thoughts are transformed. To quote Taussig, this is not a question of animating matter but a 'question of being moved, *again*'; a 'question of being *touched*, again' – it is a rebirth of mimesis: 'copy fusing with contact'.[60]

During the reconstruction of the Frederiksgave site, all visitors, both formal and informal, were well received. If officials such as Danish ministers or people from the fund financing the project visited the site they were welcomed by the Chief of the village and his elders, who made a *durba* – a traditional ritual to accept the visitors and show the village's collaborative spirit. During several of these visits, I had the chance to hear the Danish architect talk about the site and the reconstruction work. He told visitors about the work, and how he and his Ghanaian colleague had interpreted patterns of decay and had thus been able to reconstruct the site. Curiously, standing there in the burning sun, it seemed from our attentiveness that we were all so absorbed in the stories told by the enthusiastic architect that, for a moment, we almost did not feel the sweat springing from our overheated bodies. We were completely engrossed by the size of the sand grain used in the construction, the burning of the shells to produce lime, the wonderfully dense West African '*borassus* timber', as the Danish architect named the fan-shaped palm tree, which could resist all sorts of termites and rodents. A high-ranking official visiting the site later exclaimed: 'I never thought that lime could be so interesting'. The architect was truly a wonderful storyteller, and it seemed we were all spellbound by his narration. Indeed, we participated in the magic of mimesis; our thoughts were transformed by touching the lime, seeing the timber and listening to the architect.

For me, the highlight of the tour and the most poetic moment was when we slowly climbed the small hill and approached the western part of the building. Here, the only surviving parts of the original walls suddenly rose high above the rest of the collapsed building. The architect said that two fig trees had self-seeded in the organic matter accumulated on the flat roof. By counting the growth rings on the trees he had been able to estimate that they were around 140 years old, and with this information he could infer that the building was abandoned to the forest shortly after the Danes left. Within a short time, cracks in the lime plaster caused by the tropical rain and heat of the day had started appearing, and the house had slowly become dilapidated. This, in turn, was an opportunity for the two self-seeded fig trees, which could then increase their growth via the organic matter, a sort of clay that was used as mortar between the stones. Drawing the nourishment and water accumulated in the clay, the trees grew and began to embrace the western part of the building. The architect thus explained that the two fig trees were both protecting and destroying the walls. Everybody in the crowd nodded, and probably imagined the huge trees that were reduced to imprints on the old recovered wall.

In the beginning, the architect told us, together with his men he was trying to figure out what was going on in the mixture of vegetation and building. Upon further exploration, they saw that some of the trees' huge roots were peculiarly horizontal, with sudden 'unnatural 90-degree bends', and some had strange edges due to their attempts to find nourishment and water in the cracks or wherever possible. With an impressive sense of poetry, the architect now looked at the visitors and said that, with such unnatural forms and shapes, he knew that the trees and the roots

> tried to tell us something, they tried to communicate with us. But in the beginning we were stupid and deaf, not blind but deaf, we did not understand the language of the roots. It was really funny and interesting, and suddenly we said: "now it is there, the western tree is actually beginning to whisper, this root is beginning to whisper". This was at the same time as I and my colleague [...] were measuring everything, we hung plumb bobs and stated "but it fits in with the plan that the root has, it is a little bit flat on the one side, it fits precisely with the wall it hits if we hang a plumb bob" and then we knew, then we could just state that the wall really had been there. And like this we could slowly build it up and finally or later in the process we made jokes with it and said "now, now they talk" and later again "now they are actually shouting at us!

FIGS 3.5 and **3.6** Photos of the recovered wall where the two fig trees have protected the building from collapsing, 2008, Sesemi, Ghana.

We were all laughing, and I was probably not the only one to be completely gripped by the story of the architect learning to first just hear the roots whisper and later understand their language. Actually, these talking roots became key to the understanding and engagement of the Danish architect, and therefore also to my understanding of the site. The story showed the double nature of the reconstruction work – a duality that is not a problem unless magic is excluded as part of the reconstruction. The reconstruction was an external decoding of the site, but it also incorporated sensuous internal relations with materials. But the architect's story also raised new questions. Apparently, none of the crucial characteristics that helped him to hear the talking roots had anything to do with audibility. Instead, he used tools like rulers and a plumb bob, which both need the eye to interpret the measurements taken and the verticality of lines. Why did he say that, in the beginning, they were deaf but not blind? And why did he need his ears when it seemed as if it was his eyes that determined his actions and interpretations? Are there other forms of listening than phono-centrically?

Apart from simply rejecting any significance in the architect's choice of words, saying that it was just a coincidence and that he had perhaps confused the senses, one could argue that he was engaging with particular ideas of the senses rooted in a long Western tradition, and particularly in the Cartesian division of body and mind.[61] Here, participatory qualities are often ascribed to the ear and observational qualities to the eyes.[62] Whereas the ear is thought to be involving, intuitive and active, the eye is reflective and analytical[63]; it observes from a distance. This function of the eye was implicit in the previous chapter's discussion of how surveying is an 'anti-conquest', understood as a non-interfering external practice of the observer. Instead of radically separating the senses from each other, though – which in this case would mean separating the audible from the visible – one could focus on their intimate relatedness.[64] From this perspective I suggest that the Danish architect, in order to investigate the building, had to move beyond the observational and decoding function of his eyes in order to understand the roots. He had to engage with the roots by drawing the world into him in intuitive ways that the distant reflective eye could not comply with. Or, conversely, it seems to be a matter of actively submersing in the sounds in a way that a reductionist understanding of the sight could never offer. For the architect, it was not only a matter of observing or breaking up the roots, the stones and the lime into atomistic units. Instead, it was a matter of letting the material world do its bit, of alerting his intuitive sense in a way that could synthesise the whole sounding board of the building, traditionally the domain of the ear (i.e. intensifying all his senses). The external relation between subject and object had to be given up in order for transformation to happen.

Returning to the Danish architect surveying and investigating the buildings with his ruler, we are reminded of his delight in having received 'messages', as he called them, from the original builders. Instead of seeing his work in individualistic terms, he emphasised its social relation that took the form of messages from the previous builder, provided and amplified by his ruler. But in the case of 'the talking roots' we might have to expand our notion of dialogue partners still further. The challenge of reconstructing the buildings could certainly not be the job of a lone individual – it could not even be a solely human affair. The roots, as we read in the quote above, played a vital role as engaged actors. At first they communicated in ways that were not audible and thus not understandable to the architect. He needed to engage in the sounds, to explore and measure the sources producing the sounds. And, when engaging, the 'things' he explored were not merely emerging and understandable to the eyes. Neither was it principally a matter of making an external assessment of form viewed from afar. Instead, he was engaged in sounds understandable to the ear, as internalised social activities (with fuzzy edges) that behaved more like prosthetic extensions than as external units to be assembled from the outside. It is worth noting that, in the quote, the architect says that the roots talked as the building was being measured. In this way, he indicates that the talking roots in some way related to the measuring, but he also chooses his words in a way that offers an understanding of a parallel process: listening to and looking at the ruler and plumb bobs. He does so in a way that makes these elements relate in some undeterminable fashion. One could say that he leaves a great amount to be decided by the ear, that is, following Ingold, to intuition and the 'whole' picture.[65] The more they understand, the more 'it fits' together, the louder the roots talk. The job of reconstruction, then, is not just to be decided by an external survey that could be undertaken by the eye. Pressing onto our senses, the roots spurred a participatory engagement, activating more senses than one and acting in themselves as anything but the passive dead matter animated by constructionism or the technical and equally passive matter in need of no animation found in a materialist perspective. The singing roots are a case of transgressional sensuality where it might just as well be the eye that can hear and the ear that can see. This was, however, a view that was challenged by the Ghanaian architect and his understanding of reconstructing a building, as we shall see below.

ORGANIC BUILDINGS AND CREATIVE CURES

One afternoon at the reconstruction site in Sesemi, I sat in the open shed with both the Danish and the Ghanaian architect. We were slightly tired after a long morning in the sun. Lazing on our wooden stools, we sat and digested our canned mackerel and biscuits while chatting. We were talking about their thoughts on the buildings and on the talking roots. The Ghanaian architect said that, to him, buildings were like sick patients that he had to cure. First you come up with a diagnosis, then you find possible causes, then you treat the building like a sick patient, he explained. At first, the Danish architect did not comment on this. When I asked him if that was also how he perceived buildings, he said that, for him, this was too imprecise, he was more interested in the 'The course of damage and the images of damage' – he wanted a more holistic approach and not merely a narrow focus on isolated elements. He then added that, in Denmark, professionals talk about 'understanding the house'. Immediately the Ghanaian architect smiled and replied 'a building cannot talk' – clearly he thought that the Danish architect, whom he respected, was going too far at this point. The Danish architect answered: 'If I go to a doctor, then he receives me holistically, he is already working even before I have told him what's wrong. You come to a house, and you're already working, finding solutions'. The Ghanaian architect found his colleague's explanation far too vague and difficult to work with. Instead, he looked at me and explained that when he makes investigations he works with a certain SWOT model. Enthusiastically he took my little notebook and wrote an 'S', and explained that it stands for 'Strength'; he wrote down the word. He did the same with all the letters so that the words 'Strength', 'Weakness', 'Opportunity', 'Threat' appeared in my notebook in easily readable hand writing. He then elaborated each letter: 'the 'S' creates jobs for people' – I had now got my notebook and pencil back, and under his finicky writing I added the keywords vertically in order to economise on the horizontal space. Later, when

I was interpreting my cramped vertical writing I came up with the following: 'S: strength/create jobs for people, W: weakness/erosion, O: opportunity/more money will come, T: threat/too many tourists will put pressure on the facilities, and the felling of trees is a threat, along with erosion'. The Ghanaian architect then explained that, since a building cannot talk, you have to find the problem and recommend a cure – you give it treatment. If the trees are the cause of the problem, as the two fig trees were for the reconstruction of the Frederiksgave buildings, then you fell the trees.

To the Ghanaian architect, reconstructing the house meant dividing up the problem into pre-given ordered categories. The SWOT analysis seemed to be a structuring figure that he could use whenever he encountered a dilapidated house. It had similarities with both the ruler and the Munsell Code in that it shared their universal aspirations and potential global outreach. However, the SWOT analysis that the Ghanaian architect came up with that particular afternoon on the site differed from the kind of analyses that the Danish architect was coming up with. Although the ruler contained ideas of being applied neutrally to the world, we saw how it also had a creative side. Through the ruler, the Danish architect could receive 'messages' from his former compatriots. The SWOT analysis likewise contained ideas of being applied neutrally, as a structuring factor, to the case at hand. But it also had a creative element – it was not just a detached model for analysis to be applied to the world, but was itself a perspective which, through sensuous mimetic relations, shaped the analysis. It was a model that could transform or displace the Ghanaian architect through sensuous mimetic relations. By using the SWOT analysis, the architect was not only able to find technical solutions to the building, but could also receive messages from people living nearby; in a highly structured way, he could be informed of their needs and concerns. By listening carefully, or maybe intuitively that very afternoon, since a SWOT analysis had never been included in the project design, the Ghanaian architect was able to receive messages that reflected the workers' and villagers' concerns, namely attracting jobs, tourists and money into the village. These concerns were not, however, of primary concern to the project planners, particularly not the Danes involved, who labelled them as 'side-effects'. The Danes' interest was more in line with that of the Danish architect: that of receiving messages from the past and getting to know 'our common history'. One might say that in the project plan, contemporary needs and concerns regarding jobs and tourism had nothing to do with the original. Indeed, the interests of the two architects reflected different communities. The Frederiksgave site was apparently valued differently. These different concerns and ways of creating value at the Frederiksgave site will be the focus of the next chapter.

During my fieldwork and analysis, it became clear that Frederiksgave is not a self-contained thing to be reflected upon from a distance – not even from a symmetrical axis or from a universal history. Norton Wise writes about the role of images in scientific knowledge production. Quoting the botanist Linné, who is said to have exclaimed: 'Whoever derived a firm argument from a picture?',[66] Wise regretfully suggests that images have often been thought of as either 'much too powerful, likely to lead to the deceptive excesses of imagination rather than the calm reflections of reason, [or], on the other, as much too weak, capable of illuminating only the surface of things rather than their deep structure'.[67] Images are either thought of as deceptive, derailing the object of study, or too weak to penetrate the surface. In this chapter, we have seen a variety of images: maps, architectural drawings, models and sketches. Instead of deceiving us, I argue that these images constitute and transform the Frederiksgave site in multiple ways. Realising the need for transformative magic as a component of reconstructing work that explodes the notions of copy and original, of constructionism and materialism, is one way of anthropologically qualifying common heritage.

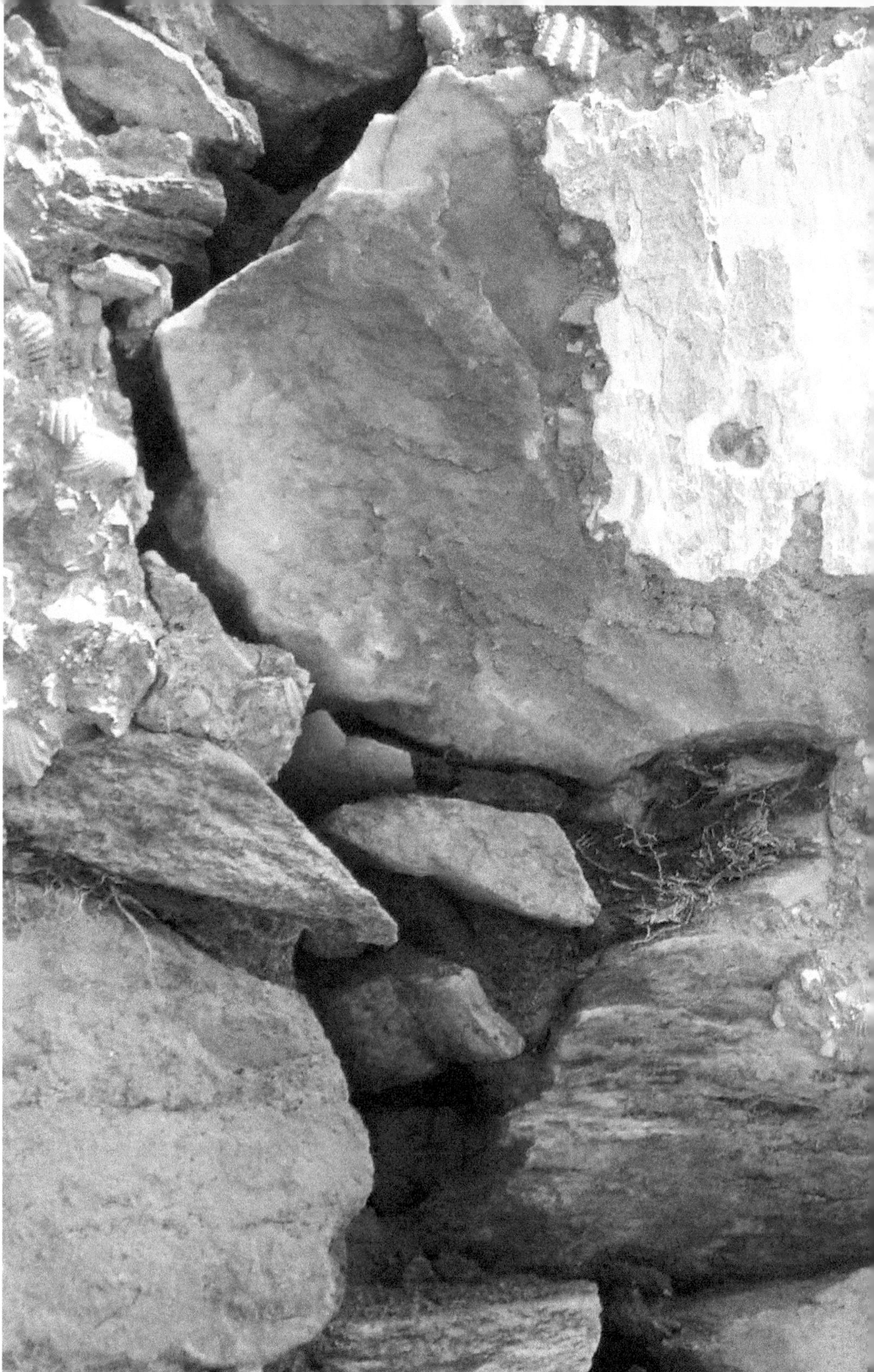

4

VALUING HERITAGE THROUGH THE FETISH

VALUE AND POWERFUL MATERIALITY

'I'M GOING ON A CRUSADE THIS MONDAY,' SAID THE FAMILY FATHER AND Christian priest with whom I lived, while we explored a former Danish fort in the present-day coastal village of Keta in Ghana. His straightforward attitude was in stark contrast to my immediate reaction. I was desperately trying to rid myself of images of stereotypical brownish European medieval knights in armour, men and women perishing at the stakes and in holy wars. After a few seconds, I managed to ask him what he meant. He looked at me as if I was ignorant: 'A crusade, you know a crusade...'. I stuttered: 'Ehh, yes, I know crusades, but to me crusades are something that set off long ago from Europe'. 'No, no, no,' he replied. 'We have it too, crusades are still very important. We have to get rid of Satan's work... those fetishes and fetish priests and their false faith [...], the evil spirits can only be chased away by prayers and destruction!' I had seen fetishes in the area, small white clay figures looking, to me, like small figures out of Star Wars. Whenever I had asked about these figures, people had laughed and/or looked somewhat perplexed and answered shortly that they were 'fetishes, traditional religion'. What the priest had planned for the coming Monday was to drive to nearby villages and 'spread the gospel'. He had on several occasions succeeded in converting people, he said. And he told me about his feats, often considered dangerous because they involved contact with fetishes and, thereby, with Satan. A successful crusade achieved conversion and the destruction of the fetishes, he added, and then he told me of his greatest achievement: the conversion of a fetish priest and the ensuing burning of a huge room filled with fetishes. Immersed in rhetoric about the importance of preserving material cultural heritage, I asked a somewhat stupid question: 'Do you really destroy them?' 'Yes, of course!' he replied enthusiastically. I continued in the same vein, 'Don't you save some for the National Museum in Accra?' As if the situation was not already awkward enough, this question caused the priest to regard me with a very severe face: 'No, they must be destroyed, they are evil!' In reply, I asked, 'But why do you care so much about these fetishes and their destruction when you are a Christian and know that they are false faith?' Instead of answering, he asked, 'Don't you believe in them?' 'Well, I don't really think so,' I replied and the conversation drew to a close.

This opening conversation introduces the overall theme of this chapter, in which I engage the notion of the fetish to explore ideas about the powers of material objects and the values they are seen to embody. In the previous chapters I have explored Frederiksgave by bringing to the fore particular aspects of the project that detail how the Frederiksgave site was emerging as a common heritage project through quite particular means and in quite particular ways. I did this, first, by presenting a reading of the cultural political climate that produced it, then by considering the design of the project on the part of the planners and their ideas about cultural encounter, and then by focusing on the tools, drawings, ideals and techniques involved in the authentic recreation of the building, and the mimetic relations that were accordingly brought into play. Here, I move on to look at the ways in which the Frederiksgave site was analysed, constructed and, I suggest, *naturalised* by the project makers as a particular topographic feature and a significant piece of nature, engendering particular valuations and ideas about powerful materiality. In short, I look at how Frederiksgave comes to work as a materialisation of value, that is, a valuable heritage site.

During my several stays in Ghana, I heard about fetishes every now and then. I do not know if it was a coincidence, but somehow the fetishes always seemed to be present in proximity to former Danish buildings. Historical sources in the archives had informed me that fugitive slaves could seek refuge with the fetish priest and gain the protection of the fetish if they were dissatisfied with their slave owners.[1] This could be a reason why fetishes were found close to Danish sites. The tension that the fetish created among the Danes and their slaves is palpable in the old documents. A particular realism seems present when Balthazar Christensen, an expatriate Dane of the 1830s, notes in his diary that the master, especially if he is 'white' (in Danish: *blank*), cannot tyrannise his slave, since the slave can simply run away to a 'fetish place'.[2] However, Balthazar adds, this was not always a good deal for the runaway slave, since being a slave of the fetish was not easy work either. Historically, the fetish suggests an ambiguous presence that seems to occupy an interesting if awkward space in society. The fetishes I encountered during my fieldwork took very diverse forms. For example, several people I talked to mentioned 'the fetish' by pointing to a lagoon, a mountain, a spring, a cannon from a European fort, while other used the term to refer to clay figurines in families' courtyards, in shrine houses, in public spaces or in an old abandoned village. In a conversation with three guides from the National Museum of Ghana in Accra, I was told that many of their friends and relatives thought of their job as quite peculiar. With a smile, one of the guides generalised: 'Many Ghanaians think this is a strange place'; they all burst out laughing and then one continued: 'To keep all these old things in a place like this is strange, some even think that there are fetishes inside', and again they laughed.

In an article on collections and visitors in small British museums focusing on the everyday life of 'ordinary folk' in a particular area, Sharon Macdonald has touched upon the idea that for 'old things' to count and be treasured as museum objects a certain fetishisation of the objects is required. The fetishisation of everyday life is a social process whereby mundane material objects can be 'turned into a collector's item',[3] i.e. fetishised by being ascribed certain values. From the opening quote above and other fieldwork experiences from Ghana there is reason to push this statement a bit further by exploring not how mundane objects become fetishised, but how some of the former Danish museum and heritage objects and places work as fetish objects, and were seen by visitors and, more importantly for my present purposes, by heritage makers, as powerful in themselves and as materialising certain given properties, and therefore calling for careful and deliberate practices of maintaining these 'natural' qualities. It was also on account of these qualities that the museum guides mentioned above found it unlikely that any robbers would dare to break into the museum at night. The 'strangeness' perhaps also explained why few Ghanaians visited the museum in Accra – 'a fetish house' as one of the guides suggested with a smile. When I asked if they themselves were not affected by working in such a place, they agreed that maybe in the beginning it was strange, but then they went on to say: 'We are educated Christian people, it's more traditional people who believe in that sort of thing'. Much like the crusader who opened this chapter, the guides at the National Museum of Ghana thereby tapped in to a schism in Ghanaian cultural politics.[4] One position sees tradition and the past as positive and noble resources inspired by Nkrumahist ideas of national enlightenment and the growth of 'African personality'. Birgit Meyer labels this tendency 'the cultural politics of Sankofaism'[5], referring to the Akan symbol of a bird looking back – the same symbol used on the key exchanged at the inauguration ceremony, as described in the Introduction. Another position, though, holds a different idea of tradition, one that is apparently widespread among people belonging particularly to charismatic and Pentecostal Churches, and which we saw reflected in the opening conversation about the Monday crusade. In the view of these Christian groups, tradition and heritage are features that must be overcome, as they are seen to stand in the way of the Christian message, rather than serve as repositories of value.

The Ghanaian museum guides' view that the ascription of awesome, fetish-like qualities to museums is a thing of the past (although nevertheless somehow powerful) was not shared by all. A fieldwork experience one late afternoon in January 2009 at the Frederiksgave site in Sesemi demonstrated this. Together with one of the men who had worked at the site and who was now the caretaker, I visited the museum exhibition in the main building, along with some Danish archaeologists. As always in the afternoon, we were surrounded by children who had returned from school. Suddenly, two men and a woman I had never seen before entered the site accompanied by some men from the village. They were representatives of a family whose daughter had injured the caretaker by throwing a stone at him a few days earlier. On behalf of the family, the visitors had come to apologise for the incident, which had caused a visit to the hospital and a few stitches. In low voices, they exchanged some words and money with the caretaker. With the conflict settled, and given that they were now at the site, the caretaker invited them to see the exhibition in the main building. Since I rarely saw Ghanaian guests visiting the Frederiksgave site and the exhibition, I was excited and curious to hear what they thought about it. However, after spending a few seconds in one of the two small rooms flanking the central hall, the visiting woman ran out of the main building, obviously agitated. I followed and caught up with her. People were laughing. At a safe distance from the building, I managed to exchange a few words with her – she did not like the museum at all. It was apparent that she did not want to talk to me about it; somebody added that she did not speak English that well. People around us continued to laugh, and all of a sudden switched to the local Ga language, which I did not understand. It was awkward – the woman was still agitated, people were laughing, and I was eager to find out what it was all about. A few minutes later, some of us gathered in the open shed. My curiosity was met only with a few fragmented sentences: 'She doesn't like it…it's no good…this small room…the gun…slaves,' and a lot of laughter. These were moments full of tension, and the conjunction of laughter and fear, silence and half-told explanations, produced palpable uneasiness. No one, least of all the upset lady, was able or willing to tell me what had just happened. It seemed that this was not so much a matter of language problems and my not speaking Ga; by her agitated body language and her unwillingness to actually speak, the lady clearly succeeded in communicating both to me and the other people around. I was in no doubt that her encounter with the building and exhibition produced a need to flee. What was at stake was that the Frederiksgave museum, evidently, was not just *any* old thing. This was a view shared by the project makers who in the process of reconstruction strove to accommodate particular qualities thought to be both inherent in and vital for the Frederiksgave site. A kind of circularity is again at play here: certain inherent qualities make the site appear as common heritage, and these qualities must be respected in the heritage practices for the site to maintain them.

These incidents with dangerous and powerful things, buildings and spaces made me curious because they somehow mirrored ideas about materiality and topography that the project makers often referred to. The persistent attention that people involved in the heritage work at Frederiksgave paid to materiality and topography called for analytical attention in my exploration of the Common Heritage Project. In particular, this analytical focus is meant to explore how materiality and topography appeared as vital parts of the naturalisation of the Frederiksgave museum as a heritage site of common interest, and how particular valuations affected as well as constituted the site. What I will show is that thorough analyses of the landscape, of building materials, and of the maintenance requirements stipulated by the project planners were intimately related to, if not coincident with, the valuation of the site. This approach gives rise to two related questions that direct this chapter: how is heritage valued as the 'Frederiksgave Plantation, Common Heritage Project', and how is this, in turn, valued as heritage?

In addressing this issue, my path leads me through particular understandings of materiality that relate in various ways to the etymology and historical ideas of the fetish. In other words, I draw here on the history of the fetish as a prism through which to analyse how material objects and topographical features both expressed and created value at the Frederiksgave site, and how the common heritage site came to life through this double movement of describing and producing. My primary guide is a series of articles entitled *The Problem of the Fetish* (1985, 1987, 1988) by William Pietz, in which he explores the concept of the fetish. Rather than being an intra-African phenomenon as it is often thought to be,[6] the emergence of the fetish was dependent upon the conjunction of a commodity ideology and two different religious ideologies each founded in non-capitalist societies.[7] As such, the fetish was a product of trading relations between African and Christian feudal and mercantile capitalist social systems, where it grew out of very different notions of value.[8] I find Pietz' insistence on this here-and-now quality of the fetish appealing – that these cross-cultural spaces were not societies or cultures in any conventional sense. The fetish

> must be viewed as proper to no historical field other than that of the history of the word itself, and to no discrete society or culture, but to a cross-cultural situation formed by the ongoing encounter of the value codes of radically different social orders.[9]

What I would like to emphasise here is the attention to the situations producing the fetish. According to Pietz, Karl Marx likewise appreciated the notion of the fetish precisely because it was able to describe the power of specificity, singularity and historical consciousness, thereby pointing to the illusion of natural unities.[10] By confusing the singular with the general, the fetish could appear as an *a priori* entity that had erased all the (e.g. human) energies it was constantly made up of. Pietz suggests that by taking a point of departure in these heterogeneously structured encounters, it is possible to explore how the fetish grew out of very different notions of the social value of material objects, a theme I will return to (especially at the end of the chapter). Conducting part of my fieldwork on the West African coast where the notion of fetish popped up, as we have already seen, there was clearly analytical purchase in literature on the fetish – at times also termed 'the religion of materiality'.[11] In my view, Pietz' trilogy of articles can thus offer new theoretical insights into issues of the materiality of cultural heritage, which has too often been reduced to an arbitrary instrument of social relations and discourse. Through the history of the fetish we learn about the development of a word, the meaning of which has always revolved around oppositions such as manufactured/natural, material/spiritual and referential/substantial – dichotomies that take centre stage when discussing the value of cultural heritage projects such as Frederiksgave. In this sense, the fetish is an apt concept with which to explore ideas such as authenticity that have been central to heritage studies. Why not use the fetish to explore some of the particular types of materiality involved in the Frederiksgave heritage project?

Following Deleuze, Pietz goes so far as to suggest that the fetish might radically revalue and reverse the tradition of Western philosophy.[12] As an affirmative term, it can challenge a so-called Western philosophical tradition founded on a radical separation, often even hierarchisation, of materiality and spirituality.[13] The notion of the fetish entails not only the possibility of transgressing this fundamental philosophical divide, but also of dealing with a materiality that is untranscended.[14] In dealing with untranscended materiality, the fetish points to a paradox: it is *both* a figure that transcends the divide between the material and the spiritual *and* untranscended, implying that the effect and meaning of the fetish is inherent *in* the fetish – a point I will return to later. Embracing this paradox in projects such as Frederiksgave may guide us in developing a new vocabulary to capture the materiality of heritage, which seeks to move beyond images of transcendence and representation – an ambition also mentioned in Chapter One. It may allow me to come up with a generalisation about cultural heritage that is not an abstraction (such as the sentence 'cultural heritage is a physical manifestation of universal value'). Instead, my analysis of cultural heritage remains in place, as it were, even as I grapple with its value.

The particular uses of the fetish explored by Pietz go back in time to the fifteenth century when the first Portuguese merchants traded with African kings along the West African coast. They built lodges and forts near coastal villages from where they could trade gold, ivory and slaves for Europeans goods such as beads, brassware and textiles.[15] The notion of the fetish evolved in these particular socio-historical spaces dominated by trade. It was through mercantile relations that ideas of the fetish developed in the sixteenth and seventeenth centuries via the Portuguese term *feitiço*. From the very outset, then, the concept of the fetish emerged in cross-cultural encounters. In Portugal, *feitiço* signified amulets and small relics of saints,[16] and the term was used for characterising often innocent magical practices and witchcraft performed by the poor – a poor man's magic.[17] But, as we shall see, the term 'fetish', as it came to be known on the African coast, has a long and interesting etymological background that can be traced back to Roman uses around the beginning of the first millennium. These particular uses, and the etymological development that attended them, give us tools to understand how and why ways of treating and understanding materiality seemed tremendously important in the Frederiksgave project. Like the priest's fetish crusade described in the opening paragraph, bad faith was lurking round the corner and needed to be eliminated. With these introductory thoughts in mind, I now turn to the history of the fetish in more detail.

MANUFACTURED AND NATURAL GOODS AT FREDERIKSGAVE: TRUE AND FALSE HERITAGE

Derived from the Latin verb *facere*, 'to make', Pietz traces the word 'fetish' 2000 years back to the Latin adjective *facticius*, meaning 'manufactured'.[18] Here it appears for the first time in written sources, specifically in Pliny's *Natural History* to describe particular commercial relations. It was thus used to differentiate manufactured, man-made commodities from natural, given commodities. The latter were understood as the product of purely natural processes, not altered by human effort. Pietz mentions an Arabic aromatic gum that could be collected from the ground, and which in Pliny's time was distinguished from a similar but processed and therefore manufactured gum from Cyprus.[19] Interestingly, one can still see traces of this rather persistent division between the man-made and the natural in the UNESCO distinction between natural heritage and cultural heritage.[20] The difference in mode of production seems to be *the* difference separating cultural heritage from natural heritage. On the UNESCO official website, represented by small green squares and yellow circles scattered around the globe, with a high concentration in the northern hemisphere, one can thus locate the selected natural sites (180) and cultural sites (704) worth safeguarding. Since 1992, however, this division has been challenged or maybe rather softened by the introduction of a notion of 'cultural landscapes', depicted by small yellow-green icons and described with the statement that 'cultural landscapes represent the 'combined works of nature and of man'.[21]

The 2000-year-old division of commodities into either manufactured (*facticius*) or natural was slightly changed by Pliny himself to also connote a distinction between the *appearance* of a manufactured commodity and the appearance of a *naturally* made commodity. For instance, commodities that were functionally identical could differ in appearance according to the character of the product. As an example, Pliny mentions the blue colour of mined flower of copper as different from the synthetically produced blue of the manufactured mineral.[22] In a commercial setting, this visible difference invites a discussion of distinctions in value: is the artificial good as valuable as the natural good (or vice versa)? The appearance and character of goods becomes an index of different values. This distinction is obviously relevant to notions of fraud – what is actually expected and exchanged in the commercial trade? The morally neutral division of the manufactured, the man-made and the naturally produced, then, was displaced by Pliny himself into a hierarchisation of values such that the naturally produced became the 'authentic' and the 'true', whereas the manufactured became the 'unnatural' and the 'deliberately false'.[23] In consequence, fraud emerges when the authentic natural material is copied or manipulated via man-made processes. In the following, I take manufactured to be synonymous with artificial. In this early understanding of *facticius* or *facticium,* the concept therefore not only means manufactured but also humanly altered with the purpose of deceiving, in that on closer inspection the commodity is not the substance that its appearance promised.[24] Fraud, as thought of in relation to appearance, invites analysis of an object's component parts – is it *facticius* or genuinely natural?[25]

Regarding both the production mode and the character of the product at Frederiksgave, – i.e. the dilapidated and reconstructed building – various professional heritage workers at the site undertook a thorough analysis of the component materials. As we have already seen, authenticity was important to the heritage workers engaged at Frederiksgave. In addition to magical time travel through architectural drawings and antique tools, authenticity was also thought to be obtained through particular practices to do with qualities of the artificial and natural products, and with mixing these together in the right doses. Here it is necessary to anticipate what will follow and note that it would be more precise to say that the Roman understanding of natural goods as raw materials to be collected by humans – i.e. non-humanly altered goods – was, in the case of the Common Heritage Project, extended to imply materials that related to nature and time in a very specific manner. Partly, as we shall see, this was because the materials chosen for the reconstruction had to be of the same kind, or work *with* nature instead of trying to alter nature. It was also partly because what the Romans valued as natural products unaltered by humans could in the Frederiksgave case be extended to mean products that were valued for being unaltered by time, in the sense that the materials should ideally take us back to both the time and the place of the original Frederiksgave plantation. By this I mean that, in order to reconstruct the cultural heritage site, a virginal (unaltered and unspoiled) year when the building was originally constructed was settled upon as the natural and given goal that the reconstruction should make us reach, implying that there was only one point and time of origin to be imitated by the heritage site. Reconstructing the site was a way of completing the building as it was in the selected 'year zero' of 1831, rather than 'altering' it to account for its appearance in any of the 173 years between then and when the reconstruction began. The reconstruction should not be made fraudulently artificial, but rather be made as if merely collected from a specific place and point in time, and from there naturally extended into the present. My point here is that what should be understood as authentically natural products, then, are indeed humanly altered, but in particular ways that follow the distinction between fraudulently artificial (*facticius*) alterations and authentic natural extensions. Let me explore what was more precisely meant by artificial and natural goods, or 'materials' as I shall call them here.

Although the year of the construction of the Frederiksgave buildings is difficult to define because of the long construction process, the Frederiksgave Plantation and Common Heritage Site booklet and posters give it as 1831.[26] 1831, then, was fixed as the point of origin from which alterations, decay and reconstruction could begin and be recapitulated. For example, remnants of two walls indicate that two small rooms had been erected on the veranda on a later occasion. Even though the Danish architect was not too enthusiastic about conserving and securing these two ruined walls built after 1831, he accepted it because the Ghanaian archaeologist convinced him that it would be good to maintain the remaining walls 'for pedagogical reasons', to show visitors how the walls were constructed, as the Danish architect explained to me. Today, therefore, two rough brownish walls (not whitewashed), each approximately one metre high, divide the white veranda into three sections – the brown walls follow the symmetry of the building and are not seen before one enters the veranda.

In line with the pedagogical ambition conveyed by the Ghanaian archaeologist and coordinator, a sequence of four smaller squares of wall was left un-whitewashed on the back of the building. Together, these wall sections show the process of constructing the house in its different stages of completion: in the first square are rhombus-shaped stones, the size of a foot, glued together with mortar. The next two squares expose rough and smooth plastering respectively. The little series culminates in a well-plastered wall which, if it were not meant as a pedagogical example, would be ready for the whitewash that covers the rest of the building. Finally, part of a larger original wall is also kept un-whitewashed. This wall seems to date from the original building, and has miraculously been conserved by the protection of the two huge fig trees described in Chapter Three. The wall was kept rough for 'demonstrative reasons', as stated on the

FIG. 4.1 The veranda with rough brownish wall, 2008, Sesemi, Ghana.

FIG. 4.2 Sequence of four unfinished squares at the back of the main building, 2006, Sesemi, Ghana.

poster: 'Why this rough wall?', exhibited nearby. Both the architect and many visitors (myself included) have stepped close to this rough wall to let our eyes analyse it meticulously, while our hands slid over it to point at a familiar form, often that of a seashell. These displays function as windows to the past, and collapse time to allow visitors to directly explore the original materials, such as the burnt shells that the mortar was made of.

These pedagogical tools, I suggest, illustrate a more general feature of the reconstruction of the Frederiksgave site, namely the issue of diminishing the gap in time between then and now by extending what was once there, rather than altering it. Like Pliny's distinction, the reconstruction work was about collecting natural authentic pieces and downplaying their manufacture. In other words, it was a matter of willingly disregarding the lapse in time (1831-2004, when the reconstruction project was initiated) in order to extend the past into the present and future. It is important to note that extension should not be understood as 'us' constructing history via extension, but rather as history extending itself into the present under the professional guidance of the planners of our common reconstruction project – a point I will return to later.

A group of key people from the National Museum in Denmark explained the gap in time, beginning after the Danish King sold the Danish possessions in 1850, as follows:

> Two hundred years of Danish presence was irreversibly over [...] In addition to Danish toponyms and a long list of descendants with Danish family names, the Danes left six Danish forts, a long list of plantations and merchants' houses behind. The darkness of history swallowed Frederiksgave for almost one hundred years – until the ruin was described and surveyed in the middle of the 1940s by writer Sophie Petersen and drawer and architect I. B. Andersen, and later in the middle of the 1960s by architect Niels Bech and geographer Henrik Jeppesen.[27]

In this quote, the notion of 'the darkness of history' can be seen as a way of describing in writing the lapse in time between the Danes leaving and their return. The dark jungle which with time had literally taken over the place consigned the Frederiksgave plantation to an oblivion in which time was thought to stand still until it was set in motion and illuminated once more, emerging through the intervention of the National Museum, with its descriptions and records. Of course, since the villagers living close by knew of the place all along, the illuminated rediscovery must be understood in a very particular way, namely as a consequence of the idea of settling on the year 1831 as the point of departure containing *the* common history to which we can be brought back through various techniques such as measures, drawings and written text.[28] For all the apparent dynamism entailed in the exhibited and written attempts at bridging the gap between then and now, the dynamics are perceived from a specific position in space and time, with 1831 set as a year zero to which we can work to return. In a sense, then, the heritage work appeared to stop and start history. From this perspective, the two brownish walls that were later added to the veranda could be seen as interrupting, in more ways than one, the smooth backtracking to year zero constituted by the whitewashed surface. They came to disturb the point of origin (1831) by indicating that the building had been altered in another past – an alteration that with the newly reconstructed building was neither eliminated (by tearing down the small brown walls) nor incorporated (by rebuilding and whitewashing the walls), but allowed for in ways that somehow seemed awkward. When tourists visited the site they often questioned the brown walls, not immediately understanding the pedagogical ambition. Like two small brown teeth in an otherwise perfect white denture, the remnants seemed to mock the whitewashed building by showing the fragility of naturalising a specific point of departure as both the end and the beginning of history. The ruined brown walls expressed a tension between reconstructing and securing the building, and they showed that a reconstruction could have been done differently. As such, they were expressions of the choices and rejections I have explored throughout, as they interrupted the Frederiksgave site as an inevitable and continuous entity. Seen through the vocabulary of Pliny, the ruined brown walls are artificial in relation to the year zero, which in contrast is the natural year for the whitewashed building.

The idea of building on top of a ruin can also be seen through the distinction introduced by Pliny – modified as I explained above – between natural collected goods as equivalent to an unaltered point of origin and manufactured goods as equivalent to alterations in the point of origin. 'Just to walk around in exactly the same building as they once did is fantastic,' commented the former Museum director when substantiating the reasons for building on top of the ruin at Frederiksgave. By choosing to reconstruct on the plot of the existing ruin, the people from the National Museum were well aware that they were indirectly challenging the Venice Charter, which recommends stopping reconstruction when conjecture begins;[29] they knew that it was a 'rather unorthodox decision'.[30] A group of Danish archaeologists visiting the newly inaugurated site actually lamented the new structure, arguing that they clearly preferred to sense 'the presence of history'[31] by way of a ruin – this sentiment, they told me, was not as strong in a renovated building, even if it was located on the actual plot of the original building. As these statements indicate, there was a clear tension, particularly among the project planners from the Danish National Museum, between reconstruction and conservation at the Frederiksgave site. For the people from the Ghana Museums and Monuments Board in charge of cultural heritage in Ghana it was not considered a problem. But for the Danes involved there needed to be a balancing of the original against the newly added, in order to turn Frederiksgave into a proper cultural heritage site.

The project of not altering the original building at Frederiksgave seemed to be an impossible ambition when the National Museum chose to reconstruct on top of it. The planners had considered following the Venice Charter by securing the ruin and erecting a copy of the main building alongside it. But building on top of the ruin was also supported in pedagogical terms.[32] Early on in the project, the Ghanaian and Danish partners, had agreed that a ruin 'did not make much sense in Ghana', as the Ghanaian architect told me. He continued, 'Ghanaians would not understand a ruin' and, for this reason, it was right to reconstruct on top of it. Even though this plan deviated from the National Museum's practices in Denmark, as key people from the museum told me, the Danes' enthusiasm for the reconstruction process was profound. Their engagement and energy mirrored their delight; clearly, choosing to build on exactly the same spot created a feeling of authenticity, as reflected in the director's enthusiasm regarding the possibility of walking around in exactly the same building as his predecessors.

The location was apparently seen as making the heritage project naturally extend common history into the present, rather than being an artificial alteration, as it would have been if built at a different location. By deviating from the articles of the Venice Charter, both by reconstructing on top of the ruin and by using new materials (since anastylosis was not possible), the materials chosen for the reconstruction were seen by the project makers as acceptable alterations in accordance with a special game with nature, a game that extended or revived the site from the selected point of origin.

For instance, the sequence on the back of the building described above collapsed the building processes between then and now – it was another way of overcoming the passing of time, of overcoming the 'darkness of history'. It blurred the gap in time so that it became impossible to tell the past from the present, impossible to tell who built in the way that these sequences revealed, because 'we' in the present had constructed Frederiksgave exactly as 'they' once did and vice versa. And, with such linearity, the four sequential squares could be seen as emphasising the idea that today's reconstruction was seen as a more or less given and natural result of the past construction. The sequence functioned like a recipe to follow by exposing the already given process; one might say that it was a sequence that denied its own sequentiality. It unveiled what was already there to further display year zero, until now engulfed in 'the darkness of history'.

Fourteen archives had been visited in Denmark, but unfortunately, no drawings of the buildings making up the Frederiksgave plantation had been found. Even though an architectural drawing would have been valuable, and an obvious way of rebooting to 1831 by following old guidelines, the Danish architect loved the detective work of finding out what the site used to look like. For the architect, it was a quest for the natural, i.e. the original building, and a denial of the artificial, i.e. a distortedly manufactured building. He liked the fact that solutions were not obvious and that 'things didn't really fit at first'. At one point we were having a break in the open shed at the site. He explained that it kept him alert to continually think of new solutions to the problems he encountered at the reconstruction site. He likened his job to a pack of cards and, laying his pipe down for a moment, he bent over the wooden table in the shed. Excited, I also bent over the table, my senses sharpened. He folded his hands as if holding a pack of cards and then, with his thumb, he scrolled through the fictitious cards. Suddenly, his thumb stopped and he took out a card with the words 'Nine of hearts, *that's* how it should be, not two of hearts' – he exclaimed. His demonstration reminded me of a magician fooling an audience, but this ability to find 'the right card', he told me, came from forty years of experience. It was not something that could simply be learned from books – the ability came from sensing, measuring, constructing and exploring various other old constructions and the materials they were made of. This situation demonstrated that, in the eyes of the architect, it was possible to 'get it right' – that there was one natural solution. For all the subjectivity involved, a key seemed to be attainable from a finite pack of cards. The right cards would make for a true reconstruction, finding a natural solution to what at first appeared unknowable.

The situation described above points to an interesting and productive ambiguity regarding the Danish architect. As we have seen, on the one hand, a true cultural heritage project attempts to let the buildings speak for themselves; the project extends and completes buildings as they used to be, with the help of professionals as 'midwives' bringing to the world what is already made. In one way, then, the Danish architect is a neutral replaceable medium, facilitating a natural process, merely by 'choosing the right card'. But in another way he is completely crucial as he is the one with enough personal experience to make the right choices. His forty years of experience make him – and only him – choose the right card from the many that may at first appear right but which are wrong. As such he is irreplaceable, and much more than a medium at the service of nature and history. Apparently, he is a prerequisite for constructing heritage both as natural and artificial history, to go back to Pliny's distinction. In other words, Frederiksgave was rescued from 'the darkness of history' both by itself and by a seasoned professional.

During fieldwork, other instances of finding the right card illustrated the (often blurred) distinction between the natural and the artificial. Analyses were conducted by a variety of professional heritage workers engaged in the Frederiksgave project, as archaeologists excavated and examined the artefacts and the ruined parts, while architects were invited to investigate the ruins and choose which materials to use to renovate the building – a high-priority issue that attracted a great deal of attention, including financial. A Danish historian was engaged to find letters, diaries and official documents regarding the Frederiksgave plantation in the archives, and along with the rest of the professional team he was to advise particularly the Ghanaian archaeologist and coordinator on which artefacts to exhibit and which stories to tell at the site.

Since only a few dismembered parts of the original building were available, anastylosis was not an option, as I have already mentioned. Choosing other materials for the reconstruction was therefore vital, and this turned out to be a matter of finding materials that related to nature in particular ways. Archaeological excavations were undertaken both inside the three buildings and in the surrounding area. The artefacts found were cleaned, photographed, measured and identified according to material and chronology, before being given a number that could identify in which layer and where they had been found. In collaboration with the archaeologists, the architects conducted 'archaeological surveys of the buildings' in order to study the original appearance of the main building, and the old building materials used. Part of a wall was studied; the clay, stones and the plaster used were analysed and identified and, again, numerous photos were taken from various angles and distances. Rubble with traces of wood imprints was investigated, and remnants of layers of the whitewashed lime were counted through a magnifying glass. And what could not be thoroughly analysed in Ghana was sent to the National Museum's laboratory in Copenhagen as samples. Indeed, the findings were analysed in the etymological sense of breaking them up into smaller parts. Likewise, the two architects conducted investigations to 'interpret the patterns of decay', as the Danish architect put it: the building was measured, roots were listened to, eyes observed the plants growing on the building, and the knife picked into the materials, as described in the previous chapter. Due to termites and the humid tropical climate, no wooden parts had survived. By means of written sources partly provided by the Danish historian, however, the Danish architect was able to find out that in the construction of roofs expatriate Danes had used a particular sort of tropical palm with a high concentration of acid that supposedly made it inedible to termites. All these analyses were enthusiastically performed in order to find out what materials had originally been used and to ascertain the appearance of the building – what it had looked like when originally built in 1831. All of this was documented in detailed reports written by the Danish architect. It seemed that being there at the original place, combined with all the sensuous analyses of the materials, could bring the participants in the reconstruction process closer to the time and feel of the original Frederiksgave, as also argued in Chapter Three. But this reconstruction process seemingly produces a paradox: the more 'we' in the present know about how Frederiksgave was originally constructed, the less the present reconstruction appears as a creation – we have to create it in such a manner that it is merely uncovered. The original materials, in a sense, talk for themselves – as truly historical objects. Detailed knowledge of these historical objects seems to turn what 'was done' when reconstructing the buildings into obvious, natural facts. In the words of Pliny, one could say that by knowing how it was once constructed, today's reconstruction becomes less artificial (*facticius*) – less a matter of man-made creation than one of collecting and uncovering Frederiksgave's history from the darkness of time and the wilderness of the jungle.

In the following, I will go into more detail with regard to how the reconstruction materials and exhibition artefacts were chosen and handled, and how this process oscillated between displaying heritage as a natural given and as a man-made artificial object.

CONSCIENTIOUS WORK WITH NATURE: TECHNIQUES AND MATERIALS

From his work first as a carpenter and later as a specialist in old buildings in Denmark, the architect of Frederiksgave had acquired a huge knowledge of Danish fauna and flora. In Ghana, he was eager to learn about tropical species. He talked to local people and had samples of plants sent home to specialists in Copenhagen. He was fascinated by the skills of adaptation and knowledge that had been required of the earlier Danes, and as described with regard to Wulff's House in Chapter Two, he praised the more than 150-year-old 'hybrid buildings' that evolved on the coast for being smartly designed and composed.

I, for my part, was completely fascinated by the architect's huge knowledge of building materials and of the etymology of words regarding flora, fauna and handicraft. Just as Pliny the Elder in his *Natural History*[33] had divided his thorough and detailed description of nature into several books, our 'lectures' – as the architect named our conversations – followed the same structure. We went through a variety of materials, talking about their characteristics, their etymological meaning, and their relations to other materials. This resulted in lectures on the oak tree, on lime, on sand, on linseed oil, on wooden tar, on lacquer, and on densely woody charcoal such as palm nuts, to mention but a few of them, all dealing with 'natural products' as the architect collectively referred to them. In this way, we talked what at times seemed to be a strange and chaotic reconstruction site into an orderly meaningful cosmos, as had Pliny's *Natural History* 2000 years before. We spent hours talking about lime and mortar and other substances pertaining to 'natural history and technique', as he framed it. In the shade of the tool shed, the architect told me about the size of a grain of sand, its shape dependent upon where it is collected, whether it has sharp edges from lying peacefully on the bottom of a lake, or if it is rubbed round from being tossed in the rough sea, and how an angular shape is relevant to its binding strength. He showed me how, in Denmark, he had learned to make an easy check of the quality of sand by mixing a small portion of sand with spit in his hand, thus getting an idea of the concentration of clay and sand. We found some sand at the site and tried out his low-tech quality check. He could easily see my enthusiasm and, jokingly, before we were interrupted, we agreed to save 'the next private lecture'. In the evening, we continued on the subject of lime and, as our bodies began to be cooled by the night, he told me about the cooling qualities of a particular material: well-slaked lime made from burnt seashells; about its exceptional capacity for transmitting air, resulting in a quick cooling down of buildings – a capacity much needed in a tropical climate with large variations in temperature in any one day. He explained how farmers in Denmark had taken advantage of the antiseptic and anti-static quality of lime by whitewashing their stables and houses annually to kill all bacteria and prevent dust from accumulating on the inner walls. This hygienic atmosphere was later imitated in city apartments and in suburban villas, where the fashion among residents was to have white walls and wooden floors pigmented slightly white, as he also told me. The Danish architect pointed out that it was not just a matter of aesthetics; actually, he did not care that much for aesthetics in the first place. Instead, he was more interested in good techniques; it was the technically good move that caught his interest. He then went on to talk about an old technique for increasing the strength of coloured lime by adding buttermilk, and how this ingredient covered the small well-slaked lime and pigment grains and made them stronger because of the milk's adhesive qualities. In the process, I curiously asked hundreds of questions and thereby gave him the opportunity to talk our common work and shared nature into order. For example, I asked why, given this benefit, buttermilk had not been added in rich quantities to the lime used at the site? To this he replied that 'It is about finding the right dose', and he explained that it was not just a matter of making it strong and impermeable. It was about 'whitewashing layers of lime that were so technically weak that they were strong. That is conscientious work with nature'. He lit his pipe and explained: 'It's about working *with* nature not against nature'.

By using Pliny's distinction between artificial (in the sense of products altered by humans) and natural (products collected by humans) as a source of inspiration, we can set the ideas of the Danish architect to work and thus explore how the Frederiksgave plantation (the object recovered from history) was conceptualised as both a natural and a man-made artefact. Pliny's distinction, however, is not exactly the same as the distinction made by the Danish architect. The architect was interested in techniques that were indeed performed by humans, but so as to 'conscientiously work with nature'. What unites the 'natural products', as the architect called them, is that they are all working with nature and produced through techniques that work with nature (e.g. lime, buttermilk) and/or are ready to be gathered and hence unaltered by humans (e.g. oak, sand). By activating a version of Pliny's distinction between natural products and artificial products, it becomes clear that distinctions were made at the Frederiksgave site; authentic nature and the right treatment of it (i.e. to work conscientiously with nature) were seen as opposed to the fraudulent artificial products working against nature. 'Natural products' should therefore not only be judged by whether or not they have been altered by humans, but also by the ways in which such alteration is carried out. This gives rise to a few questions that needed to be resolved in the Frederiksgave reconstruction. What are good techniques and products, as opposed to fraudulent and bad techniques and materials? What did it mean to work with or against nature in the context of the Frederiksgave reconstruction? In what ways was the heritage seen as prone to fraud? How do the techniques and materials affect the valuation of Frederiksgave as heritage in the eyes of the people involved? These questions turn cultural heritage into a matter of finding true and good ways to deal with the materials used in the reconstruction, and of finding the right 'dose' of human intervention. Above we saw how the architect was an ambiguous figure: on the one hand he was almost superfluous, just a neutral medium, but on the other hand he was important because his life experience qualified him to predict how both nature and history might fulfil themselves. It seems as if cultural heritage inherits its value by appearing unchanged, and the role of the heritage worker is to let both history and nature speak, since the products and materials involved already have the solution, the potential of fulfilment within them, if it is conscientiously recovered.

THE APPEARANCE OF NATURE: MAINTAINING COMMON HERITAGE

This coupling of perspectives on nature with ideas about what should be considered authentic as opposed to fraudulent seemed vital in the Frederiksgave project. People visiting the site should not be 'cheated by modern materials such as concrete and emulsion paint' as a key person from the National Museum once told me. As in Pliny's time, appearance can reveal the character of the product and be tied up with a kind of valuation system.

As an example of work against nature, the Danish architect mentioned emulsion paint. This artificially made product was clearly not one of his favourites. He likened living in buildings painted with emulsion to 'living in a plastic bag'. If painted onto a permeable substance, such as for instance lime mortar, stone or clay, which were the components of most of the old European-built constructions on the African coast, then the emulsion would form such a strong protective layer that it would start flaking off the building (because of the potential difference of permeability of wall and paint). Lime, on the other hand, would be weak enough to enable permeability, but strong enough to protect the building from sun cracks and rain. The architect acknowledged that the poor indoor climate ensuing from the emulsion's impermeability could be handled by introducing yet another technical solution, for example, expensive energy-guzzling machines that could renew the air – one solution giving rise to another problem, as he expressed it. Indeed, the architect's ideas about nature were combined with a critique of how we had organised our modern society. He suggested using technically elegant solutions that did not interfere with nature – as he said 'nature always has the best solutions'. He lamented the fact that concrete and emulsion were generally the most sought after materials in Ghana. When we visited Ghana's UNESCO-listed heritage sites, the forts and castles along the coast, we noticed the lustrous surface and the peeling walls characteristic of emulsion paint on former lime structures. Renovation had been done with what the architect defined as the wrong materials. In the village of Sesemi where the Frederiksgave site was located, colourful concrete houses had sprung up to replace old brown mud houses. To many of the people living in Sesemi that I spoke with, the colourful houses were clear signifiers of status, and even thinking about choosing to live in a cluster of mud houses if one could afford to construct a brightly coloured concrete house with aluminium roof and a surrounding fence seemed incomprehensible. The Danish architect was clearly of another opinion; he treasured 'natural materials rather than artificially made bull-shit' as he once jokingly put it when alluding to the Ghanaians aspirations to live in modern houses. Just as important, as noted above, he treasured a thorough knowledge of the qualities and characteristics of the natural materials, and as a mantra he repeatedly told me: *'You may just as well work with nature as against it'*. Of course concrete, as a burned mixture of lime and clay, could also be seen as a product of nature. But the reason why the Danish architect rejected it in the renovation of the main building was, first of all, that it was not the original building material and, secondly, that it did not fit well technically with the other original materials. Emulsion received an even harsher evaluation; it was rejected for the same reasons as concrete but, in addition, its propensity to work against nature was repeated several times by the Danish architect. As if ranked, emulsion paint seemed to be a more artificial, and thus a normatively worse product, than concrete – the latter was actually used in the erection of a full copy of one of the buildings, probably a stable and/or kitchen, built a few metres alongside where it used to be. Like the other two buildings, the concrete structure was whitewashed, but modern facilities such as a small kitchenette with running water, toilet and electricity had also been installed in the building so that it could be used as a reception and potential store for fresh drinks and souvenirs, in addition to exhibiting the archaeological artefacts.

If the priest quoted at the start of this chapter was on a crusade against fetishes and idols as dangerous objects and signs of backwardness, then the architect could similarly be seen as fighting materialities that he considered to be 'bullshit' in arguing against a modernity that eradicated techniques and knowledge developed over generations. The sign was thus reversed in the architect's crusade: it was a struggle for history or tradition and against a modernity that compromised techniques true to nature. One might say that to the architect the technological and artificial modern 'stuff' had to be eradicated because of its false treatment of nature. Or rather, expressed in a self-fulfilling argument, history (up to destructive modernity) had been seen to work with nature and, as such, both nature and history appeared as naturally given phenomena that could be uncovered through proper, qualified procedures. However, not everyone renovating old buildings shares the Danish architect's views that modern techniques necessarily distort history and nature.

During my fieldwork, I had the chance to meet a Dutch architect who had been involved in an EU project that had sponsored the renovation of ancient European-built buildings and some of the fort structure in Elmina, in the western part of coastal Ghana. As an experienced worker with heritage in rather poor countries, he had judged – rather pragmatically, as he said – that it would be better to paint the renovated houses with emulsion instead of the original whitewash. He argued that emulsion lasted longer and only needed repainting every six years, as opposed to the well-slaked lime used for whitewashing buildings, which needed a brush up at least every second year to look nice. Furthermore, he argued that emulsion was a material that the Ghanaian and other local craftsmen knew and used in their daily work. He told me that even though the well-visited UNESCO site, the Elmina Castle, had recently been whitewashed to look its best for the celebrations of fifty years of Ghana's independence, it was looking grey and spotted after less than a year. He had therefore concluded that, even though it may not be correct in terms of the originality of the houses, it would be better to paint the houses with emulsion. In all, the Dutch architect had thought it rather difficult to engage the people living in Elmina and the owners of the houses in terms of seeing the value of authenticity and of this part of history, as he expressed it. In the very next sentence, he pointed to issues that apparently seemed of much higher priority and interest to the Elminians, such as schools, sanitation, jobs and so on. The colours chosen for the historical houses were not the original combination of white and beige colours, either. Together with the other partners involved in Elmina, he had suggested these traditional European colours at a meeting, as these were the colours originally chosen for the houses. However, an architect from Namibia who was also present had presented pictures of various Mediterranean pastels, and clearly the Elminian owners of the houses preferred these colours to the more neutral but original ones. All the renovated houses were therefore now painted in very bright colours, too bright for the Dutch architect's taste but, as he said, 'it's their houses, they're the ones who live in them and look at them each day, why should I insist?' Vividly recollecting all the 'lectures' and discussions I had had with the Danish architect, I asked his Dutch counterpart where the limit should be set when choosing materials that were alternatives to the original ones. With this question, I was probing the issue seemingly so essential for the Common Heritage Project, namely the distinction between original and new materials, and authentic and fraudulent appearance. The Dutch architect responded that his tolerance level depended upon whether it was relatively easy to make amends for the use of alternative materials by approximating to authenticity. For example, he argued that one could easily repaint the houses in the original colours if someone wanted to, whereas old wooden window frames would be more difficult to replace. Interestingly, he did not mention the more radical move of scratching off the emulsion paint and whitewashing the buildings in the original colours. Instead he talked about the houses having a similar appearance to the authentic ones, while not necessarily staying true to the authentic materials.

Using the same distinction as Pliny's example with the fraudulent artificial (*facticius*) gum, the Dutch architect had considered keeping the emulsion but painting the houses in their original colours in order to give the houses an authentic appearance. Yet an authentic appearance was not in line with the wishes of the house owners, and so the situation changed. Well aware of the original whitewashed buildings and their colours, the Dutch architect thus indirectly pointed to a space for negotiation and adjustment within each project, not allowing for a particular understanding of nature to decide the course of reconstruction. Projects, in his view, were processes rather than products. To him, heritage seemed obviously to be a relative and social affair – adjustable to the present-day lives lived at the sites. It was more important to adjust to such a lived life than to maintain strict ideas about authenticity and natural techniques in order for history to be unveiled. In other words, the Dutch architect introduced a different kind of commonness from the one explicit in the Frederiksgave project, namely a commonness stemming from the needs and wishes of the present-day Elminian citizens and owners of the houses. With the slogan 'Building on the past to create a better future' the heritage project in Elmina had, in addition to renovating old buildings, also worked from an explicit ambition of assisting the city with a ten-year development strategy. By collaborating closely with the local authorities on identifying the needs and wishes of the people of Elmina, the heritage project was much more in line with the numerous development projects in Ghana, where communities were engaged. Such an inclusive approach was, as also mentioned before, apparently never an ambition for the planners of the Frederiksgave project. Apart from whatever interest the people of Sesemi had in taking part in 'a common history', their interests were mainly labelled 'side-effects' by the Danish project planners – as we shall further explore in Chapter Five.

Interestingly, the Danish architect had a similar argument in relation to where his tolerance level was. In response to a critique raised by some Danish archaeologists of building on top of the ruin, he talked of the possibility 'of taking off the hat' of the main building, explaining that one could, in theory, remove all the new materials used for renovation in order to return the site to the original ruin. This ruin, as the architect stressed, had been virtually unaltered, simply strengthened, secured and built upon. It had been strengthened by clearing out 2-3 centimetres of old mortar made from clay in the remaining stone construction, followed by filling in with a new and stronger mortar made of lime and angular river sand. PVC tubes also now made up the inside of the columns on the terrace, in order to strengthen the rather weak pillar construction. And in order to stabilise the building, it was secured by being tightened to a huge subterranean steel reinforcement bolted to the cliff upon which half of the main building stood. This construction, the architect told me, 'was not interfering with the building', but was merely a construction that would guarantee that the building did not 'run down the slope', as he jokingly explained. The Frederiksgave site was thereby constructed with different considerations to the Elmina project, which achieved commonness by paying attention to present-day local considerations. The considerations at Frederiksgave were also local, but local in a different way. Apparently these concerns were not negotiated in consideration of the village's present-day local life, as was the case in Elmina. Instead, they referred to the local environment and to the local life of 1831. Instead of the kind of commonness sought in Elmina, the Common Heritage Project found commonness in a shared Danish-Ghanaian history and nature to which local buildings had to adapt then and now. In this sense, commonness is part of the absolute value of cultural heritage – it is a universal good. Universal in the sense of being given as a natural site for 'our common history' which, curiously, is a point in time rather than a process. As a given common good, the reason for paying attention to it appeared obvious and unquestionable. No argument other than taking care of our common history was needed, and whatever else the project accomplished became 'side-effects'. Concerns for the stability, conservation and durability of the newly-constructed building could be accommodated with unobtrusive modern materials. The space for negotiation was to be found in different spheres from those at play in the Elmina project – in an internal sphere in the building and in the archives, rather than in an encounter with living people. Maintenance, however, did not necessarily imply unobtrusive techniques, as we shall see.

Even though it was a high priority, the whitewashing of the Frederiksgave building the following year became the subject of some misunderstandings. Many of the young men living in the village had, under the direction of the Danish architect, participated in the first whitewashing of the buildings immediately prior to the inauguration of the site. Based on this experience, guidelines had been produced in order to eliminate any misunderstandings in the further process of maintenance. Together, the Danish architect and the Ghanaian architect had written a page-long instruction on how to whitewash the building in the future. Bags of burnt seashells with which to make the lime had been left in the tool shed at project end, together with a barrel of well-slaked lime. This would secure proper maintenance of the surface of the buildings for many years to come – a maintenance that sustained the possibility of returning to year zero (1831) and extending it into the future. One or two of the former workers from the village had been asked to look at the water level in the barrel every now and again, to ensure that the lime did not dry out. When I arrived with the Danish architect a year after the inauguration, the surface of the Frederiksgave building looked bizarre. It was spotted and had cracks in its surface. Upon making enquiries, the Danish architect learned that there had been a celebration in the village, for which occasion the village council headed by the Chief had asked for a brush-up of the building. It was this, according to some of the villagers, that had turned the building greyish and dirty-looking. The Danish architect could infer from the cracks that now spotted the surface that they had mixed the lime with too little water, and probably whitewashed the house in full sun, thereby not allowing for the necessary slow drying process. Furthermore, unlike emulsion paint, lime has to be whitewashed in very thin watery layers, preferably at sunset. It seemed that the workers had painted the house as if they were painting it with a nice thick emulsion. Obviously, the Danish architect was disappointed and he could not really understand how they had got it wrong – they had done it a year previously under his instructions, and he and the Ghanaian architect had left a clearly written guide. As a ray of comfort, we discovered that they had only whitewashed the façade of the building, the side facing the village; the work against nature and history had thus done limited damage. But the building had nevertheless been altered; the materials may have been right, but they had been used in the wrong doses. The procedure for natural maintenance – the extension of year zero made possible by the well-slaked lime and its proper use – had not been followed. Instead, the house appeared mistreated, a mistreatment that was not of the 1830s, but due to other habits, interests and ignorance and, indeed, to interference with nature. Visitors could be fooled by this alteration, because it was not the authentic properly whitewashed building that they saw, but a mistreated copy. Paradoxically, and as previously mentioned, the more careful the heritage work is, the less visible the human intervention becomes. One could say that, by reconstructing the original after the manner of the original builders, the actual reconstruction process fades away, as do the ensuing attempts at maintenance – these practices are ideally invisible as processes, because they are only needed to keep a year zero and a given product stable. The main building at the Frederiksgave site is not to be understood as a new construction, but as an extension emerging through the various Danes who visited, surveyed and documented the site in order to bridge the gap of 100 years of darkness, as stated by people from the Danish National Museum. The point here is that even if the place gained value as a cultural heritage site from this conscientious work with nature and by collapsing the gap between then and now, such a point in time and place needs proper maintenance. Maintenance, then, is ideally a matter of not interfering with nature and history. Rather, the issue is simply one of cultivating the already given and charted, as captured in the idea of a single moment of origin: in this case the year zero of Frederiksgave, identified as 1831. Indeed, the bumblings and failures of the project show us that an expert's design – here supposedly a non-misunderstandable set of guidelines for whitewashing – cannot control its subsequent life. The various ways of treating the building indicate that it is not just a copy of history and/or nature, even if this is the vision of the project planners. Instead, they show the various practices and ways of valuing the project. Thus the awkward encounter between the Danish architect and the mistreated house points to an important aspect of the heritage project, namely that there is a certain fragility entailed in working with a point – in this case the year 1831 – in that it causes all maintenance and human involvement to be interferences, for better or worse. As analysed in Chapter Two, encounters also seem obstructed by conceiving of heritage work in this way, or at best reduced to minor interferences having no generative potential. Only a very particular encounter seems to be allowed for, namely an encounter with a point of origin

(1831). By leaving no room for other encounters, multiple valuations of the site are reduced in number – reduced to 'side-effects' or to negligence.

IDOLS AND REFERENTIALITY: APPROXIMATING THE CREATION AT FREDERIKSGAVE

Above, we saw how a Roman use of the word *facticius* was used to distinguish artificial goods from natural goods, and how this distinction could be fruitful in exploring the emergence of a heritage site in Ghana where both nature and materials were key elements for the people involved. Having examined how the Common Heritage Site obtained its value as such by skilfully handling an already given history and nature, let me now look at the development of the etymology of the word 'fetish'. This will allow me to further explore how the site accrued value, and how the materiality of cultural heritage is seen to become effective and valuable in the words of the people involved.

From a Roman commercial setting, Pietz moves on to track the etymological roots of the fetish in an incipient Christian religious setting. In this new context, instead of denoting or suggesting the opposition of artificial fraudulent goods to natural genuine goods, the concept is related to the theme of the body, the soul and the sacramental objects.[34] The notion of idolatry, understood by members of the early Christian Church as the worship of any manufactured religious object that does not point to the true God, seems to be produced in these complex relations of material bodies, spiritual souls and sacred objects. *Facticii*, one of the etymological roots of the fetish, was the term used to characterise the manufactured character of these false man-made objects. Worshipping such objects was regarded as spiritual fraud and classified as idolatry in early Christianity. Matter, Pietz argues, was seen to be 'an improper medium for acts of worship'.[35] Whether the practice in question was bodybuilding or artistic sculpture, the concern for the early Christians was not to seek to surpass the work of God. Instead of worshipping external forms, the early Church prescribed inner faith and the soul's free will as proper Christian faith. The unmotivated free verbal utterances that characterise the human worshipping of the divine creation were voluntary acts of true faith which, in substance, were not material but spiritual and eternal. Relations with the divine could be made through the spoken word, which was distinguished from the worldly human realm where we are left with the craft of resemblance. God was understood as the only true creator, and humans were doomed to act within the material world of mere resemblance. But resemblance had various meanings. Pietz notes that resemblance in a Judeo-Christian understanding was thought to be 'an essentially material relation and as such inherently improper for representing spiritual models'.[36] Instead of being a result of free will, materiality was thought of as being only referential, secondary and of lesser value. This understanding differed from what Pietz characterises as a Greek philosophic tradition (Platonic and neo-Platonic), where material resemblance was thought of as a matter of how successfully an individual or an object embodies the virtues of its type – meaning the degree to which a unification through a reflection of the soul's 'substantial resemblance' to the godhead could be reached – a resemblance which, when realised, would appreciate that it emanated from the One.[37] As Pietz explains, resemblance for the Greek mind is:

> the relation between material entities and their eternal ideal forms. In Christian thought the logic of image and resemblance explains the truth within the material half of the creation only [...] resemblance neither expresses the true relation between the earthly and the divine nor describes the logic of the spiritual half of creation (which is explained by a logic of identity and voluntary relation – even notions of the 'imitation' of Christ are based on the idea of enacted identification rather than mimetic reflection).[38]

At this point, an analytical experiment might prove productive. As we have seen throughout, the Frederiksgave site was discussed by the planners very much in terms of authenticity, commonness, true appearance and closeness to original materials, design and topography. As has become clear, paradoxes emerged with regard to all of these issues: the recreation of an original, authentic building was the project's starting point and its end goal – but this is a contradiction in terms. If we focus on the distance between the human material world and the divine spiritual world then we might liken the spiritual being to the point of origin at the Frederiksgave site, this being the creative point from where everything emerges. We might then ask whether cultural heritage as it was practised in the reconstruction of the Common Heritage Project was pointing to the tragedy (mere resemblance) or rather to the potential of materiality (embodying the virtues of its type)? How successful were the different strategies adopted to reach the point of origin through technologies such as detailed studies of the site and of the archaeological artefacts, the architectural measures and proportions of the building materials, and investigations in the Danish National Archives? In other words, did the reconstruction process follow what might generically be called a Greek or a Christian reasoning? Did the planners and constructors, like the Greeks, understand the reconstruction as a matter of embodying the virtues of its type – that is, as a matter of substantial resemblance between the material reconstruction and what it had been in the past? And is this implied in the idea of working with nature? Or did they rather understand the reconstruction as referential, and thereby always already a tragic project due to its incarceration in materiality, while still being as close as one can get to the past? Was the reconstruction an issue of coming to terms with the fact that resemblance with or imitation of the past can only be enacted identification through the verbal act of the free will, rather than embodied mimetic reflection, as Pietz expressed it? Is it a matter of referentiality when the Danish architect stresses the need to work with nature, or is it implying an embodiment? All of these questions arise out of my attempt to understand the value of Frederiksgave through the history of the fetish, the religion of materiality. In other words, I now explore how Frederiksgave *worked* for its worshippers as a particular material object.

It seemed that in very specific ways, whether through anastylosis (the use of dismembered original parts), identical location, similar materials or materials working with nature, authenticity – to employ the term used by those involved in the reconstruction – could really be attained, at least momentarily. This can be seen, for example, in the case of the treasured lime, described above. The Danish architect did not pass up a chance to talk about the lime's wonderful capacities. By worshipping the lime as the original material used at the Frederiksgave site, and for its capacity in the restoration to 'work with nature', in the hands and words of the Danish architect, the material accorded with the Greek understanding of resemblance. It did this by embodying the virtues of its type – virtues that had to do precisely with authenticity and working with nature. Neither the Danish architect nor the later visitors to the site seemed to regard the newly produced lime as a mere simulacrum, or to be in only referential relation to the point of origin of the Frederiksgave site. Instead, the lime contained virtues pertaining to an original history and nature. But if the very specific 'guidelines' aimed at capturing the virtues of nature and history were not thoroughly followed – as happened when the villagers later whitewashed the building on their own – or if the Frederiksgave site had been painted with emulsion, then the visitors would have been cheated.

A huge amount of energy and money was put into exploring the site, selecting the materials and preparing the exhibition – all in order to uncover and return to the point of origin. But the resemblance to the original plantation could indeed be questioned, and it certainly was throughout the project. For instance, the steel reinforcement was debated; obviously, it was not part of the authentic construction, but because it was apparently not interfering with the building it was nevertheless chosen in order to secure the building and guarantee that visitors would be able to meet and share a common history (and nature) at the site for many years to come. By the same token, there was a debate about whether electricity should be provided in the main building. The Danish architect yielded to arguments about using the building for meetings and educational purposes that might require electricity. However, he dismissed any idea of using electricity to illuminate the exhibition, guaranteeing that the house – with all its windows and its well-sited location – would provide sufficient light. Discussions in meetings at the National Museum focused on whether remakes of oil lamps found during the excavation of the site could be used in the event of evening functions, but this idea was dismissed since the lamps would produce too much soot in the whitewashed building. As a compromise, electricity was then built into the walls, assisted by sockets discreetly laid in small rough pieces of wood, instead of the plastic sockets of today. (In fact, electricity was only a virtual subject of discussion, since there was no electricity in the village at that stage in the project. And yet, perhaps partly in response to the project, the application for electricity that had been made by the Chief and elders in the village many years previously had finally been approved by the Ghanaian electricity company by the end of the project). These two newly added modern materials (steel reinforcement and electricity) obviously did not resemble anything from the 1830s, and so, unlike the lime, they could not directly be seen as embodying the virtues of a type. These modern additions were somehow beyond the issue of resemblance. Of course, this was well known to the project planners, and still they chose to use these materials, even though they were not strictly necessary. This could indicate that the typical virtues of steel and electricity were defined differently – not only as virtues of 'substantial resemblance'. Instead, the virtues of steel and electricity could be understood as those of creating a site where visitors could come and join in or even worship 'our common history'. From this perspective, where the 'type' is the Frederiksgave site, these materials could actually be seen as embodying, maybe even enhancing, such virtues. Both of the added materials facilitated people's experiences of a site that had not, after all, slipped down the hill, and that now, being suitably lit, could function as a place to learn about our shared past in appropriate educational facilities for many years to come. Put differently, the virtues embodied in these types were those of creating and maintaining an easy passage to or contact with a common point in history. The introduction of electricity to the building had the additional effect of making not only the past, but also both the present and the future collapse into the project, thereby elucidating yet another paradox; namely, that the return to year zero, 1831, might also accelerate a current development by bringing electricity to the village.

Introduced on the basis of proper knowledge and technical skills, the new materials could facilitate engagement with the past, or even embody it – as expressed in the previously mentioned quote: 'Just to walk around in the very same building as they once did is fantastic'. In other words, materiality with certain qualities was what made up the heritage, and if it were treated as such (as common cultural heritage), then it was treasured for those material qualities. Once again, we see here a peculiar circularity in the valuation of the common heritage site. It seems that, even though they were clearly non-authentic, the new materials gained value by being seen from a Greek perspective that posits materiality as a potential of embodiment and not a tragedy of resemblance. However, in the Frederiksgave project there were indeed also expressions that could be understood in a Judeo-Christian way. On the main posters introducing the site to visitors, it is stated that the main building and the small annex 'have been reconstructed, both in appearance and in materials, as close to the original as possible'[39], and the neighbouring poster states that

> By way of surveying and careful examinations of the material, combined with an architectural analysis, it has been possible to reconstruct the building as it most probably looked in the 1830s and 1840s.[40]

Reconstruction is here presented as a matter of approximation. Through meticulous and professional work, the reconstruction takes us as close as possible to the original. It is only an attempt, never promising a complete unification through substantial resemblance, even though professionals have examined and analysed the place. We have to make do with a referential resemblance – only a 'secondary' history of what it really was in the past.

The furnishing and setting up of the exhibition, too, might be understood through such Judeo-Christian reasoning about materiality. When setting up the exhibition, the furnishing of the building was thoroughly debated among people from the National Museum. Proposals were made in Denmark and then presented to the Ghanaian coordinator for comment, either via emails or on trips to Ghana. The people working on the exhibition in Denmark (including me) were eager to hear his comments and thoughts, and wanted him to put forward ideas and produce text for the exhibition, nurturing the collaborative spirit of the project. It was decided that selected archaeological artefacts should be exhibited in the concrete annexe building, but that the main building should be furnished only with copies of artefacts. The idea of making copies was eagerly discussed, since the Danish National Museum usually only exhibits original objects. But how should the museum act in a small Ghanaian village on the outskirts of Accra? Since the place could not be secured according to the National Museum's standards, a repatriation to the site of the collection of Ghanaian items now in Denmark was not an option. These Ghanaian items were part of a rare and highly treasured early collection of everyday items shipped to the National Museum in Copenhagen in the 1830s and 1840s. The collection had been acquired upon a request made by the former director of the museum to the last Danish Governor on the Guinea Coast, as the area was then called, in the period of Frederiksgave's operation – a time when letting laymen collect items and send them to experts in Europe was common practice.[41] Some of the people involved in the project thought that it was a shame to deviate from the museum's standard and exhibit copies; still, all agreed that this was the only option, since any repatriation would demand too much security and too many facilities to ensure a stable climate and proper protection.

It was agreed that, for the Danish artefacts, copies should be bought in auction houses or from second-hand dealers in Denmark – in line with the Judeo-Christian understanding of resemblance as material and therefore secondary. The copied artefacts were mainly selected with the aid of an inventory that had been made in relation to the auction when selling the Frederiksgave plantation in 1850, which had been found in the Danish National Archives. The copies were also inspired by the highly treasured early collection of everyday items kept securely in storage rooms at the National Museum in Copenhagen. Under close instruction and supervision from the Danish historian, I was hired to find and buy the 'Danish' items at auctions and from second-hand dealers in Denmark, while a Danish trainee was engaged to hire Ghanaian handicraftsmen to make copies from pictures of the treasured everyday artefacts in store at the museum – indeed a referential and second, third or even fourth-hand job.

The Danish historian explained to me that Frederiksgave's heyday coincided with a furnishing style known as 'Empire', named after the French emperor who was a trendsetter at that time in Western Europe. Even though, according to the Danish historian, you could not expect the highest fashion on the African coast, you could imagine out-of-date furniture being sent to the coast. I was therefore to look for Empire-style furniture that did not have too much decoration. The Danish coordinator, the historian and I thoroughly studied the inventory and the diaries that the historian had found in the Danish National Archives. Copies of Danish drawings made on the African coast from the 1800s were also circulated in meetings at the National Museum. For example, a French prince visiting the Danish Fort of Christiansborg in 1843 had made a water colour painting of a

FIG. 4.3 Aquarelle made by a French prince visiting Christiansborg, used in the exhibition at Frederiksgave. Courtesy of the M/S Maritime Museum of Denmark.[42]

lunch, which we meticulously studied as evidence of what the furniture would have looked like. However, looking at the picture, it was difficult to focus on the design of the chairs: other things were going on, and the painting added other layers to the idea of a common past. Looking at the drawing, my eyes constantly moved to the social interaction between the almost naked black waitresses and the white men in full uniforms.

In other words, it demanded a very specific and decisive gaze to focus on the chairs in the picture. Nonetheless, I succeeded in finding two chairs in Empire style that looked somewhat like the ones in the drawing. Again, lots of differences must be ignored in order to create resemblance via small conjunctions of sameness.

Some months later, when the container from Denmark was opened in Sesemi, the Chief of the village spotted the antique chairs that I had bought for the exhibition. According to the Danish architect who was present, he solemnly sat on one of them, spreading his legs as Ghanaian tradition prescribes, and contentedly exclaiming: 'I am the first African Chief to sit on this old chair'. I knew that there were close links between stools and leaders in Ghana; even the new presidential palace was being built in the form of a traditional Ghanaian stool. So when I heard the architect's account, I could not help think of the famous old Asante stool that is still a vital part of the Asante King's power. When colonising what later came to be Ghana, the British had taken the royal stool as war booty and exhibited it in the British Museum. In 2007, the Chief of Sesemi was somehow inverting this story by taking the opportunity to sit on old European chairs and exhibit them in his village. I would suggest that the Chief's reaction to the chairs was not a matter of referentiality, as if the chairs were understood as copies pointing to an original point at the beginning of the nineteenth century, nor were the chairs being used as a secondary image or symbol of his power. Sitting on the chair was rather a way in which he could manifest his unique power as Chief via old European objects. Exclaiming that he was a unique African Chief while sitting on the chair, he was embodying the virtues of its type – virtues that had to do with power, colonial rule and his chiefhood.

The secondary role of matter, and the idea that immaterial acts were the only true way to worship a Christian God was, according to Pietz, a theme discussed within the Church itself at the time the word fetish was developing in the fifteenth to seventeenth centuries.[43] This renunciation of material objects did not mean that there were no sacramental objects within the Christian Church – there were crosses, images of saints, Eucharist wafers, and so on. But, as stressed in a Catholic catechism from 1975, what was important was that all these material objects demanded voluntary active participation based on faith – they 'are not some kind of fetishes that work magically by just being had or worn or said'.[44] At least as importantly, however, what distinguishes these material objects from idols is that they are accepted by the Church institution. In the case of Frederiksgave, too, one could talk about significant institutions sanctioning the heritage objects – whether copies or originals. Old national institutions such as universities, archives and museums legitimised and approved the project – and they did so, as far as possible, in accordance with international institutions such as UNESCO. It was not an individual affair, but rather a matter of communicating a common past in accordance with institutional standards. Just as the Catholic Church could transform bread into the body of Christ, so the National Museum and the heritage workers involved in the Common Heritage Project worked to turn 'a pile of worthless stones' into a valuable heritage site.[45]

> As a consequence of the sacramental objects being different from other superstitious objects, given that they are based on voluntary verbal acts and endowed with sacred power by the church institution, the objects' power was, in the early church, seen to be independent from their manufacturing.[46]

As Pietz remarks, there is no Christian Daedalus in Christian thought:

> Humans can manufacture (facticii) images as idols, but they cannot endow them with any true relation to God [...]. Humans can manufacture but not create, and they cannot endow a body with a soul.[47]

But are today's heritage workers such as historians, archaeologists and architects modern equivalents Daedalus? Or are they manufacturers of cultural heritage that can be worshipped because proper institutions have approved them and sanctioned their sacred power to take us to a given point of creation?

In order to explore these questions, we need to consider the mode of production at the Frederiksgave site, and not settle for a dismissal of heritage as idolatry. In the history of the fetish concept, the Church's ideas about idolatry cannot explain what came to be termed witchcraft and vain observances[48] – both practices where materiality and mode of production took a central role.

CROSS-NATURAL EQUIVALENCE: WORKING IN A COMMON NATURE

During the early Middle Ages, a new form of non-cultic worship emerged that attempted to obtain desired results or effects, or to prevent particular things from happening, through the use or mediation of certain objects.[49] Pietz identifies witchcraft and the related notion of vain observances as characteristic of these practices, which were more related to the material world than a spiritual world.[50] In Portugal, the first European naval trading nation to appear on the Western coast of Africa, witchcraft was termed *feitiçaria*.[51] Witchcraft worked via physical actions that sought to interfere with the laws of nature through various combinations and doses of essential material ingredients.[52] According to Pietz, the effects of the material mixture were seen only as products of mechanistically correct combinations and doses of the ingredients.[53] Most importantly, these mixtures of various ingredients had to be combined with spells and voluntary verbal pacts with evil forces, as the Church framed them. So, just like the idols and sacramental objects, witchcraft depended upon some immaterial voluntary verbal act in order to be efficient – even though the act was not institutionalised. Thus no powerful novelty, as Pietz further remarks, could come from the material objects alone; nothing indeterminately new could happen via the material world, according to Portuguese witchcraft. The objects were only made efficient by being measured and mixed in the right doses and combinations, together with verbal invocation.

These ideas and, not least, the vocabulary of witchcraft, vain observances and Christian understandings of the relation between materiality and spirituality, were among what the Portuguese brought with them when they arrived on the African coast in the fifteenth century. Their mission was primarily to trade, as described above. The Africans highly treasured the Portuguese goods, along with other African religious objects, and the early Portuguese traders therefore soon termed all these venerated objects *feitiço*. The Portuguese distinguished between African idols and *feitiço,* understanding the former as freestanding statues and the *feitiço* as rightly proportioned and ritualised powerful objects worn on the body.[54] It is interesting to note that, instead of inventing a new term or calling these treasured objects by an African name, the Portuguese seemed to recognise them as belonging to the same phenomenon known in Europe. In other words, a sort of 'cross-cultural equivalence' existed – at least to the Portuguese who documented the encounters in various texts. Yet Pietz modifies this equivalence and argues that, in the fifteenth and sixteenth centuries, witchcraft was not a well-discussed issue in Portugal, which might have given it some looseness in its definition, and thus be a reason for choosing the term in Africa – it was not to be interpreted in a strict sense, since the Portuguese merchants might not have either dared or wanted to trade with witches.⁵⁵ Therefore, *feitiço* might have been understood by the early Portuguese traders more in the sense of harmless and vain observances, and 'poor man's magic'.⁵⁶

The religiosity demonstrated by the various African groups trading with the Portuguese could not, however, be sufficiently captured by an old European Christian vocabulary. Over time, it became clear that *feitiço* was not an adequate term to describe this religiosity, which was apparently intimately related to precious material objects. The Africans' religious behaviour wasn't something that the Portuguese could understand as the true worship of God, since it was not based on a relationship to a non-material power to be related to via the free will. Neither was it idolatry, which captured the material object as a passive referential image governed by ideas of resemblance. Finally, it was not really witchcraft either, since what the Portuguese merchants saw lacked the element of a linguistic pact that in European witchcraft accompanied the mechanistic relations to nature.⁵⁷ The term used for the Africans' practices, therefore, changed over the years, and the Portuguese *feitiço* changed to a middleman's term, *fetisso*, thereby removing both Europe and Christianity from the word. *Fetisso* subsequently became increasingly associated with religious practices in Africa, causing it to drop out of Christian religious discourse – and, misleadingly, be understood as an intra-African phenomenon.

As the Portuguese word *feitiçaria* changed first to *feitiço* and then to *fetisso*, its meaning also evolved. It no longer characterised merely 'the same phenomenon' (witchcraft as practised in Portugal) just with different content – a classic relativistic figure, as described in Chapter Two. Instead the word came to describe a different phenomenon, *fetisso*, that emerged through heterogeneous encounters on the African coast. However, as we have seen, the role of encounter was subsequently either forgotten or ignored, and the concept came to designate something inherently African, as also mentioned in the introduction to this chapter.

At the Frederiksgave site, I will suggest, the early relativistic figure of cross-cultural equivalence was inverted – at least by the project planners. Here, the same material – the physical structure or nature of present-day Frederiksgave, which collapsed with history and nature, as we saw in the previous chapters – had various names, as I will explore further in the next chapter. The name 'Frederiksgave' was far from shared among the people engaged in the site. For instance it was called 'Frederiksgave plantation', 'the thing', 'tourist attraction', 'fort', 'Common Heritage Project', 'slave centre', 'Danish Fort' or 'museum'. The site thereby also invoked a classical relativism – but of a different equivalence to the Portuguese-African, namely of what I would call a cross-*natural* equivalence. While the early Portuguese-African encounter could be framed as having the same culture but materialised in various ways, the Danish-Ghanaian encounter could be framed as having the same nature, but literalised in various ways. In what sense, then, did the project participants work from an idea of '*more or less the same nature*'? With all the different names used to characterise the site, one could indeed argue for some sort of loosely defined understanding of it. And, certainly, all these words were used ingeniously in different contexts. However, the project planners', particularly the Danes', repeated cry for 'education of the guides' as a solution to the 'wrong history' that was continuously appearing at the site with regard to the transatlantic slave trade seems to indicate a limit to the looseness of nature permitted. For instance, when a Danish journalist called the inaugurated museum a 'fort' in a Danish newspaper, it caused the Danish coordinator to react, as she explained to me. The problem seems to be that, by naming the site 'a fort' and linking it to the transatlantic slave trade, the nature of the place is altered – it is not the same nature – not even '*almost* the same nature'. Therefore, any words that alter the site's already given nature and history (i.e. of Frederiksgave being a plantation using locally enslaved people as its workforce) should be eradicated. The other terms – 'the thing', 'tourist attraction', 'museum' – even though rather imprecise, did not alter the nature of the site; as curious abstracted symbols they floated above a real world of phenomena. We find a similar argument, but with history instead of nature, in the case of the Danish words still present in Ghana: *kalkun* (turkey), and *gaffel* (fork). They were also permitted because they did not alter history; rather, they confirmed a non-compromising and innocent version of the past, where cultural exchange was a matter of folklore. In this light, the Frederiksgave site appears as an intra-natural phenomenon where a frictionless point in history and nature can be uncovered.

THE FORCES OF MATERIALITY: UNTRANSCENDED HERITAGE

Over the years *fetisso* (or 'fetish', in English) came to designate powerful materiality,[58] describing the 'novel divine power in material objects and bodily fixations within the contingency of worldly experience'.[59] Even though this particular understanding characterised the emergence of the fetish concept on the West African coast 500 years ago, the challenge of understanding the vitality of the material world is longstanding and ongoing in the Western philosophical tradition.[60] Whereas idolatry, according to Pietz, was seen as performing a (wrong) law and a (wrong) faith, fetishism as it developed in West Africa came to be seen as an accidental and completely lawless and natural process.[61] To the Europeans, what their trading partners in the south venerated seemed completely arbitrary. The Europeans back then could not find any rules defining what came to be venerated as a fetish. Sometimes it was a lake, at other times an animal or an object. By the turn of the nineteenth century, the celebrated European philosopher Hegel argues that the Africans were worshipping

> the first thing that comes their way. This, taken quite indiscriminately, they exalt to the dignity of a 'Genius' [...]. [I]n the Fetich, a kind of objective independence as contrasted with the arbitrary fancy of the individual seems to manifest itself; but as the objectivity is nothing other than the fancy of the individual projecting itself into space, the human individuality remains master of the image it has adopted. [...] it is merely a creation that expresses the arbitrary choice of its maker, and which always remains in his hands. Hence there is no relation of dependence in this religion.[62]

This quote points to an interesting differentiation between a so-called objective independence and an individual's arbitrary fancy. But, by quickly dismissing the objective independence of the fetish and turning it into a cabinet of mirrors, Hegel could be criticised for missing an important point in the material character of the venerated object. By understanding the fetish as a human projection, he does not leave any agency to materiality, which Peter Pels, for instance, sees as a vital characteristic of the fetish.[63] The fetish, for Hegel, is a passive medium resembling what Pietz characterised as an idol. Hegel sees the fetish as nothing but an image of human intentions, a mirror of our individual hopes and wishes – arbitrary and changeable, as these by definition are. I will return to the idea of the arbitrary character of the fetish, but for now I will concentrate on Hegel's disregard for the material independence of the fetish, which allows him to see only the fetish's dependence on humans and not the other way round. In his attempt to show the Africans' inability to think strictly and consistently, Hegel perhaps misses some interesting points about fetishes. As we shall see below, the relationship between humans and the fetish, and particularly the role of the individual's power over the fetish, is something that has been carefully discussed by recent scholars.

In the early writings on fetishism, such as Hegel's, the idea of the fetish was inscribed in a racial discourse whereby it was believed that the physicality of the fetish was a sign of the African's inability to worship an abstract being.[64] Interestingly, this normative and hierarchical thought resonates in Ghana today. In the introduction to this chapter, for example, we noted the tension between, on the one hand, the minister's belief in traditional fetishes (a belief that leads him to destroy them), and on the other hand, the attitude of the three young women working at the National Museum of Ghana, who while recognising traditional belief in fetishes, as modern Christians consider these beliefs passé and are therefore able to work in a museum containing fetishes. During my fieldwork in Ghana, I heard several Ghanaians argue that traditional thoughts and belief in fetishes were actually hampering the country's progress – further evidence for the existence of tensions over powerful materiality. As noted above, the idol was pointing beyond itself, indexing an immaterial being, whereas the fetish gained its power from its material embodiment. Yet Hegel's quote above exemplifies a prevalent understanding of the fetish as indexing human intentions – an understanding that makes Deleuze state that taking the fetish seriously might potentially reverse the Western philosophical tradition.[65] My point here is that this difference between a thing being what it is (a material embodiment), and its being a material embodiment pointing beyond itself, mastered by its human maker, has consequences for how we analyse and theorise the particular form of materiality that makes up cultural heritage, and hence also for how we value that heritage.

In an article entitled 'Fetishism', Roy Ellen has pointed to 'an inner ambivalence as to whether it is the objects themselves which effect material changes in some mysterious way, or whether it is some spiritual force which is represented by or located in (but separate from) those objects'.[66] Among anthropologists at the beginning of the twentieth century there was much confusion regarding the concept of fetish, which, according to Ellen, led anthropologists to abandon the idea altogether. The confusion was about whether the fetish was material or spiritual in character, and in the twentieth century this confusion among scholars ended in a reduction of the fetish to a derogatory term only to be connected with the religion of 'primitive peoples' who lacked the power of abstraction, resulting in their worship of objects from the perishable material world. Nevertheless, in the edited volume *Border Fetishism* (1998) Peter Pels takes up the challenge and summarises the confusion as concerning the difference between the *spirit of* and the *spirit in* matter. In an attempt to explore the agency of materiality, Pels discusses Appadurai's often-quoted introduction to *The Social Life of Things* (1988). Pels argues that by reducing a thing's agency to something that can be understood and explored only methodologically, Appadurai disregards materiality as a radical other that cannot be mediated by humans.[67] For Appadurai, things necessarily get their meanings from human transactions: 'things have no meanings apart from those that human transactions, attributions and motivations endow them with'.[68] Inspired by Pietz' three articles, Pels suggests instead that materiality can 'talk back' in two ways:[69] it can either be others talking through the material object, or it can be the object itself talking back. He terms this difference as one between the spirit *in* matter as opposed to the spirit *of* matter.[70] Spirit *in* matter is a derivative agency obtained through 'an other' enlivening or inscribing agency into matter, just as – and here I agree with Pels – Appadurai seems to understand things. It should be said, as Pels also recognises, that Appadurai's focus on commodities automatically accentuates the human agency in exchange situations.[71] Matter as a derivative or referential idea points, in Pels' terminology, to an animistic tradition – the material object is animated by something external to itself.[72] As discussed above, such referentiality was also characteristic of idols in Pietz' terminology. But fetishes in Pietz' view are not idols or false gods 'but rather quasi-personal divine powers associated more closely with the materiality of the sacramental object than would be an independent immaterial demonic spirit'.[73] In Pels' terminology, fetish is the spirit *of* matter, i.e. an agency internal to the thing in question – to the fetish object.[74] Here Pels is following Pietz' ideas of the fetish as being characterised by its 'irreducible materiality'[75] or its 'untranscended materiality'.[76] Pels writes, '[t]he fetish's materiality is not transcended by any voice foreign to it: To the fetishist, the thing's materiality itself is supposed to speak and act; its spirit is *of* matter'.[77] As a consequence of this powerful capacity, 'the fetish is an object that has the quality to singularise itself and disrupt the circulation and commensurability of a system of human values'.[78] It is an 'other thing'[79] that talks back. The fetish is not a neatly controlled pedagogical illustration to be (de-)activated at will.

Even though Frederiksgave was reconstructed in order to teach and communicate our common past – as justified, for instance, by the choice of building on top of the ruin – the learning process did not just follow smooth illustrative lines; it seemed as if there was more at stake. A model of the buildings accompanied by informative posters could have been erected beside the original site, but the project planners chose to reconstruct on top of the ruin. This indicates that there was something highly fascinating about the topography, the materiality and the ruin that influenced their 'rather unorthodox decision'. It seemed that Frederiksgave was not just any building: it was, in Pels' vocabulary, an 'other thing' talking back. Apparently it evoked something else apart from just the opportunity for education via a referential constructed model or a poster. In the case of the director, topography and materiality even aroused feelings of awe. So, too, for the frightened woman who visited the site, even if with different sentiments. In this case, it seemed as if the materiality and topography caused her to quickly exit the building, evidently arousing fear in her. Here one could indeed talk about a materiality that talked back.

What I argue here is that all these examples point to the important insight that each moment of intense material or topographical experience in the Frederiksgave project seemed to be made up of both referential stories and untranscended effect at once. We might consider Frederiksgave both as having 'quasi-personal divine powers' and being a freestanding idol to be worshipped; it was both something to admire and worship from a distance – preferably from the symmetrical axis – *and* something that could be embodied by 'walking around in precisely the same building as they once did'.

OTHER THINGS — HERE AND ELSEWHERE

By stressing that the fetish is an 'other thing', Pels points out that it is different from already accepted processes by which things are characterised by their exchange value and their use. Even though the fetish can be a commodity, it is an 'other' commodity, and it is differently valued. This makes Pels insist that

> its singularity is not the result of sentimental, historical or otherwise personalized value: The fetish presents a generic singularity, a unique or anomalous quality that sets apart from both the everyday use and exchange and the individualization or personalization of objects.[80]

In relation to the Frederiksgave site, one might say that its singularity, being reconstructed on a unique location, is a result precisely of sentimental, historical or otherwise personalised values, thereby disqualifying it as a fetish. However, the examples of fetishes Pels comes up with in the following sentences, such as velvet, fur, blue jeans, old shoes, underwear, and so on, could all be explained as powerful materiality; they are fetishes precisely because of their history – in other words, their power could just as well be explained as being a result of sentimental, historical or otherwise personalised value. Pietz, on the other hand, seems to have a different and less radical idea of fetishes. He writes that they

> exist in the world as material objects that 'naturally' embody socially significant values that touch one or more individuals in an intensely personal way: a flag, monument, or landmark; a talisman [...] a city, village, or nation [...]. Each has that quality of synecdochic fragmentedness or 'detotalized

totality' characteristic of the recurrent, material collective object discussed by Sartre.[81]

Putting 'naturally' in quotation mark calls for attention. Pietz explains it with reference to the fetish's ability to make metonymic relations, and refers to the French philosopher Jean-Paul Sartre's idea of 'detotalized totality'. 'Detotalized totality' is Sartre's paradoxical figure developed in order to rethink collectivities as something other than a direct unity of consensus. As *pars pro toto*, a metonymic quality, the fetish (as a part) is embodying a greater collective whole, a totality or, to be more precise, socially significant values – just as the flag can be seen as embodying the collective nation. But if we recall Pietz' (and Marx's) attention to the historical dimension of the fetish, that it is 'always a meaningful fixation of a singular event',[82] then this collective whole of socially significant values can never be self-identical. On the contrary, being based on 'recurrence', a concept developed by Sartre,[83] totalisation can only be reached momentarily as a detotalised totality – an idea that we noted in Chapter Three, when Taussig challenged the idea of (pure) imitation through the sensuousness of mimesis. Sartre clarifies that, as a material and social organisation, a city acquires its 'reality from its ubiquitous absence. It is present in each of its streets *insofar* as it is always elsewhere'.[84] At first, the quote might seem like an oxymoron or a collapse of logic: the city gains its reality from its absence. But instead of a collapse in logic, I would argue that it is an alternative to abstract thinking where the concrete manifestations (e.g. streets) can be added together to form an independent and abstract idea of the city. City and street are not separate entities, with one hierarchised above the other. Rather, they take part in each other. This means that the city is present in its particular streets but it is also always elsewhere. No street can capture the whole city, and we might add that no city can capture the whole street; there is always more to the street than the city, just as there is more to the city than its streets. Similarly with the Common Heritage Project; here, the collective 'common heritage' is a material and social organisation that, I would argue, gets its reality from its ubiquitous absence. This means that it is present in all its stones, lime, pages in a diary, and so on, yet it is always also another place. And the stones, lime and diary pages are also always more than this 'common heritage'. Above, I have argued for this in the case of the name of the place. The alternative names, while naming it, were also pointing beyond, to something other than the Frederiksgave site. In avoiding being captured as a whole (a city, a common heritage) and in refusing to be reduced to a mere collection of parts (streets, walls, lime, archives, etc.), the 'detotalized totality' of Frederiksgave is as total as it can get.

The reason why I find this discussion of the fetish useful for my analytical purpose is that it provides an alternative to ideas of the materialities of the world being reduced to a matter of human instrumental relations – a social life of things. However, the idea of spirit in matter, the fetish as an untranscended object, does not capture the work of common heritage either. My fieldwork continuously made it impossible to uphold such an either/or view of the materiality of heritage. The actual encounters in the here-and-now made the heritage site's work cut across such a divide; materiality gained power and worked through people, history books, the particular moment, the UNESCO charters, the architect's ruler, and so on, all at once. The point is that in order to qualify common heritage such as the Frederiksgave site, I need to let this complexity remain and instead focus on the here-and-now whereby the Frederiksgave site emerges as both a referent and an untranscended object to such an extent that the divide ceases to make analytical sense. Materiality indeed talks back – we need only recall the singing roots of the previous chapter – but it depends on someone listening professionally for a distant history to be uncovered in the present.

If we explore the Common Heritage Project through the lens of the fetish, it can be said that the fetish was awakened (the magic was generated) when investigating the lime with a knife, when looking at the maps through a magnifying glass, when decoding old Danish handwritten sources in the Danish National Archives and when walking around in the building. From these sensuous relations a cultural heritage site emerged. And it is these sensuous engagements, I suggest, that produce part of the power of the cultural heritage site. The sensuous mimetic faculty that is at play at the Frederiksgave site awakens the fetish. How, then, does this relate (or not) to the issue of Frederiksgave as a site materialising the universal value of common heritage? Once again, I draw on the fetish history to explore this matter.

TRINKETS AND TRIFLES – 'THE MYSTERY OF VALUE'

In the early European-West African mercantile encounters, the question of value became pertinent; what was valuable and what was the right tally in these heterogeneous encounters became pivotal questions. The trade, by definition, centred on translating and transvaluing objects, and thus raised questions of the social value of material objects. In return for the precious metal, the Europeans offered what they often referred to as 'trinkets and trifles' or 'trash' to their trading partners[85] – a view that has recently been contested by the archaeologist DeCorse, who has carried out excavations in Elmina, the first Portuguese trading station on the West African coast.[86] In the old diaries and official documents, it seemed shocking and completely ridiculous to the European traders that many of the 'trinkets and trifles' they traded were praised as powerful and valuable material objects by the Africans; they wondered about '[t]he mystery of value'.[87] At times, the European traders even expressed contempt for those who valued and worshipped 'trifles'.[88] They pondered over the ignorant and confused Africans not knowing the 'true' value of things. One can easily imagine how the Europeans, but probably also the Africans, stood and rubbed their hands with glee after having exchanged glass pearls, brassware and clothes for gold. And, not least, why rich sponsors in Europe were willing to invest huge sums in the dangerous and costly voyages and, particularly in the eighteenth century, why African traders sold huge numbers of slaves in return for European goods. However, ideas of cross-cultural equivalence regarding magical objects were slowly abandoned.

The arrival of the Dutch in the sixteenth century, and subsequently the British, Germans and Danes, to mention only some of the Protestant European nations seeking fortune via the Atlantic Ocean, gave rise to new understandings of materiality. The Dutch Calvinists in particular, according to Pietz, had very different ideas about materiality to those of their their Portuguese competitors. To the Dutch, the African fetishes were seen as homologous with the Catholic sacramental objects dismissed by Protestantism.[89] As a result, the Dutch merchants ignored the above-described Catholic division between idols (referential materiality aspiring to a spiritual being) and *feiticios/fetissos* (efficient materiality). To the Dutch, and to Protestants in general (who did not accept any mediation by either the papal authority or sacramental objects in relation to God) both idols and fetishes were understood as deflected spirituality, and therefore wrong. The Dutch and other Protestants thought that the African's worshipping of material objects was false, even ridiculous. As a consequence, debased gold came to be known as fetish, in this way connoting unpleasant and suspicious trading situations,[90] rather than a religious situation. The Dutch understanding of the fetish was closer to the Roman Pliny's distinction, used in mercantile situations, between the artificial (*facticius*) and the natural, than to thoughts on idolatry whereby materials were understood to refer to a divine being. In Pietz words, the 'material objects came to be understood as proper to economic as *opposed to* religious activity'.[91] Trade became a secular, disenchanted affair, and religion a spiritual affair, and the two, ideally, did not intersect with each other. According to Pietz, a new understanding of nature and the natural powers of the material evolved as well. This new understanding stressed the

> fundamental impersonality of material happenings that was the basis of the new 'enlightened' definition of superstition as the personification of impersonal natural forces, accompanied by the attribution of end-oriented intentionality to chance events and to objects randomly associated in contingent experience.[92]

Belief in the impersonality of natural forces, and the denial of end-oriented intentionality to chance events, created an idea of an 'enlightened' mind. Together with new technologies (e.g. modern navigation aids) and a new commercial consciousness produced by new forms of economic organisations (e.g. the Dutch West Indies Company), material objects became the focus of attention in the relations between European and African merchants on the coast. '[T]he truth of material objects came to be viewed in terms of technological and commodifiable use-value, whose 'reality' was proved by their silent 'translatability' across alien cultures',[93] as Pietz argues. If material objects had other meanings and values then this was to be understood as a given culture's deception and lack of reason.[94] Material objects were understood as universally impersonal entities, independent of their substance and function. To the enlightened European mind, any notion of fetish went against a thinking based on 'natural reason and rational market activity'.[95] What for the Europeans was based on pure technological knowledge was understood by the Africans as involving supernatural agency. This led the European merchants to conclude that their trading partners had false ideas about causality. And therefore, the argument went, the Africans could not estimate the true value of things. Following this line of reasoning, one of the expatriate Danes, Ludwig Ferdinand Rømer, gives a very interesting description of a fetish house in his account of life on the Guinea Coast. He terms it 'the Negro's curio cabinet' – a term that is most likely intended as derogatory, since the curio cabinets so fashionable in the sixteenth and seventeenth centuries were considered outdated in the eighteenth century,[96] when Rømer wrote his account. Rømer calls the items 'foolish trinkets (I do not know what else I can call them)'[97] or 'knick-knacks'.[98] By bracketing his hesitation or inability to name the objects, it could be argued that Rømer is emphasising that he is dealing with a phenomenon unknown to him – in other words, an intra-African phenomenon. The fetish houses, Rømer writes, are always round,

> and inside you see a thousand kinds of worthless objects, hanging up or lying in it. A clay pot, standing in a corner, contains red earth in which there may be a feather from the tail of a cock. Sticks tied together with thread or raffia are placed on the wall or sides of the hut. [...] Indeed, you cannot count all the bric-a-brac they keep in those places.[99]

A few paragraphs later, he writes as if the clients visiting the fetish priest in the house are being fooled. Placing himself in an enlightened position, he asks them, 'why don't you lift your heads a little [...] and open your eyes, in order to see'.[100] Like his contemporaries, the Englishman William Smith, or the Dutchman Willem Bosman, both quoted in Pietz' text,[101] Rømer points to the contingency of the things chosen and also to what is of prime interest to my analysis: the deceit, the blindness of the Africans – 'why don't you lift your heads a little [...] and open your eyes, in order to see'. Rømer continues that if one wanted to know about the religion of the 'Blacks' one had to be on the coast for several years without anyone seeing us laugh at their ceremonies, or, when they answered our questions, without a European ridiculing them. If we do this, and say 'it is nonsense', etc., they then answer, 'That may well be – believe what you will!' And they will even laugh with us.[102]

One can easily sense the disrespect, not to mention the awkwardness emanating from this quote. In order to obtain knowledge about the Africans' religion, one has to hide one's laughter. And if one speaks honestly, raising a disagreement, they will only settle the discussion, potentially agreeing, potentially not, leaving the question unanswered and, as if establishing a momentary meeting point, they laugh with the Danes – and avoid similar encounters.

Reading this old description immediately reminded me of an incident I experienced during my fieldwork in Ghana. On a late afternoon in November 2008, I was sitting with a group of people from Keta, the easternmost coastal city housing ruins from Prindsensten, a former Danish fort. We sat at the end of the sandy road outside the Chief's office, under a tree facing what was once Prindsensten. I enjoyed these afternoons; the people seemed very interested in politics, and our repeated attendance seemed to be a sign of our pleasure and engagement in listening and discussing various issues with each other. As we had done the previous two weeks, we discussed issues of British colonialism, poverty in Africa, Barack Obama, corruption, chiefs, local and governmental elections, immigration and, of course, the fort – 'a tourist attraction for the city', as the people of the town called it. This afternoon, the discussion revolved around the fort and what to do with it. Suddenly, one of the pacesetting men raised his voice and stood up. He looked down at me, and in his loud voice he asked me,

> C'mon Nathalia, why is he [the Danish architect] standing there looking at that wall for hours? Eh? Standing there with his pipe [and he imitated smoking a pipe so characteristic of the Danish architect, and all of us listening started to laugh], scratching the wall with his knife [he raised his index finger and bent it in the air], looking closely [he took my arm and moved it close to his eyes to study it. We all laughed, and in a high voice he shouted:], why? Tell me why? If it were the Americans, then they would just have rebuilt that

thing quickly so that tourists will come. But the Danes, eh, eh, eh, [shaking his head] they are just looking, they are so slow!

The people around nodded approvingly and expressed agreement, while we nearly fell over laughing: I found it funny, because in that setting I too could see the humour and inefficiency of 'the Danes', despite my fascination with the detailed attention the architect paid to the materiality of the old Danish sites. By imitating the Danish architect and his apparently strange interests, the man articulated 'the mystery of value' described above. In contrast to the Danish architect and, with him, the Danish National Museum, the speaker was not interested in the lime, the oyster shells, or the detailed surveying of the building– these things did not turn it into a 'fort', a 'tourist attraction'. No, instead he suggested following the Americans, known for their mercantile ingenuity, and just rebuilding 'that thing' as fast as possible in order for it to attract tourists and, with that, money for the impoverished town. Humorously, he questioned what to many Danes from the museum seemed to be the universal value of heritage. But he did more than just question: like Rømer, he asked the Danes to look up and see. He asked us to see that the Danes' fetish house – the fort – was full of trinkets and trifles, and not precious lime, sand, measures, etc., as they falsely thought; the value lay elsewhere – in the pockets of the thousands of tourists who would come and visit the fort because of its history and its location on the West African coast.

The European merchants clearly could not make sense of what their trading partners treated as fetishes; it seemed completely random. An important characteristic of the fetish was that its power rested on its ability 'to repeat its originating act of forging an identity of articulated relations between certain otherwise heterogeneous things'.[103] But the European traders could not identify this repetition and stringency. The arbitrariness of defining what the fetishes were produced a paradox to the Europeans, namely that social order in Africa was apparently generated by a solely 'natural and lawless process'.[104]

I encountered similar accusations or implications of arbitrariness during my fieldwork, but this time it was not expressed by European merchants, but by many people living close to the former Danish buildings. In general, the

Europeans' interest in the old European constructed buildings, and the energy put into studying and possibly renovating them, was, as in the instance described above, a mystery to many Ghanaians, who prioritised spending their scarce resources differently. For instance, I participated as a fieldworker in an excavation at a former Danish fort, Fredensborg, on the Ghanaian coastline. Before the archaeologists started digging, they talked to the Chief of the city, explained their interest and asked for permission to dig in the grounds. Permission was granted, but several people from the village looked at us as if we were mad, and asked the archaeologists or myself whether we were digging for gold. Why else should we trouble ourselves with the hard and unpleasant work of digging into what had until recently been a public toilet? The Danish archaeologists said that this was a typical question in gold-rich Ghana, but that in Denmark too they had been asked this treasure-hunting question. They explained their purpose, and invited people to come and look at the work and the artefacts. The people seemed to appreciate our inclusiveness, but did not seem convinced enough about our drive to bother.

It was likewise in Sesemi, where the Frederiksgave site was reconstructed. It took a long time for the Chief of the village to be convinced that the Danes would actually reconstruct the building. He was polite, and arranged 'durbas' [official rituals] where he and his group of elders all dressed in traditional clothes and performed rituals to confirm their goodwill and willingness to cooperate. But until the Danish architect started hiring workmen from the village and actually commenced the reconstruction work, he was not convinced that the project would in fact be realised. Shortly after the inauguration of the Common Heritage Site, I talked to him about the project. It was a Sunday, there was a relaxed atmosphere in the village, and people were slowly returning from the churches in the area, still dressed in their Sunday best. I found the Chief relaxing alone on his porch. He was constantly smiling, and seemed to be very satisfied with everything. The small village at the end of the road had for one day – the inauguration day – been the centre of the world. With all this hype, the challenge for the Chief now, I was told by some people living in the village, was how to manage all the invitations from chiefs in the area to be guest of honour at their social arrangements. How would the Chief afford all the gifts that such a position traditionally demanded in Ghana? For the moment, however, he was not worried about such challenges. Instead, he threw back his head, looked up at the sky and exclaimed: 'It's a miracle'. I was not prepared for such an expression, and asked what he meant by 'miracle'. He explained: 'All these big people coming here to Sesemi; before nobody knew about Sesemi, now they do, it's fantastic,' and he added, 'We can only give thanks to God'. Then he showed me a paper produced for the church-based celebration of the commissioning of the site. It looked like the official invitation to the inauguration: on the front page there was a copy of the drawing of the architectural façade of the building, but instead of welcoming you to the inauguration it read: 'Thanksgiving Service in Commemoration of the Commissioning of the Frederiksgave Plantation and Common Heritage Site'. None of the Danes from the National Museum or otherwise involved in the project had been invited, or had even heard about this commemoration service. Nor had the people from the Ghanaian ministries or the Ghanaian university been invited to attend. It was an internal village affair, and not thought of as a common event. Bringing the Common Heritage Project to the church seemed to be a new and surprising movement – at least to me. This was the first time I had heard about the project in such religious framing. It was not so much a matter of being Frederik's gift, as the name denoted, nor a gift from the foundation granting money to the project, or from the Danish National Museum to the University of Ghana, as was officially stated. To the Chief of the village, it was 'a miracle' and 'a gift from God'. In the New Testament, miracles are illustrated as what happens when water is turned into wine or when waking the dead. Similarly, following the words of the Chief, a miracle could mean suddenly turning a pile of stones that perhaps reminded people of a difficult past into a prestigious building attracting notables from all over. One could also point to the arbitrariness with which miracles happen. They do not follow any law and order, at least not known to humans, and the only thing we can do when they happen is to wonder and give thanks to the Lord, just as the Chief and the villagers were doing.

With these incidents during fieldwork at the former Danish ruins (the slow-paced attention to materials, the excavation/gold digging and the reconstruction/ miracle), it should be clear that the value of Danish-built structures is not given once and for all. The people living close to the sites were difficult to convince of our enthusiasm for the ruins and the importance they materialised. The Chief's declaration of a miracle showed that to him it seemed completely arbitrary that his village had been chosen from among many just as important ones; this choice certainly seemed to be completely out of his hands. The movement of turning water into wine, or ruins into highly valuable artefacts, was later commented on in the article written by many of those involved from the National Museum: 'Before the excavation the villagers viewed the ruin as an overgrown and worthless pile of rocks, but in the course of the last three years the buildings have become a living testimony to the times of their ancestors'.[105] However, to the writers themselves, it was never a question of turning something worthless into something valuable, of turning water into wine, but more of rediscovering what for centuries had lain in oblivion in the dark jungle. Clearly, and as opposed to the villagers, the people from the National Museum worked on the assumption that they already knew the true value of things. Importantly, this self-assuredness meant that the diverging views of the heritage objects and places on the part of, for example, the people living in the village, did not really interfere with the course of the reconstruction. The project, as also discussed before, was never geared toward inclusive community practices, since Frederiksgave was merely seen by the project makers as an extension of a common past with inherent value, to be uncovered and constructed by responsible – and affluent – agents. The project simply followed History, Nature, laws, order and international charters as best it could.

ENCOUNTERING MYSTERIOUS VALUE — THE MATERIALITY OF HERITAGE

In this chapter, I have explored in great detail the history of the fetish in order to analyse the powerful materiality of heritage and the mystery of value, thereby showing how heritage works and is valuated. Drawing on Pliny, I explored the distinction between natural and artificial goods, and showed how in the reconstruction process this distinction was continuously both challenged and upheld. The Danish architect emphasised working with nature in order to let history speak for itself. Commonness at the site was, according to the project planners, found in the sharing of one single universal nature and history (naturalised history and historicised nature), and this was what had to be uncovered if heritage was to be authentic and true. Professionalism, the right techniques and materials, were thus vital for creating the Common Heritage Site. Invoking the history of the fetish, we saw how questions of the material and the spiritual shed additional light on the reconstruction of the Frederiksgave site. At issue in the history of the fetish was the distinction between materials as resembling or embodying the original creation. At Frederiksgave, we saw instances where both of these logics were enacted, and my point is that common heritage is made of materials that at once resemble the original and embody the virtues of its type. This is essentially a discussion of what a thing is – whether it is controlled by a human maker or has agency in itself. The Frederiksgave planners, in their care to let the objects act in accordance with nature, worked from a curious mix of these two positions. At first, the idea of the fetish as untranscended materiality, an 'other thing', or a thing in which the effect is only inherent, seemed a good way to analyse the power of heritage objects. However, in my view – and based on what took place at the Frederiksgave site – the idea of the untranscended seems to contradict the generative power of encounters. If we follow Pels' argument about the fetish being an untranscended object, we risk rendering it a given entity, a nature 'out there', not talking back as much as talking past. Sartre and Pietz, on the other hand, retain the paradoxes inherent in the term 'fetish' and how it is understood, without letting these fall into confusion – as, according to Ellen, had happened among anthropologists at the beginning of the twentieth century. With the notion of detotalised totality, Pietz points to the incompleteness of the fetish, but he also points to its historicity, that the fetish is a fixation of a singular event. Only in the sensations of the here-and-now can the fetish gain its power and value. Likewise with the Common Heritage Project, it was sensuous moments of engagement with material and topography that made the site valuable. This was a value that, as we saw, was not pre-given, but rather pointed to awkward moments and to a mystery that has a certain degree of circularity and indeed a paradoxical character to it: the common heritage has inherent value, but still needs to be created in particular conscientious ways to preserve and maintain this value. My fieldwork material thus kept questioning the translatability and universal worth of heritage, showing the mystery and multiplicity of value. To the project planners, the Frederiksgave site presented a universal history to tell that did not include it being a fort, as some would have it. To others, the value of Frederiksgave rested in the pockets of future visitors, rather than in the reconstruction of a shared past. In short, the Frederiksgave site was commonly valued in different ways. In this way, the bumblings and failures marking where both pure referentiality and untranscended materiality were challenged could be seen as vital parts of the value of common heritage. An important dimension of heritage, then, is that it works in ways that point beyond the discussion of spirit *of* and spirit *in* matter. The friction between these ideas of the material qualifies cultural heritage, and suggests a specific and mysterious materialisation of value.

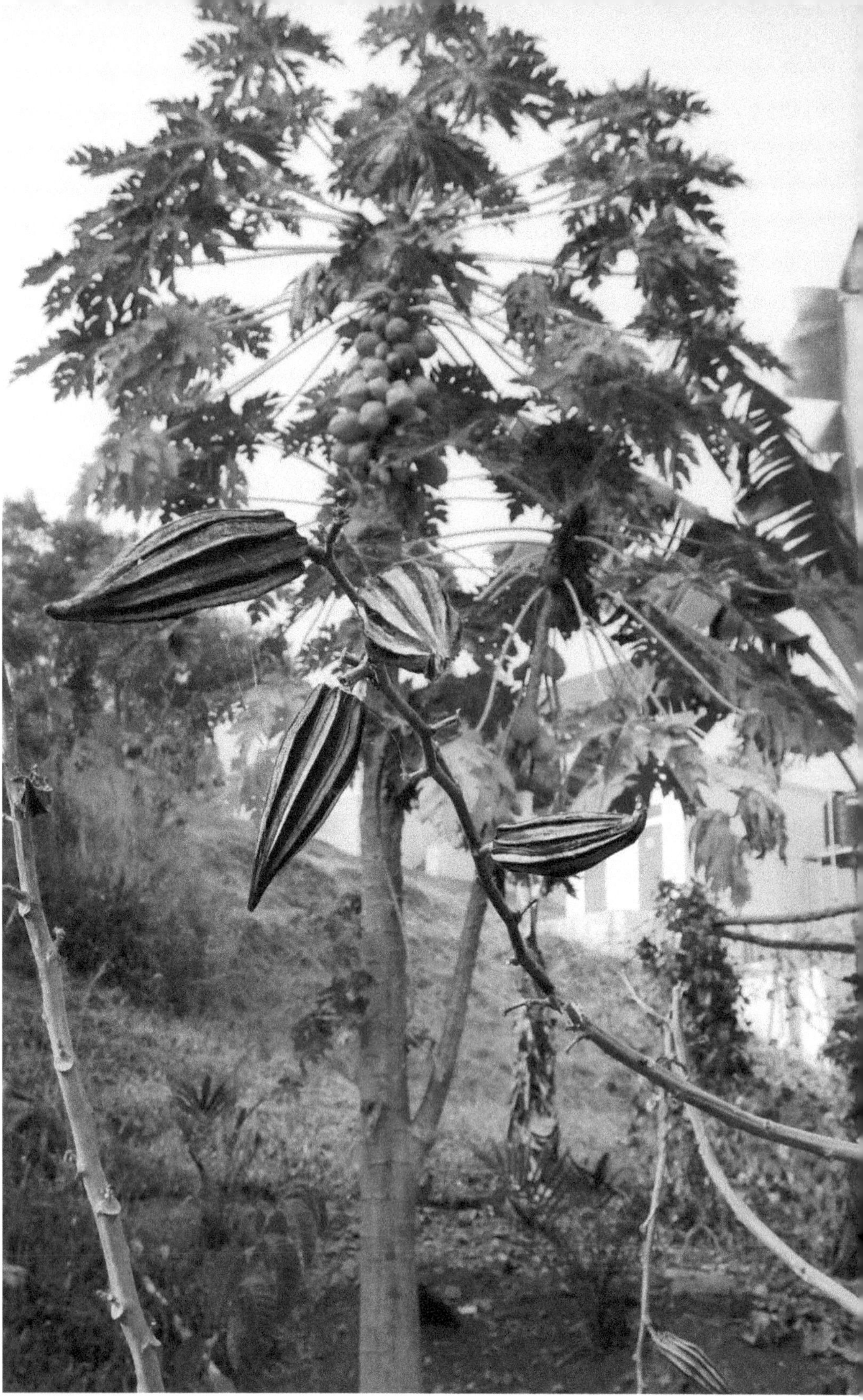

5
QUALIFYING HERITAGE THROUGH POSTCOLONIAL MOMENTS

POSTCOLONIAL MOMENTS: NURTURING CONTINGENT SYMMETRY

'WITH THE EXHIBITION IN THE MAIN BUILDING THE AIM WAS TO SHOW similarities as well as differences between the African enslaved workers and the Danish masters, and this was done by telling stories about the working and leisure life of both parties at the plantation.'[1]

Written jointly by most of the Danes involved in the Frederiksgave project, this quote informs us of the thoughts behind the exhibition set up in the newly reconstructed buildings. It shows how a dual figure of similarity and difference was used for structuring the exhibition at the Frederiksgave site. Moving on from the previous chapters' exploration of the project design, architectural drawings, tools, materials and values, I now turn to the life of the 'finished' exhibition and plantation site of Frederiksgave.

Here I will discuss the kind of comparative work entailed in the Frederiksgave project – referred to as a cultural encounter and a common past – by drawing on Verran's notion of 'postcolonial moments'.[2] This notion, which I bring to bear generally on common heritage work, first appeared in her book on Yoruba numbers in Nigeria,[3] and was further explored in an article on different firing strategies in the Australian bush, where Verran analyses the collaboration between landowning Aboriginals and scientists to suggest that postcolonialism is about making differences realisable and not seeing futures as mere repetitions of pasts.[4] What interests me here is that thinking about the postcolonial in this way suggests that recognition of differences can allow for a new way of understanding symmetry as a dynamic *quality*, rather than a more or less stable relation between given entities. This is important because it was exactly this kind of dynamic approach that I have suggested was present but not always prioritised in the Frederiksgave project, by its construing symmetry as a relation between essentialised apolitical entities, and displaying this as a cultural encounter between distinct groups 'having' a common history.

As Verran shows in her article, the strategies of the two groups with whom she worked, Aborigines and scientists, differ profoundly. This became clear in practical, unpredictable encounters and has, over the years, often caused conflicts and misunderstandings. However, even in such a difficult and almost impossible situation, possibilities for dialogue and seizing 'postcolonial moments' still arise. Paraphrasing Stuart Hall, Verran sees these moments as 'occasions for theorising, for telling differences and sameness in new ways'.[5] This is not the postcolonialism conveyed, for instance, in the classic *The Wretched of the Earth* (2001) by Frantz Fanon, where the formerly oppressed, via their newly gained voice, reverse the relations by proactively emphasising their differences from former oppressing colonisers. At stake here is not an epochal or genealogical notion of postcolonialism where subalterns' possibilities of finally speaking back are the issue. Neither is it simply a matter of having moved beyond colonial asymmetry, as the Frederiksgave project makers seemingly saw it, and which caused them to design their project, in spite of its relation to the precarious theme of slavery, as a neutral cultural encounter and a matter of uncovering a common and given history. A postcolonial moment is not about 'retrieving a lost purity by overthrowing and uprooting an alien knowledge tradition'.[6] Reversal of roles is not the issue. Instead, a postcolonial moment provides an analytical opportunity for reconfiguring particular fields and interrupting existing orthodoxies in open-ended ways. More generally, it is a matter of realising that differences are not already given as properties of distinct entities or parties, but are something that we constantly make[7] in agreeing to speak.[8] To employ this approach in heritage work, however, takes an effort and a measure of courage.

The attempt to make differences (between, say, ideas about events in the past) realisable in a shared here and now implies that they are not delineated once and for all, nor externally related to each other across borders of predefined entities. Such an understanding implies that rather than looking at, comparing or collecting various things (in the plural) as anthropologists have often done, things are to be understood as comparisons in themselves.[9] Things as they appear to us are thus always made up of relationships to what they are not, i.e. what a thing is different from and what it compares with in and of itself. In other words, what appears as a thing – for instance, a heritage site – always also entails what it is not, because other possible comparative relations exist that would make it appear differently. The point here is that sameness has to be seen as already always implying difference. Sameness in a postcolonial moment is an effect, and thus about a symmetry established by the very fact that all parties contribute to and are produced in the ongoing making of a (differentiated) here-and-now (which can – and does – of course imply inequalities). Postcolonialism, in Verran's words, is about enabling 'difference to be collectively enacted'.[10] In my words, it entails allowing for a commonness in heritage work that does not imply the levelling of difference through the implicit mobilisation of certain logics of sameness posited at the outset.

In the previous chapters, many situations in which the Frederiksgave site emerged as 'common heritage' were explored in great detail. These situations were of various kinds, and the presence of awkwardness and tension was often explicit; awkwardness has thus been a faithful companion in analysing what went on during the reconstruction, where archaeologists, archives, architects, universal aspirations, forks, trees, drawings, rulers and whitewash (among many other agents) kept encountering one another and thereby bringing Frederiksgave to life. So far, my focus has been mainly on the emergence of Frederiksgave as a common heritage site during the phases of design and reconstruction. Accordingly, I have primarily looked at the Frederiksgave project as articulated and practised by the project makers, among whom the Danish planners have taken centre stage, because they were for the most part the ones most concerned with the heritage work and also those to whom the (universal) worth of Frederiksgave was most apparent. In this chapter – which is also a conclusion in the sense that it reflects back on the previous chapters – I broaden the scope a little to focus on moments of fieldwork that mocked the project planners' vision of Frederiksgave as an object of universal nature, common interest and aligned value. Using the notion of postcolonial moments, I take the opportunity to more actively propose possible alternative ways of qualifying heritage work latent within the project. The idea, then, is at once to reflect on what has gone on so far, and to do so by engaging with still more relations. Throughout the chapter, I will raise a number of questions that arise from my field, not necessarily with the aim of answering them, but so as to offer suggestions as worked examples of alternative ways of going forward. It is in doing this that I also begin to modestly propose and activate the potential of an ethnographically informed generative critique of common heritage work.

First, I want to show that the project's main and explicit idea of turning the Frederiksgave site into a common heritage site tended to background other issues that kept popping up during fieldwork. I thus want to explore some of the other concerns that were also generated in the mocking situations of the reconstruction project, the 'side-effects' as they were tellingly often termed by the project planners of the Common Heritage Project. As also discussed in Chapter One, I see this focus on mockery and unexpected outcomes as an interesting way to contribute to an anthropology of heritage, because it allows us to explore heritage as a fundamentally emergent and collective enterprise, and not as the result of compromises between given parties, hegemonies, technical solutions or degrees of historical accuracy.

Second, and accordingly, I want to develop a vocabulary that might give us tools to understand encounters in common heritage projects that sidestep the language of pre-given entities meeting, subsuming each other, or even colliding, as was characteristic of the notion of cultural encounters analysed in Chapter Two. Instead we can make better use of the encounters as privileged sites of analysis, as generative moments where entities (such as pasts, people and history, as well as heritage sites) are *produced* as outcomes. This might pave the way for a positive critique of common heritage, resting on creative invention rather than deconstruction, as discussed in Chapter Three.

Third, and in direct consequence, I want to suggest that we can learn something very important for further common heritage projects by staying with these awkward moments, instead of attempting to resolve them to arrive at heritage in the singular. This was one of the reasons why I detailed the complex history of fetish in relation to Frederiksgave in Chapter Four. Nurturing postcolonial moments will help with such ambitions, and for this reason, I see them as vital to my overall aim of qualifying heritage and developing an anthropology of common ground. This lens gives us an opportunity to work creatively and by way of improvisation with common heritage, instead of (as was a dominant feature in the plans for the Frederiksgave project) to dismiss, ignore and explain away awkwardness, or moments that challenged the initial design, purpose and story of the project. The actual process of collaborative common heritage making does not allow for such genteel and transcendent ideas of common heritage as given, and everything else as deviation.

In the following, I will discuss the ideas of sameness and difference expressed between Ghanaians and Danes in the project, but which could have been more actively brought to the fore. I ask several questions. How are the sameness and differences that the people from the National Museum mentioned to be understood? How might the notion of contingent symmetries come into play when, clearly, the relativist idea of cultural encounters did not do away with claims to universalism? In what ways could moments of tension in the course of the life of the Frederiksgave project perhaps have been developed more fruitfully and courageously, and have allowed for the continued existence of different perspectives and interests produced and emerging in the course of the project? In other words, what might heritage be and become when seen as a product of encounters in a postcolonial moment as I have described it? In order to address these questions, let us first take a closer look at some of the posters exhibited at the site.

POSITING SAMENESS AND DIFFERENCE: EXHIBITING LIFE IN COMMON?

In one of the three rooms in the main building are exhibited an old writing desk holding a goose quill, along with two small crocks for ink and sand, and a copy of a letter from one of the expatriate Danes. A display case on the floor

FIG. 5.1 Part of the exhibition in the main building, 2007, Sesemi, Ghana.

contains, among other things, an almost full-size gun of the 1800s. Three display cases contain objects and text related to the theme 'Work', as is stated in slightly bigger font on one of the posters.

The case introducing 'Work' also displays a copy of a hoe and a machete from the 1830s-40s. Under the heading, it states the following:

> The work conducted by Danes and enslaved plantation workers differed considerably. The enslaved workers on Frederiksgave worked for the plantation owner from 6 to 10 a.m. and from 2 to 5 p.m. four days a week. The rest of the week they cultivated allotted plots of land for their own subsistence. The Danish officials worked from 8 to 12 a.m. and from 2 to 5 p.m. six days a week, mainly writing and copying administrative documents.[11]

Clearly, the text focuses on the differences between 'Danes' and 'enslaved plantation workers', all the while implicitly comparing the work schedule of both parties. It is a comparison *between* two given entities – a plural perspective – and consistent with the relativist stance discussed in Chapter Two. Another poster in the opposite room is called 'Leisure time', and focuses on the similarities between 'the local people' and 'the Danes':

> Although the daily work tasks differed considerably between the local people on the Gold Coast and the Danes, many of the leisure activities were similar. Apart from sleeping and personal hygiene, time was often spent together drinking, eating, smoking, and playing various games. The slaves liked to perform music and dance, occasionally with the Danes as an audience. The Danish officials spent time reading books from a small library at Christiansborg.[12]

Under the text, various artefacts, such as games, miniatures of both a bed and a straw mat used as a mattress, and musical instruments are exhibited, along with accompanying texts informing the visitor about the different lives of the Danes and the local people at the site. For example, it is stated that

> Most of the Danish authors writing accounts from the Gold Coast praised the cleanliness and hygiene of the people on the Gold Coast, in contrast to the European habits of merely stripwashing oneself and the wide use of perfume.[13]

Overall, the posters in the exhibition provide information on the differences and similarities between Danes and the people of the Gold Coast: they were all humans, yet they slept on different beds; they all worked, even if different hours and with different working tools; they all drank, albeit different alcohol; and they all played, even if different games. As stated in the introductory quote from the article written by many of the Danes involved in the project, this dual figure of differences and sameness runs intentionally through the exhibition. The lives of the Danes and slaves or local people on the Gold Coast are sharply separated, though their similar and common human activities are also stressed. At first glance, then, the exhibition might be seen as presenting symmetric relations between the two parties. But how are we to understand these relations when looking through a lens of postcolonialism in Verran's sense? What I suggest is that by taking their point of departure in two groups – Danes and enslaved workers – 'symmetry' is presented as given rather than contingent. People are reduced to data in an already established system, rather as in the Linnean system discussed in Chapter Two. The posters exhibit two already given groups, meeting every now and then in what was characterised as a cultural encounter.

If we recall Figure 4.3, the illustration depicting Danish and French men in uniforms and the lightly dressed female black waitresses, we will recognise a similar non-meeting within the same frame. In a sense, the illustration almost becomes a caricature of the parallel lives of both parties; one (ob-)serving the other. The 'black' waitresses and the 'white' men remain separated, living different lives even in encounters such as that enjoyable moment – just as they do on the posters exhibited at the Common Heritage Site. What I suggest here is that sameness and differences are enclosed within parallel lives. This is not necessarily a matter of a given ('racial') hierarchy. As we saw from the information about personal hygiene, the roles could be reversed so that the colonial Danes appear foreign to Danes today. Here one could perhaps talk of a reversed colonialism whereby visitors can learn that the Danes/Europeans were not as clean (and hence, one might add, civilised) as the Africans, who took proper care of their bodies. This rather specific and intimate information about hygiene might be surprising to visitors: either you are left wondering quite why this intimate information was chosen as a theme for a poster, or your ideas about who has traditionally been associated with the 'civilised' virtue of cleanliness are reversed. Maybe the choice to exhibit this subject was made for pragmatic reasons. Following a request from the former Director of the National Museum to the Danish Governor on the African Coast, everyday objects including hygienic artefacts were collected and sent to the newly opened ethnographic museum in Copenhagen in the 1830s-40s. These objects are now kept in storage rooms at the National Museum of Denmark. These old collected items could therefore function as templates for copies to be made in Ghana for the Frederiksgave exhibition. Maybe the project planners found this information interesting to communicate, particularly because it followed the cultural relativist idea of separating the two groups while evading clear-cut hierarchisation. However, in my view, by positing the two groups populating Frederiksgave when it functioned as given entities, the posters occasion mere description, rather than allowing the encounters between the Danes and the Africans to effect a meeting of the two parties; in other words, in this case the exhibition does not seize the opportunity to nurture a postcolonial moment in Verran's understanding. Differences and sameness were confirmed as given and stable by being posited.

Of course, a setting with slaves and masters is already, from the start, sharply divided, and it might appear inappropriate to highlight any possibility of symmetry. However, a focus on interaction that may have blurred the picture, thereby explicitly giving rise to frictional situations, has been left out of the exhibition, and this to me amounts to a subtle form of colonising, in that the parties are already assigned unchangeable roles in the so-called cultural encounter – i.e. as mere data in an already given system. In this light, one might say that recognition of contingency is a precondition of symmetry – of being allowed to *become* a part of the shared past, thereby contributing to its production instead of merely filling it out – for both parties. Thus, rather than a contingent symmetry, the exhibition communicates a universal history entailing a given relation – sometimes hierarchical (in unexpected ways), sometimes not – made up of parallel lives from the point of view of invisible authors. This universal history informs visitors about the distinct lives of a homogeneous group of Danes and a homogeneous group of local people from the Gold Coast, who happened to be engaged on the same piece of land.

So what could have been done to nurture a generative perspective on both the present and the past? How might the exhibition have been designed so as to show the continuous and always incomplete production of entities such as Danes and local people – with whatever hierarchies exist between or among them at any point in time? How could the symmetry, understood not as a matter of equal representation of given positions but as a shared and ongoing activity of *producing* entities (and their pasts and futures), have aided the making of a much sought-after commonness of the past?

One artefact that could have pointed to some sort of awkward interaction, where the roles of people were not already charted or colonised by a universal story, was a whip. Exhibiting such an artefact at the site was briefly debated when planning the exhibition. The Ghanaian coordinator suggested that a whip should form part of the exhibition. According to the Danish coordinator with whom he communicated, he argued that the overseer working on the plantation might have used a whip to force the enslaved plantation workers to work. But the Danish historian was opposed to the idea, because there were no signs either in the archives or from the excavations that such a tool had actually been used at the plantation. Records show that whips were used in the sugar plantations of the former Danish West Indies (today's US Virgin Islands). But plantations in Ghana, the Danish historian argued, were different from the plantations on the Caribbean islands. Importantly, to the Danish historian it was a question of historical accuracy and evidence, rather than an attempt at repressing the 'Danish evil' of the past. As discussed in Chapter One, the project planners were well aware that the plantation in Ghana entailed a 'dark heritage' of using enslaved workers, but while not shying away from addressing this, they wanted to do so in accordance with what they perceived to be historically accurate data. In this light the whip, according to the historian, was simply not accurate data in the system of History. However, this appeal to historical accuracy was interestingly balanced with a relativist view of history. Commenting on the suggestion that the whip be displayed, he said, 'the more they [Ghanaians, personified by the Ghanaian coordinator] take ownership, the better […] it is their history, and they have the right to that […]. One cannot own the history'. Again, we see an interesting mix of universal and relativist ideas. Having said this, the historian also expressed an awareness of the financial issues involved, since tourism in Ghana is a huge sector, attracting many African Americans to visit the forts along the coast and other sites related to the transatlantic slave trade. These potential tourists might be more interested in visiting a place that was more in line with what they expected and which entailed a strong symbol of oppression, such as the whip. Thus, economic factors might have been among the Ghanaian coordinator's concerns when he suggested exhibiting a whip. But before exploring these factors, it is useful to return to the dual figure communicated in the exhibition.

In the historian's statement, we see an implicit separation between 'their history' and 'our history'. Again, these two histories are presented as running parallel to each other, rather than meeting and thereby jointly contributing to a symmetrical making of the shared past. Such a symmetry, according to Verran, is based on 'infra-sameness' rather than 'meta-sameness' – that is, a sameness that is internal to the things related and therefore also structured according to the particular encounter, rather than based on a third and distant meta-point of view from where one can observe the sameness of two given entities. With the vocabulary of infra-sameness, Verran gives a name to the possibilities for creating encounters built on 'a sameness that is good enough merely for a few here-and-nows'.[14] She thereby pays attention to provisional encounters of 'infra-sameness'. At issue here is a 'modest symmetry',[15] practised in the joints of the concrete. In the case of the Frederiksgave project, to focus on such modest symmetry is not to make the irresponsible claim that the enslaved workers at Frederiksgave had opportunities equal to those of their Danish masters, and that this should be reflected in the exhibition. But it is to claim that one way of practising common heritage work in an exhibition could be to let the possibility of violent oppression remain a live issue. Rather than the exhibition universally settling on the depiction of specific kinds of oppression on the plantation, a 'small' agreement and/or acknowledgement of oppression could have been nurtured in (modest) here-and-nows. Might one have exhibited a whip so as to nurture such an uncolonised moment?

More specifically, in terms of what the exhibition could have displayed to nurture a modest symmetrical commonness, one could imagine it explicitly communicating that Frederiksgave could be the same as *and* different from a West Indian plantation; that the whip might *and* might not have been used at the Frederiksgave site. This would replace an appeal to historical records as evidence (or, indeed, to 'their history' as an alternative version). The disagreement as to whether Frederiksgave should display a whip was, in my eyes, a productive opportunity to engage differences in collaborative heritage work. The question could have remained unsettled, but instead the 'solution' was to not exhibit a whip in the exhibition, since no historical sources documented the use of such an instrument at Frederiksgave. In this way, the possibility of connecting Frederiksgave with the transatlantic slave trade – and potentially attracting tourists interested in this history – was backgrounded by way of an appeal to historical evidence. As we saw in Chapters One and Three, accuracy was an aspiration; it was about measuring lengths, widths and heights that fitted precisely with the numbers on the ruler. Like finding the right card among a pile of other cards, there seemed to be only one possibility in the exhibition's communication: to determine the 'true story' (as found mainly in archives, excavated objects and the ruin). And, like free verbal invocations, the posters exhibited had to refer to and represent that story through materials and texts.

At other times, it was the Ghanaian coordinator's ideas that were communicated in the exhibition; for instance, the word 'slaves' was changed to the less essentialising 'enslaved workers' on most of the text displayed. I suggest that the question of whether the enslaved workers at the Frederiksgave plantation shared the same harsh conditions (being humiliated and flogged with whips) as the enslaved Africans in the Caribbean can be seen as part of a more general aspiration existing in Ghana to call upon the African Diaspora and unite all Africans – an aspiration that was impeded by the refusal to exhibit a whip. Even though I never heard the Ghanaian coordinator mention the plight of the African Diaspora, he nevertheless dedicated his PhD thesis about the Frederiksgave plantation to these and other enslaved people. In its preface, he states:

> This work is dedicated to the memory of the enslaved Men, Women and Children whose history is the subject matter of this study and to the millions who were uprooted and transplanted in the enslaved world of the African Diaspora.[16]

Although it was not explicit, the planners of the exhibition in Denmark had no doubt that, in addition to commemorating the once enslaved people of Ghana, the transnational African Diaspora was somehow present in the setting up of the exhibition. The Danish historian told me that early on in the project he had discussed with the Ghanaian archaeologist and coordinator whether slavery on Danish plantations in Africa could be understood as analogous to slavery in the Caribbean – an issue they seemingly did not completely agree upon. As we shall see, fieldwork experiences point to this unsettled relation between the plantations and the larger issue of slavery.

During my periods of fieldwork, many festivals and ceremonies were held along the Ghanaian coast in support of the official Ghanaian agenda of inviting the African Diaspora to Ghana. In a former Danish Fort in Keta, I saw a poster headed: 'Panafest. Emancipation day '07. Joseph Project. Theme: reuniting the African family'. The Ghanaian Ministry of Tourism and Diasporan Relations had initiated the so-called 'Joseph Project' in 2003[17] and made the poster for the 200-year celebrations of the abolition of the transatlantic slave trade. Similarly, the fiftieth anniversary of Ghana's independence was celebrated in 2007, the same year the Frederiksgave exhibition was set up. Two officials from the Ministry explained to me that the biblical story of Joseph being sold by his brothers had been their source of inspiration for the project. They were now hoping for reconciliation between 'black brothers', as they expressed it while showing me photographs from one of the ceremonies at one of Ghana's large European-built castles. The project's official web page explains: 'The Joseph project is Ghana's invitation to the Diasporans to make the return journey, to reconnect with the land of their ancestors and their brothers and sisters in the homeland'.[18] When I asked the officials to elaborate on this, I was told that the 'black brothers' nowadays arrived mainly as tourists from North America.

A group of young and well-educated Ghanaians working in the Ghanaian museum and heritage sector told me that this reconciliation between 'black brothers' often created very ambivalent feelings among the people involved.[19] They told me of an incident in which some Ghanaians had laughed at crying African Americans commemorating their enslaved forefathers, and of another in which they themselves, as workers in one of the big castles, had felt marginalised because some of the African Americans behaved as if they owned the forts and castles along the coast, insisting on their right to visit them without paying entrance fees. But on the other hand, they added, the African Americans did bring a great deal of money into their economically poor country. These were indeed difficult situations. The explicit aim of uniting all Africans pointed to a postcolonialism that entailed other differences than those between European colonisers and African colonised, and which could not be grasped by seeing just two given groups.[20] But by talking about 'black brothers', the Joseph Project created a unity that distinguished itself from the rest of humanity, such as, for instance, the Europeans who had been deeply involved in the history they commemorated. As such, the Joseph Project continued a racial thinking that is far from new.[21] I would argue that the Joseph Project, part of which took place in the former Danish fort of Prindsensten in Keta, was not – at least not immediately – used as an occasion 'for telling differences and samenesses in new ways.[22] Instead, its design repeated a racial representation.

Whatever the project ideal, the exhibition at the Common Heritage Site was set up against an international backdrop, communicating to more than a Danish and Ghanaian audience whose past was called common; inevitably, it was about more than two nations sharing a history that can then be represented accurately and controlled in an exhibition. The African Diaspora, and other nations, apparently also entered the picture, and were present in this particular shared past. All along, as we shall see in the following, the universalising ideas embedded in notions such as 'common heritage', and surfacing in ideas about a given history and about given groups in the Frederiksgave project, were challenged by words, perspectives and objects, making it all the more striking that the project planners maintained that there was *one* (common) story to tell. The world was intruding on our shared past in ways that the Common Heritage Project could not control, and which in my opinion could push heritage work more generally in interesting new directions.

NAMING HERITAGE: WORDS OF THE WORLD

While reconstructing the site with the right materials, the right doses and the right location, copious verbal utterances were exchanged between the people involved. Many of these utterances dealt with the history of the site, either in written form or in the form of people talking together – in old and present-day Danish, and English. Ga and Twi, the two local languages, were also naturally heard, but rarely, I was told, to refer to the history of the site. Nailed to the walls, roofs and floors, pages and pages of text were hung up and exhibited. Both inside and outside the newly reconstructed building, posters offered 'An overview of the site' and information about 'Frederiksgave. The Royal Danish plantation on the Gold Coast'. And, under the heading 'Maps', both old and new maps located the site in time and space. As touched upon above, the posters communicated the lives of the 'Danes and the enslaved plantation workers' under headings such as: 'Work', 'Leisure time', 'Personal hygiene', 'Games', 'Locally made pottery', 'European tableware', and others. And, in even greater detail, one could be informed about the plantation via a small folder that could either be downloaded from the Internet or, if in stock, purchased at the site.

All this written text, however, only seemed to be a small interruption in or temporary accumulation of information from all the talk that I overheard and participated in during my fieldwork. The Danish heritage workers and professionals, in particular, did a great deal of talking. Summaries and discussions of books, notes, materials, emails, laws, measures and talks with visitors and other people were considered collectively. Questions were posed, and answers ventured or left unsolved. Detailed information about what 'the Danes' and 'the local people' or 'the enslaved workers', as they were termed on the posters, had been drinking, eating, growing, playing, wearing and hunting was shared. Questions about why the Frederiksgave site had not turned into a successful plantation, how the slaves were treated and how often the Danish expatriate men visited the place were debated. Whether they had had an enamelled coffee pot to brew the new grown coffee, as a Danish historian visiting the site suggested from her knowledge of the Danish National Archives, was discussed. There was no limit to the level of detail and information explored by the professional heritage workers engaged in the project. But, as a common credo, all the professionals agreed that here, exactly here, was (the spot of) our common history; here it was possible to walk around in our forefather's footsteps; here history unfolded. The discussions notwithstanding, all were convinced that Frederiksgave manifested the past in the shape of a former plantation of common interest. By just being there, we were all somehow *doing* the credo. But outside of the community of enthusiastic heritage professionals, not everyone praised the principle. The people living in Sesemi did not tell a story of the 'Danes and the enslaved plantation workers' – not at all, as I rather quickly came to understand. It seemed that for them the place evoked different footsteps to walk in and thereby made other histories emerge.

Early on in the project, people from the National Museum had bought a video camera because they were interested in documenting the reconstruction work at the site. No one had really used it, so during my first fieldwork in Ghana

I thought that I might give it a try. I filmed how the workers mixed the mortar, how they carried the stones on their heads and how they levelled the terrain for the new building. During the recording, we laughed at the awkwardness of the camera; we probably also laughed at my female presence at the male-dominated site, at my interest in the reconstruction process and my requests that the workers tell me exactly what they were doing in different situations. Maybe we also laughed at having to speak English, a language that none of us spoke as our mother tongue, and maybe the workers also felt embarrassed by being filmed in dirty work clothes. Finally, I found two young men from Sesemi working at the site who actually seemed to like being filmed. They posed in front of the camera, and when I asked them if they could tell me something about this place, I was surprised by their story. They told me that this place had been 'a Fort' and that 'slaves had been kept here'. They pointed to a viewpoint further up the hill and said that from there 'they' (the Danish owners) could see if ships were ready to buy slaves or not. If so, slaves were brought down to the coast, chained together in long rows in order to be 'shipped over there'. I was disconcerted. At the time, the planning of the reconstruction project had already been running for some years, and the Ghanaian archaeologists had made excavations in the nearby 'slave village' in the 1990s, with assistance from the men in the village, so I did not expect such a different story from the one I had heard at the National Museum in Denmark – especially not in the midst of this *common* project. In Denmark, the Danish coordinator had told me that, with the Common Heritage Project, the National Museum wanted to tell another story than the one richly offered at the forts and castles along the Ghanaian coastline. They wanted to tell 'another chapter' in Danish and Ghanaian history, as she framed it. This was a chapter about how Danes had experimented with plantations *in* Ghana, using slave labour. But the story that the two young men told me was exactly what the Danish coordinator termed 'a prior chapter in history from before the time of the Frederiksgave plantation'; they were explicitly linking the Frederiksgave site to the transatlantic slave trade. In the video sequence, I stuttered that I had heard that the place had been used as a plantation. The two young men nodded politely and started working again; obviously they were not interested in my story, which therefore ended rather abruptly. The official story of the common heritage site advocated by the project planners was silenced and seemingly irrelevant from the perspective of the project workers I filmed. This was yet another awkward situation that, like others, did not find a resting place but was left unresolved. The workers did not exactly object to my comment about the place as a plantation; they just let it hang in the air as my own concern. Later, I told the Ghanaian coordinator about the story I had heard from the two young men, but he shrugged it off, deploring the fact that the young men still told this false story. He told me that this story was an old myth they apparently kept telling about the place.

Over the years, I had wanted to discuss this issue of addressing the link that people might make between the Common Heritage Project and the wider and still precarious theme of slavery in Ghana, because it was clear from my fieldwork that this connection kept popping up. However, rather than address the issue directly, the Frederiksgave project planners seemed to trust history to eliminate stories that were not documented in the archival and historical sources, such as that of the Frederiksgave site playing a role in the transatlantic slave trade. As a result, the pressure to educate local guides from the village, as budgeted for early in the project, was increased; the Danish National Museum felt that something had to be done; action had to be taken. In order to stop these stories, the coordinator from the Danish National Museum reacted instantly. Her response was to insist that 'we have to educate the guides'. But, for some reason, education of the local guides was never undertaken at the site. The Ghanaian partner who was in charge of this task seemed not to have found the time to do so; it did not seem to be a priority to him to align the knowledge of the guides with that found in the archival sources on which the Danish National Museum relied. Clearly, this caused frustration among the Danes at the museum, who occasionally received critical feedback from Danish visitors complaining that the guides communicated a 'false story' that did not resonate with the orthodox story displayed on the posters. Thus, from the point of view of the Frederiksgave project planners in Denmark, continuously dealing with 'the lack of education of the local guides' has turned into a problem of high priority, to be dealt with in potential future projects in Ghana. Accordingly, when considering new projects in Ghana, 'capacity building' has been suggested as an important task. In line with the statement mentioned in the previous chapters, it was 'a helping hand' and 'the least we can do' in order to safeguard a common past.

Could the various and seemingly incommensurable stories at the site be captured in, or supported by, the notion of a postcolonial moment? Do they reflect a contingent symmetry? Do or can educational activities entail moments where infra-sameness can be reached? Verran writes that aspirations to postcolonial moments imply a challenge to universalisms and orthodoxies. They are moments where the people involved understand their own metaphysics, its limits and partiality, and thereby come to tolerate rather than eliminate other perspectives.[23] Insofar as the local people's story was understood as wrong by the project planners, and as something that could be remedied by education and capacity building, their strategies pointed to one exclusive understanding of the site. This was the understanding communicated through posters and artefacts at the site – a universal story with no sender, it seemed, except history itself speaking via the archival sources and the excavated ruin. Like the ruler, history was seen as an external set of criteria. Through meticulous studies in archives, and via excavated artefacts and rubble, history could keep the Frederiksgave site in check, and supposedly true to itself. Like the metric system, education appeared as another form of universal standardisation, or as another catechism to eradicate idols, like that developed by the Church. This time, standardisation and doctrine did not come from offices in Paris or Rome, but from the National Archives and the National Museum of Denmark, and from university departments and laboratories in Ghana and Denmark. The kind of community inclusion that these ideas about capacity building entail is thus a very particular one, namely an offer to the Ghanaian collaborators to become included in the community of educated wardens of history. So great, apparently, was most of the project planners' trust in history, that they could see no problem in invoking the viewpoint of singular historical truth as a place from which to speak and act.

But as I have shown through numerous fieldwork situations, history is never just external to its subject and to the here-and-now, even if the stakeholders constantly try to make it appear as such in their universalising claims. As we learned from the architect and his ruler, history was both mediated and created at the heritage site. I want to stress here that this is not just a normative statement about history being contingent. Rather, the point is that it demands a certain perspective to make it appear as already given. It demands an effort to turn history and knowledge of it into natural entities. The point is that orthodoxies are constantly challenged in the here-and-now, and we have, I will argue, every opportunity to make the most of these challenges in heritage work.

With regard to the contradictory stories articulated at the Frederiksgave site, nurturing a postcolonial moment could have meant exploring possibilities for infra-sameness. One could have taken 'slavery' as a potential point of infra-sameness that is 'good enough merely for a few here-and-nows'.[24] Although not settling on a particular idea about the destiny of the slaves, all still agreed that there had been slaves at the Frederiksgave plantation, and thus there was a modest conjunction, and a potential starting point.

Let us take a closer look at more of the words that were shared in and around the Frederiksgave heritage project. Some time after the National Museum of Denmark had left the Frederiksgave site to the management of a Board in 2007, a postcard of the site was produced (see also figure 3.4). Immediately, the photo on it caught my eye. The picture was not taken from what seemed to be most Danes' favourite spot, i.e. from the symmetrical axis. Perfectly facing the main building and restroom, several photos, including my own, had taken me to a spot which, without words or actions, seemed valued as central by the Danes. The new postcard also showed a picture of the main building and the restroom beside it, but it was taken from an oblique angle that allowed a slight perspectival depth to the buildings. The corner of the postcard reads 'Frederiksgave PLANTATION AND COMMON HERITAGE SITE DANISH FORT (SESEMI – ACCRA, GHANA)'. In addition to being a plantation, by using the word 'Fort', the postcard also connected the Frederiksgave plantation to the huge military buildings along Ghana's coast where slaves were kept in dungeons before being shipped across the Atlantic Ocean to the New World. By naming the site as a 'fort' and a 'plantation', it appeared as a multiple figure with two or more purposes. This twist in naming the site was emphasised in both a Ghanaian and Danish newspaper article on the site. After the inauguration of the Frederiksgave site, a Ghanaian newspaper wrote that if one wanted to visit Frederiksgave, one should 'ask for directions to the 'castle' as the local people call the Danish settlement'.[25] Although in Danish one differentiates between castles and forts, the latter being military edifices, this is not the case in Ghana, where the European edifices were designated as forts and castles interchangeably. As mentioned in Chapter Four, the term 'fort' also appeared in a recent newspaper article written by a Danish journalist,[26] a fact that caused the Danish coordinator of the Frederiksgave project to react and complain to the newspaper's editor that the place had actually been a plantation, not a fort.

Again, we see the project planners maintain that there is only one history at play at Frederiksgave; what commonness entails is that there is one universal history communicated by the site. But as the postcard indicates, Frederiksgave seemed much more multifaceted when explored through fieldwork, with multiple histories and possibilities for their re-performance appearing. To the project planners, the transatlantic connection might have been false in the sense of *facticii*, a false idol, and therefore it caused them great frustration to hear from Danish visitors and myself that Frederiksgave was repeatedly linked to the transatlantic slave trade, and also commemorated as such when they were not around.

I have already mentioned the African Diaspora, and the Ghanaian interest in reconnecting with it via initiatives such as, for instance, the Joseph Project. Clearly, such relations were, on the official Ghanaian side, also thought of in terms of tourism and thereby economic gain, as seen in the coining of a Ministry for Tourism and Diasporan Relations. Attracting the African Diaspora was seen primarily as an economic asset, and thus a component of projects such as Frederiksgave – it was in this context, I suggest, that it made sense to exhibit a whip, and to call the Frederiksgave site a 'fort'. As a Ghanaian professor, Atukwei Okai, Secretary-General of the Pan African Writers' Association, poetically explains, the recognition and integration of the African Diaspora 'is like a Baobab tree that goes in search of its roots in order to water them'.[27] One relevant question, then, is whether the African Diaspora, also seeking their common cultural heritage, would visit the Frederiksgave site if it was called a plantation rather than a fort. The African Diaspora seemed highly engaged in their forefathers' stories, laying wreaths in the forts' dungeons, and some even tracking down their DNA in order to locate which African region their ancestors had come from, as some African Americans told me at the former Danish fort of Prindsensten in Keta. Would a story about a small plantation with Danish masters and African slaves *in* Ghana be of any interest to them? A place that even claimed to be different from plantations in the Caribbean, and where no whip was exhibited even though, together with chains, it was an archetypical symbol of the oppression and violence experienced by enslaved people in the Caribbean. Could the African Diaspora be interested and attracted to the site via a direct link in the form of a name: by using the term 'Fort' as suggested on the postcard, instead of 'Plantation'?

The huts that were later constructed to show the houses of the enslaved plantation workers were given different names too. In reports, applications and daily conversation they were called 'slave huts' among the Danes from the National Museum. I was therefore surprised when I later heard the workers from the village refer to them as 'summer huts'. Both the Ghanaian architect and Ghanaian archaeologist called them either 'traditional huts' or 'African huts', with a preference for the latter. This term was then adopted by the few Danes who were still slightly involved in the project after its inauguration in 2007. The word 'slaves' was apparently not appropriate with regard to the huts. The naming of the huts might point to difficulties in relating former residents (i.e. enslaved people) to the village. In Sesemi, the villagers most often called the Frederiksgave site 'the thing', 'this thing', 'Danish Fort', 'museum' or 'tourist attraction'. It should be mentioned that the expression 'the/this thing' is used very often in daily talk to signify words one does not know in English or has forgotten in the spoken moment. However, the persistent use of the phrase reminded me of Macdonald's description of how the Nazi heritage in Nuremberg, analysed in her book 'Difficult Heritage', was talked about among Nurembergers in a local newspaper in the 1950s as 'the *Erbstück* – 'heritage piece''.[28] On that occasion in the 1950s, almost no one mentioned the past purpose of the Nazi buildings, only the cost of the buildings and the potential savings gained by keeping them were discussed. In Sesemi, I suggest that calling the heritage site 'the thing' might also be a way of framing the site in an open and undecided manner that does not mention the past use of the building, unless via the name 'Fort', linking it to the transatlantic slave trade. In a recorded interview, one of the men from the village explained:

Villager: 'they [the project planners] give a little history concerning this thing [nodding in the direction of Frederiksgave]. [...] Until last Thursday [official inauguration of Frederiksgave], when that small booklet came, when I read it I saw that the <u>whole</u> history that we were told, is actually what goes on. But what is a little different is they say that [...] because they are going to make it as a tourist eh, excuse me [disturbed] when they start the whole project, the only thing that we have changed a little is that they say that [...] that place was used as a sl, eh, as a slave centre. It won't be fair [...] for the blacks to hear of that slave, this thing because when you are talking of slaves, our forefathers and then, ancestors, were used in that slave trade [...] when you just tell me that this place is a slave centre that means that, I know that ah, my foref, eh, my ancestors were taken to this site, so I wouldn't be happy [...] to go there and have a look. So they started saying that 'it's a plantation house', so we have to take it as a plantation house, that place was used as a farmhouse, they plant coffee and pineapple and so forth. So okay we were using that, but when we use the name slave attached to this thing they say 'no, no, no, no, no'.

Nathalia: who said no, no, no?

Villager: okay it was <u>that</u> from the beginning, [the Ghanaian archaeologist] is saying that, but later, when this project started, they were saying that it is not a slave this thing but ehm, it's a farmhouse [...] But [...] until the day this place was commissioned, then the Director to the National Museum of Denmark, [...] in his speech he just mentioned both, the farmhouse and then slave plantation.

Nathalia: you didn't like that?

Villager: no, no, you see, okay we got to know that then it's the <u>real</u>, that okay they used slaves here, and then both, the plantation farm and the slave work and then the this thing that they have done there [pause], then okay they bought twenty five slaves, men and women, to work for them. They got to, okay from the book they have written that some of the slaves too were sent to America [...] so that means that it's true that they used to buy slaves and this thing there. So that's from where we got that small history. When people come then we just explain it to them that this is how the whole place start to being. [...] Anybody that comes [says it's a slave]. But this last year, when we were about to start this work then they started to change it saying that it's a farmhouse, you see?

Nathalia: yeah, but why did they change?

Villager: well, some say they don't want people to know that this place was used as a slave, you see? [...]

Nathalia: so they changed it into plantation, farmhouse

Villager: yes, yes, farmhouse, but after [...] I sit down and think 'ah, this thing, from the beginning they were saying it's a slave centre and then they have been buying slaves from here to America and so forth and then, why then are they saying it is a plantation house? You see?

Nathalia: yeah

Villager: so eh, I was worrying on that this thing, until last week, when the whole thing, when I saw it's in the booklet and then I saw; ah it's really both the farm plantation and then the slave work, so they just do the two. But what they say is that for the beginning, the first person that came here to start building this thing, the idea is to make a coffee plantation [...]. So after the plantation then they say that the Portuguese, Spanish, and so forth they started buying the slaves. So those here too got interest in the slave work, so they started buying the slaves you see'.

In this rather long and painful fragment, the crucial point seems to be the tensions regarding which stories the Frederiksgave site is supposed to tell and how to name the site. The villager ponders how to relate the site to slavery. An impression of not being the one who writes or tells the history of Frederiksgave is also conveyed. The history is something that he and his co-inhabitants are informed about in bits and pieces every now and then from authorities, including people from universities and national museums; it seems to be out of their hands. However, he clearly communicates that part of the history told at the site is 'not fair to the blacks'. According to him, the villagers did not like to be connected to slavery through blood, since it is painful and shows them in an unfavourable light. The villager seems to discuss how to refer to the place and what to make of its changing names; perhaps preferring 'a farmhouse', he also labels Frederiksgave as a plantation, and even as a slave plantation, dismissing the notion of slave centre, even though this name was about 'in the beginning'. All the way through, it is a little unclear who 'they' are – the people who change the names, inform about what went on, and object to certain labels are both villagers (occasionally identified as an 'I'), Ghanaian project workers and Danish heritage professionals. Surely, history does not speak for itself here, nor is anyone its given spokesperson.

'Farmhouse' seems to be a neutral word for the villager, since it connects the place with the present-day agricultural activities in the village. The word 'slaves', however, seems to my interlocutor to be best connected with the Americas. At the end of the quote, it sounds as if the place started out as a plantation for farming the surrounding land, but then the Portuguese and the Spanish (known in Ghana for being unscrupulous slave traders, even after the ban on the trade) started buying slaves to send to the Americas, thereby producing a market for them. Via these economic interests, the villager suggests, the Frederiksgave site became involved in the transatlantic slave trade – which according to Danish jurisdiction was illegal after 1802.[29] In this view, Frederiksgave is therefore both a plantation/farmhouse and a place used in the slave trade – an idea of Frederiksgave as a multipurpose object that was not mirrored in the booklet or on the posters produced by the National Museum in Denmark. In the perspective of the villager, 'the thing' matched the text written on the postcard mentioned above, being both a plantation and a fort, and possibly other things that they/we might call it.

Macdonald points out how the city of Nuremberg is often associated by foreigners with its Nazi past.[30] For the present-day Nurembergers, such an image is reductionist and somehow understood as 'unfair'. Some argue that it was the Nazi party that chose the city and not the other way around, and as such the city appears as victim rather than perpetrator of Nazi crimes. In Sesemi, the association of being descendants of victims of inhuman conditions of the past does not seem to be welcome. The pointing out of such a victimised position was understood as 'unfair'. This was an attitude I encountered several times when talking to Ghanaians about slavery. The problem was not so much being a descendant of forefathers who *had* slaves: the problem for the people I talked to was being identified as a descendant *of* those slaves. Where in Nuremberg the difficult past had led to the question over the years as to why Nuremberg was chosen as the place for the huge Nazi party rallies, this type of question was never addressed collectively in Sesemi. At stake in the cases of Nuremberg and the Frederiksgave site is a question about the specificity of both places in the wider history of Nazism and slavery, respectively. In the case of the Frederiksgave site, the project planners knew that the Europeans exploited the people from West Africa and shipped them to the 'New World', but right here, where the Common Heritage Project was located, it was a plantation – that was how *this particular* encounter was singularly structured and perceived to be in accordance with particular evidence from the archives and the excavation. In this perspective, the differences between the conditions of the enslaved workers in Ghana and the slaves shipped to America were given and verified by historical sources. However, as we have seen from the discussions about naming the heritage site above, other relations could have been seen to contribute to the complex production of the Frederiksgave site, whereby a contingent symmetry could have been explored. The point is that with regard to the Common Heritage Project, naming the place could thus be seen as growing out of heterogeneously structured encounters, rather than designating a universal given or a natural unity. Certainly, as I have amply demonstrated in the preceding chapters, it takes a very particular perspective to make Frederiksgave appear as such a natural entity. Accordingly, 'cross-cultural equivalence' (see Chapter Four) apparently seemed difficult to achieve. I rarely heard the people in the village term the place 'Frederiksgave', which was clearly most of the project planners' favourite name for it (which is why I have primarily used this term throughout the book). If the people in the village used this name, it always produced an awkward moment where the person in question hesitantly tried to pronounce the strange Danish sounds, smiling a bit, and with his or her eyes asking me to complete the word.

Most often, as described above, it was called 'the thing', 'the fort', 'tourist attraction', 'slave centre', 'Danish Fort' or 'museum' by the people in the area – including journalists. Initially, the place was officially called 'Frederiksgave

Plantation and Common Heritage Site' but a while after the site was handed over to a board in 2007, they suggested calling the place: 'Museum of Slavery and Plantation Lifeways' – a phrase I first encountered in 2007 in a short article in a Lonely Planet guidebook.[31]

This title suggested by the board caused a person from the National Museum, still granting money to Frederiksgave, to write an email asking the former Ghanaian coordinator, now a member and key person in the board, to add the name 'Frederiksgave' to the suggested title. The argument for this was that using the name 'Frederiksgave' was a way of ensuring the continuity of the project as it had hitherto been conceptualised, and furthermore it was the name known among Danes and likewise used in the Danish and Ghanaian media. 'Plantation', the only word surviving from the original name, could be seen as indirectly linking the site with slavery in the New World and, thereby, if we are to follow the villager quoted above, turning the place into both a farm and a place for dealing in slaves – the latter association attracting overseas tourists, all the while causing discomfort among the local villagers in Sesemi. 'Museum' might be seen as replacing 'heritage' and thereby following a trend in Ghana where 'these days every chief wants to have his own museum', as a person from the Ghanaian Ministry of Tourism and Diasporan Relations explained to me. My point here is that for a common project, it has been difficult indeed to settle on a common name – significantly. the word 'common' has completely disappeared from the new title. A middleman's term, like the way the word 'fetish' emerged, has not (yet) been found, apart maybe from 'plantation', which also has its limitations, as described above. Maybe the term 'museum' is better suited to the job, being a neutral word that all can agree upon – maybe such words point to a shared interest that is good enough for a few-here-and-nows?

There are, then, important insights to be had from discussions about the name of the site. My suggestion here is that instead of striving to find the *right* name, the various namings of the site might be understood generatively as discussions that bring the site to life, and thus as an important unsettling point that could be embraced precisely to help us qualify cultural heritage at Frederiksgave. The different names (and the accommodation of different potential audiences) could be endorsed as expressions of precisely the contingent symmetry that prevails in a postcolonial moment. Calling the site a 'museum' and leaving it like that might be far too imprecise, but maybe as a *starting point* such a general term might provide a space for encounters in the here-and-now between the site and various partners with different interests, wishes and understandings. What if the names were seen, not as end points, but as opportunities to explore sameness and difference in encounters across divides? Instead of saying that there are many ways to term the site (a relativistic point of view), or of appealing to particular historical evidence to settle on the most accurate name (a universalistic point of view), one might say that the site is nothing apart from the heterogeneous points of view. This would be contingent symmetry.

WARDENS OF HISTORY?

Certainly, these (awkward, tentative, shifting) ways of handling names all indicate that the Common Heritage Project was dealing with precarious matters that have not found a stable form except in an official name. We also sensed this precariousness in the previous chapter, where I described being taken out of the building by a frightened woman in order to escape the history of slavery. Early in my fieldwork in Ghana, I met and talked with Akosua Perbi, a Ghanaian historian from the University of Legon. I had read her book *A History of Indigenous Slavery in Ghana* (2004) with great interest. In the book she explores the history of slavery in Ghana and the stigma with which this history is still surrounded in Ghana today.[32] Several of her colleagues and students at the university told me that the book was a very brave academic work, since it touched on such a delicate matter, as slavery certainly seemed to be in Ghana. Some mentioned that she could only write this book because of her family's long and well-respected position within the intellectual elite in Ghana. I had a strong sense that the situation of the frightened woman running out of the Frederiksgave building (discussed in Chapter Four), as well as the lack of a common name for the site, had to do with this delicate matter.

In a Danish-produced movie about the slave trade, another Ghanaian historian explains:

> For us [in Ghana], history is not an academic subject; you go to the classroom and study to get an A or B or C or D. It has a value. The value is, enshrined in it you find the philosophy of the people. You don't want to talk about, too much about the defeats, the ugliness. You want to talk about the victories and successes. You want to encourage the generation you are talking to. You want to encourage them to think in a certain way. To say that you see: our ancestors were great people. They were great people. They achieved this [...] so that you too have to continue with their line, so that you too achieve, you continue with this greatness. Also in some places during the slave trade, you find that many people were wrestled from inland [...] so some of those who are descendants, they don't want to talk about it. Those who were taken as slaves, they suffered a lot, and they are still asked, if you spoke to descendants of those who were taken away, they still face discrimination every single day of their life.[33]

The Ghanaian historian conveys an understanding of history as containing a perspective – a philosophy of a people – thereby foregrounding the people as writers, in opposition to the idea of letting history speak with a universal voice. Further, history for this Ghanaian historian is continuous, rather than interrupted and divided into periods or 'chapters'. It seems that the line of blood and the family's achievement are decisive for the future life of the family. If your descendants happen to have been enslaved people, it seems that this position somehow continues in the present and could make people suffer from discrimination. For this reason, it might be better if it is ignored rather than talked about. The burden of history, so to speak, is on the descendants of the once enslaved. Conversely, Ghanaian descendants of those who kept slaves, for instance the royal families, are not tainted by the inhumane practice of their forefathers; instead the focus is on their achievements and greatness.

Likewise in the Common Heritage Project, there was an implicit idea that there was a long continuous line for 'us' to engage in. For the Danes, myself included, this was a continuity with 'our' past trading compatriots and skilled builders. Interestingly, it seemed as if both the continuity *and* the distance in time were vital to the very idea of Frederiksgave: the continuity was a precondition for even engaging in the heritage work – it is after all our shared past – and, as discussed in Chapter Two, the distance in time made it possible to construe the heritage work at Frederiksgave as somehow transcending the past exploitation of enslaved workers and thus as a straightforward matter of informing objectively about a common history. The 'innocence' with which the project planners designed the Frederiksgave project – in spite of some Ghanaians' unease with the issue of slavery – made it possible to highlight without embarrassment the continuity with the former Danish presence on the West African Coast. This was also reflected in present-day expressions such as 'we had forts…', 'we were engaged in the trade with slaves…' and 'our shared past…' and so on, that established a historical continuity, but without necessarily transferring any blame. Instead of linking with consanguineous families, as the historian argued was the case in Ghana, most of the Danes engaging with the site imagined communities in the form of a nation that 'we' the Danes could link up with by means of the common heritage site.[34] However, this perceived history of the Danish part of the common past as being linked with that of the forefathers, but also far enough away from them so as to not having inherited any guilt because of the use of enslaved workers, seemed not to be paralleled in Ghana. Indeed, slavery was and is still a powerful and delicate subject in Ghana,[35] and apparently it continues to run in the veins of the descendants – something that I also became familiar with through my work with family houses in Osu, where the issue of slavery repeatedly became a pregnant one during my conversations with people, particularly when the question of who qualified to inherit part of the house had to be settled.[36] I was told both by the two historians, Perbi and Odotei, and also by people living in Accra, that after their liberation slaves had been adopted into families who took care of them over the ensuing years. In present-day Ghana, these relations could, at times, cause trouble and could even bring families to court. Knowledge of the family's genealogy became, then, a very important instrument in such trials. Given that it was such a delicate matter, it was always highly interesting and potentially fraught to see how the guides at the forts along the coast used and talked about the dungeons where slaves had been kept. The effect was especially powerful when we stood in the dark, humid and only sparsely ventilated rooms, on the uneven cobblestones, bathed in sweat, while a guide told us about the masses of people who had been crowded into the room in inhuman conditions. It always felt awful to descend into the dark dungeons or walk over the threshold and see around us the rusty bars. Once I experienced an extremely tense moment when one guide at Elmina castle guided our Danish group into one of the dark rooms. Still outside, he suddenly closed the rusty door behind us, locking us up. He did it with a smile, and the tension was only maintained for a few seconds. It was strange because immediately all my associations with the former slaves vanished like dew before the sun, and I was instantly brought to a present where my colleagues from Denmark and I became whiter than white, our racial differences foregrounded. The few moments in the dungeons were a mixture of aversion, repentance – and of course many other feelings. In this instance the guide pointed to the legacy of European involvement in slavery by playfully reversing the roles. But was this a postcolonial moment? Was it a moment of theorising sameness and differences in new ways? Was it an instance of contingent symmetry? Well, not really: rather than creating new differences and sameness, the relations were in some ways merely reversed. The 'the white people' were locked into the dungeon by 'the black people'. From the outset the entities were the same; the only – significant – difference was that the power relations at the beginning of the twenty-first century were momentarily reversed. One could indeed object to such an understanding of the situation, claiming that I overemphasise the dualism. The guide might have done it with any group of both Africans and Europeans; maybe race was not an issue. Perhaps so, but yet I will argue that the forts and the guided tours are amplifiers of differences along racial lines of white oppressors and black victims.[37] The Joseph Project, as mentioned above, might even have stressed such differences at the forts along the Ghanaian coast. Other instances, too, pointed to ideas of these apparently long-lived hierarchical relations between black and white people. On one visit to the Cape Coast Castle, some African Americans discreetly refused to follow our group of Danes.[38] Our guide later told me that this often happened, and that 'black Americans' did not want to visit the dungeons in the company of 'white people' – their former tormentors. Edward Bruner, Christine Mullen Kreamer and Katharina Schramm[39] have all discussed how the involvement of groups of African Americans in the renovation of one of the forts in Ghana created discussions about how history should be told at the site. The presence at the forts in Ghana of African Americans, Ghanaians and Europeans indeed indicates that postcolonial settings are much more complicated than the duality between 'black' and 'white' can capture.

The intense experience of the fort dungeons along the coast was apparently also imitated at Frederiksgave. Every now and then, the guides would take visitors up to the small room under the bipartite staircase and present it as a dungeon where slaves were kept. Even one of the drivers for the Frederiksgave project once took a group of Danish archaeologists and me on such a guided tour of Frederiksgave. After asking us to wait outside the first building, where we looked at the display cases with exhibited excavated objects, he gathered our small group and headed directly towards the symmetrical axis where the door under the staircase was placed. He asked us to go inside, and followed, closing the door. Even though we were only six people in the small dark room, we felt packed in like sardines. I could glimpse the white in his eyes as he told us that, 'In here they kept the slaves before they were sent over there – fifty!'. We immediately switched to Danish, and mumbled to each other that this was 'a cock-and-bull story', and that even under inhumane conditions, fifty people could never fit in this small room. From the wall sheets on display and from books we had read about the period and the place, we *knew* that it was a plantation, and that the enslaved workers lived in slave huts further down the road. According to historical sources well-known to us, this place did *not* have dungeons and was *not* part of the transatlantic slave trade as our driver tried, however unsuccessfully, to convey. Implicitly, we activated presumed indisputable historical archives in the room under the stairs to set the story straight. In the moment, the guide could not be seen as a co-producer of our shared past, only as a purveyor of tall tales.

In other words, visiting the room under the stairs with our driver who told us about the transatlantic slave trade did not awaken the fetish, to use the vocabulary of the previous chapter. That is, in the encounter with the driver's story the materiality of the place did not affect us as he might have hoped; the cramped room did not produce magic in the sense he tried to convey. The material did not become effective as a dungeon because we *knew* that another story was the truth. Using the darkness and small size of the room, the driver attached a false story to the place; it was *facticii*, idolatry. Besides, we could also calculate that our driver's estimate of the number of enslaved people kept in the room pointed to his ignorance of the history of the site. But with this obvious exaggeration and the story of the transatlantic slave trade, perhaps he was also trying to convey something else. Apart from giving us the story that had attracted thousands of foreigners to Ghana over the last three decades, and disassociating the village with plantation slavery, by his clearly exaggerated estimate of the number of people in the room he was perhaps trying to communicate a general story about the inhumane treatment of people. Instead of dismissing his ideas about the room under the stairs, we could have acknowledged it as a shared sense of inhumanity and inequality that we might all have felt when visiting the site, and that we could have agreed to speak about. This moment could have been an opportunity to explore the infra-sameness I talked about before, that is, a useful sameness that allows for differences and that is good enough for a few here-and-nows. The inhumane conditions of the enslaved workers might be an interesting starting point for dialogue, rather than, as we saw it, a conclusion settling what happened at a particular site. This would have been similar to the case discussed earlier, in which agreeing to name Frederiksgave a 'museum' might have been a good starting point for dialogue.

It was different in the dungeons at the 'real' forts and castles. Here we – myself and other Danish visitors – *knew* that these were the real dungeons. Being there and sensing the place created a contact with the past that seemed trustworthy and in accordance with historical knowledge, which was not the case with the room under the stairs at the Frederiksgave site. Many of us had actually read the Danish writer Thorkild Hansen's trilogy about Danish involvement in the transatlantic slave trade, and were, through various Danish history books and old diaries, generally well informed and prepared to visit the historical sites; we had a shared knowledge, in the sense of the 'same history' used and assumed by the project planners.

The different experiences in the two kinds of rooms – the dungeons at the forts and the room beneath the stairs at Frederiksgave – say something about the kind of knowledge that was produced at the different sites. Or rather, I would argue that it tells us that our knowledge was understood as independent of being at the sites; we did not need to be there in order to know what had happened. Being there and listening to cock-and-bull stories with far-fetched estimates did not make us change our minds – it did not produce new knowledge of our common past. Our knowledge was produced elsewhere: in books, archives, universities and museums. Like reading the ruler as an external measure that could provide us with accurate answers, reading and listening to this knowledge made us certain about what had 'truly' happened in these places in the past. Being there was mainly just a supplement to our knowledge. Its purpose was to attach sensuous experiences and images to what we already knew. And yet, as we explored in Chapter Three in relation to mimesis, one of the characteristics of a representational form of knowledge is that it makes separations between knowledge and the senses. As the singing roots conveyed to us, such a separation was challenged at the site. Cultural heritage was not something that could be observed from a distance. On the contrary, its effect was produced in encounters made up of people, material, topography, histories and so on, in the joints of the concrete. It requires a kind of orthodoxy to keep up a separation like this, and the divide involuntarily creates friction or awkward moments when encountering the world in the here-and-now. However, beneath the staircase our knowledge was indeed orthodox, in that it did not allow for interpretations that fell outside the settled logic. We *knew* that the Frederiksgave plantation had not been integrated into the transatlantic slave trade, and that the room had not been used for storing slaves. Excepting the clear exaggeration in numbers, we might have believed our driver if we had heard the same story from professionals. But expressed by a layman alone, it was not sufficient to challenge our knowledge. However, we failed to hear what other messages his propositions could have entailed, and thus to engage in a postcolonial moment. Our knowledge was not seen as an outcome but as settled information picked up in books and talks from experts,[40] only to be illustrated and represented by the actual site of Frederiksgave and the forts.

In order to understand knowledge as the outcome of encounters, rather than pre-given entities, 'an opening up and loosening'[41] may be necessary at such moments. Contrary to the idea of 'digging our heels in' mentioned in

Chapter Two, a postcolonial moment should challenge one's metaphysics, thus enabling 'difference to be collectively enacted'.[42] At Frederiksgave this would mean exploring what the site *does* as a cultural heritage site, rather than merely judging it in terms of how well it confirms the 'true' story about the plantation. With such a performative understanding, what happens on the guided tours quickly becomes rather ambiguous and not just an illustration of common knowledge, understood as a sharing of the same story.

The experience in the room under the stairs is a case in point whereby ambiguity is explored along lines of *really knowing* what happened, on the one hand, and stories linking to issues such as transatlantic slavery and the inhumane conditions in which enslaved people were kept by 'our forefathers', on the other. But it would be too simple to reduce what happened in the room under the stairs to either a matter of 'really knowing what happened' or to a 'cock-and-bull story'. However, going beyond such an either/or also requires effort. First, our clear dismissal of the driver's story as untrustworthy should cause us to think again – not to accept anything as a valid story but to question our own certainty and thereby our epistemic practices. And second, why should we do this? I suggest that it is nothing less than a matter of imagining futures; in this sense, heritage work can engage times to come as much as pasts. Importantly, possibilities for making different futures are not restricted to former colonised places; they could just as well take place in the former colonising countries.[43] For instance, the visit mentioned above to the Frederiksgave site was followed by discussions among our small group of Danes. In these discussions we talked precisely about the inhumane treatment, and felt bad that 'our nation' had been involved in such atrocities as having slaves and participating in the transatlantic slave trade. Even though we did not discuss it with our Ghanaian driver, his story somehow lived on in our discussions. After all, our knowledge of slavery was not necessarily closed down in pre-given entities, even if it had appeared so in the momentary enclosure of the room beneath the staircase. The driver had shaped our ensuing discussions – and implicitly urged us to see the challenge that such heritage can pose as one of engaging with problematic pasts rather than invoking History as grounds for dismissal and/or affirmation. Inhumane conditions seemed to be a good common starting point for engaging with a postcolonial history that enables new futures, whereas it was more difficult to allow for infra-sameness or the literal differences between 'fort' and 'plantation'. Later on the day of the visit to Frederiksgave, we likened our experience under the stairs to the other 'cock-and-bull stories' we had heard during our visits to the forts and castles. The most treasured stories among the Danes often came from guided tours at Prindsensten, which had been a Danish fort used in the transatlantic slave trade. After the Danes sold their possessions to the British, Prindsensten, like many other European forts, was turned into a prison in the twentieth century, due to its solid military construction. A newer British prison had been added to the fort construction, and had been in use until some decades ago. Unfortunately, the city in which the old fort was located had fallen victim to huge sea erosion, and as a result only two bastions, a curtain wall and some rooms built into the thick wall, remained of the Danish fort construction. Even though the coastline had moved closer to the city over the years, and a storm tide had destroyed part of the Danish-built fort, the erosion did not affect the English part of the prison, which had maintained its ground-plan and walls. But the deserted and uninhabited edifice left behind by the Danes and the British had clearly been hit by the ravages of time. Yet it was still possible to walk into the rooms, partly guarded by armoured doors and bars in the window holes.

A guide was employed by the official authority, the Ghana Museum and Monuments Board, to show tourists and school children around 'the fort', as it was called in the town. The guide did not tell us about the purpose of the newer English prison extension. Instead, he showed us around the rooms, telling horrible stories about the treatment of slaves. In one of the smaller rooms was a rather big, modern, rusty iron-made weight, of a type I had seen in old storage rooms in Denmark, where they were used to weigh big boxes and bags. Standing in this rather uncomfortable ramshackle and dirty room, the enthusiastic guide pointed to the weight and told us that the slaves were weighed there before being sent abroad. Even though it was clearly from a period after the transatlantic slave trade, many visitors, myself included, did not question the weight at that moment. We were all absorbed in the painful and awful history of the transatlantic slave trade. The fact that we were standing on the West African coast in a former fort made the sensuousness of the place affect us. It was very different from reading books or listening to professionals in auditoria and offices. Just as the architect had listened to the roots, we listened to the weight as it was invoked by the guides; it seemed to speak to us in a language that we could understand, and silently we stood still and heard about the commoditisation of people in the transatlantic slave trade. On some guided tours, however, some of the more vigilant visitors started to argue with the guides. Every time that happened, the guides slowly resigned.

The guided tour at Prindsensten could be recognised as post-colonialism in Fanon's (2001) understanding, as discussed in the introduction to this chapter; it had a dual structure of white oppressors and black victims (later to be called colonisers versus colonised). Just as when we had been momentarily locked up in the dungeons, the guides at Prindsensten spoke to our 'white' bad conscience regarding greed, commoditisation and inhumane treatment. Built on settled population groups, these moments in the fort most often missed the opportunity to nurture a postcolonial moment as understood by Verran. Both partners ('white' and 'black') seemed to avoid the dialogue.

As at the Frederiksgave site, the cock-and-bull stories at Prindsensten created disconcertment among the Danish visitors I saw there. At times, these well-prepared visitors even expressed disappointment and irritation that the history was so obviously distorted. This was too serious a story to take lightly, being a subject delicate even in Denmark, as many Danes I talked to reasoned. Many noted that in Danish schools we had not learned about the cruel, violent history of the transatlantic slave trade, and a Dane explained to me that it was because 'it did not fit with our Danish self-understanding of being a small, innocent and humane country'. So accuracy, details and expertise were treasured virtues among the well-prepared Danish visitors, as well as for the heritage workers. Visiting the various forts and castles, they tried to answer the question: what had actually happened here? Various ways of reaching the point of origin to go back to what Frederiksgave and other forts were *really* like were persistently explored among visitors and heritage workers. At Frederiksgave, having posters saying one thing but guides saying another challenged these virtues and unsettled the common knowledge that the Frederiksgave site was supposed to affirm and exemplify. Knowledge, it seemed, was often produced somewhere other than at the sites; yet my point is that generating new understandings *was* a potential when encountering the site, even if these were seen at first glance as mere supplements to our knowledge, as stated above. Again, however, it would be too simple to reduce any potential postcolonial moments to the situation in the room at the fort. True to their own ideas, postcolonial moments could, obviously, be nurtured in situations that went beyond dialogues between 'black' and 'white'. At times, discussions would arise among the Danes on the three hour-long car ride back to Accra from Prindsensten. At such moments, the atrocities of the past were discussed, and the fact that both Danes and the people from the coast at that time had been heavily involved in the inhumane trade was debated. The role of the African Americans who had painted graffiti in the dilapidated building was likewise discussed. Like the rusty weight, the stories that the guides communicated about the former Danes as greedy, lecherous people could sometimes collapse the time between then and now, and make the past stretch into the present. All these discussions had the potential to give rise to new understandings of the slave trade and of 'our forefathers', ourselves and the role of local people in the slave trade. Engaging in discussion, we raised questions of present-day poverty in Africa as opposed to our wealth and opportunities. We discussed colonialism, mercantilism, European hypocrisy and African culture and tradition and often we did not reach a conclusion; but the point is that the sites had provoked discussion – the sites had caused differences and sameness to be opened anew, discussed and settled in new momentary entities and 'truths'.

I had the chance to stay for a while in the town where the fort of Prindsensten was located. Interestingly, the same issues were debated among the people of the town in long and vibrant discussions every afternoon in front of the fort, as mentioned in Chapter Four. Here, as well, we nurtured postcolonial moments, shared perspectives, discussed disagreements and had our opinions and vocabulary changed every now and then. During my stay in the town, I followed the guided tours and became friends with the guides. While talking about the tours, they told me many details about the fort that they had either read or heard from earlier visitors. They also had a few books that visitors had donated to the place. So when I asked why they told stories about slavery in the English prison they gave a little smile and answered that that was what most visitors wanted to hear – especially the African American visitors. They did not come to the fort to hear about an old colonial prison for Ghanaian criminals, they came to see dungeons and hear about 'the mistreatment of slaves by the whites', one of the guides explained to me.[44] With such an argument, the guides indirectly told me that knowledge was an outcome of encounters. The various types of knowledge produced in the here-and-now were important to make the heritage work. However, their ideas of what visitors might want to hear often seemed pre-given, and turned the encounters into pre-structured meetings of 'black' and 'white' in which dialogue was avoided and a specific history guarded, as was the case with the weight. Sometimes the knowledge produced worked, and at other times it did not; it seemed that cultural heritage was made up of different knowledges, revealing it to be made up of complex materialisations of value.

MARGINAL GAINS AND VALUE REVISITED

During my fieldwork, I often heard the former European places along the Ghanaian coast talked of as 'tourist attractions'. As mentioned in Chapter One, the Ghanaian coordinator had been in close contact with the Ministry of Tourism and Diasporan Relations when planning the Frederiksgave project. I therefore thought that I might gain interesting insights from talking to someone from the Ministry in Accra who had been involved. One morning, I dressed in my white shirt and long trousers and succeeded in reaching the Ministry without getting too dusty and dishevelled. With the help of some friendly civil servants, I was taken to a senior official's door. I knocked on the door, opened it and behind a huge desk covered with papers and a computer sat a sizeable, smiling man who immediately invited me in. The obligatory radio standing on the table was, like the air-conditioning, turned on. Another man, presumably an employee, was sitting idly in one of the stuffed chairs placed along two of the walls. I presented myself and he agreed to talk, saying that he had half an hour. The dialogue went very well; we laughed at the awkwardness that we produced, and he seemed to like my curiosity and direct, insistent questions. With his permission I turned on my recorder. First we talked about the different European initiatives in Ghana, and he explained:

Senior official: 'As part of our plans to improve our tourist attraction, the Minister was of the opinion that we should look at all the historical things that we have in common with the European countries and I said, and I came to an understanding, because I saw how important these things are to the [European] countries, and the people from those countries, because, the people from Germany come around and they go all the way to Prindsenstown, to look at that old castle, they go there because of a common link, that that is what shows them, that their country was once one of the important countries in the west… in Ghana, or in the Gold Coast. The Dutch have been very very positive in this area, Elmina, they have taken the trouble to develop Elmina, I mean they give loans, they give grants, they give donations, for anything that goes to improve Elmina, because Elmina is one of the eh, the Dutch strong point in, when they came, in fact, last year, they invited us to Amsterdam and we went to the archives, and I was surprised, to see how they value Elmina castle, we saw the models, everything, you know, it is part of their heritage, their historical this thing, and I didn't know it was that important.

Nathalia: No, and why do you think it is so important for them?

Senior official: [Laughing] for them, I mean it shows that at a certain point in time, they were captured as one of the top powers in the world, they were then leading international trading, you know, having colonies and all those things, so historically it makes them look very powerful, are you with me?

Nathalia: Yeah, yeah, I understand

Senior official: Because, when they talk about colonial powers, they also can, because they have some places in Africa, where they were trading, and doing all sorts of things, so it is very important to them.

Nathalia: So you think it is important for them, because it reminds them of when they were big?

Senior official: Yes! It is very important!'

For the senior official, it seemed obvious that colonialism and foreign politics were vital parts of the small European nations' sudden interest in the past. This was clearly an understanding that collided with the intentions of the initiatives in the hot colonies as communicated by the two coordinators quoted in the introduction to Chapter Two. When I asked about the Frederiksgave Project, the senior official explained:

> Senior official: '[...] And the Danish connection, as I said, the Minister was interested when the, this eh Sesemi restoration thing started, because he thought if we develop it properly we can even have a lot of eh, people coming from Denmark, those places, just to see what they have done, that would be good for us because we want to increase our attractions, they have Christiansborg castle, they have things in the country that show that the Danes were here, we have names 'Isert' [a German doctor sent out to the Danish trading stations by the end of the eighteenth century] eh those, we have certain names that are pure direct eh, you know, so there are some, what we call 'the shared heritage', which we should exploit for as long as it can get our tourist product to become more attractive to more people. That it is not only the British that we dealt with, that we dealt with the Dutch, with the Danes, the so and so, we should, for a good marketing strategy we should be able to exploit these things, so the thing that has been done at Sesemi, if we handle it well, I believe people from Denmark, when they come to west Africa, they will definitely want to pass by and see what is there, naturally. For us that would be achieving the objective that we have set ourselves. So he [the Minister] was very interested when he got to know, and we went there, right from the beginning, I thought it was [he laughs again], some very wild idea, [noise] I saw it happen [laughter] you know, bringing the things and building the whole thing again, but I now see that it can be done
> Nathalia: But you thought it was a strange project in the beginning?
> Senior official: <u>Yeah</u>
> Nathalia: Yes, but why?
> Senior official: <u>Why</u> [laughter] at this time [laughter] we do, people want to come re... re... you know, I thought it was a bit, a bit eh, remote, [laughter] that eh, so

Nathalia: A bit remote the place or just to do this thing?

Senior official: To do the thing [...] but now I know that if there is anything in the historical this thing, you can develop it and create a product out of it, purely for tourism.

Nathalia: Why do you think that the Danes were interested in doing such a 'remote' thing, why do you think they did it?

Senior official: [Laughter] I think [laughter] they also want to think of their past [loud laughter]

Nathalia: When we were big?

Senior official: Yeah, why not, why not [loud laughter]'

Indeed, our meeting produced lots of laughter. I would argue that it was nurtured by the awkwardness resulting from the different ways of valuing the past that became so apparent during our talk. As a European, I might be valuing these sites intensely for their history. For the senior official, over the years European historical traces came to be seen as products, 'purely for tourism' – even remote projects such as Frederiksgave could be turned into products attracting tourists. In the previous chapter, the history of the fetish pointed to 'the mystery of value'. My point here is that this mystery is repeated centuries later in the dialogue with the senior official at the Ministry. Possibly, in his eyes, the ruin at Frederiksgave could have been termed 'trinkets and trifles' as the European traders termed goods centuries ago. The Minister, however, had already understood the Europeans' desire for and interest in their former presence on the Ghanaian coast, and actually encouraged his staff to look for 'all things' marked by the Europeans. I would suggest that the laughter in the senior official's office resonates with the joking about the Danish architect's enthusiasm and meticulous interest in old lime, clay and stones, expressed by the man in Keta (see Chapter Four). And it also resonates with the Chief of the village's exclamation that the reconstruction project was a miracle, also discussed in Chapter Four. Even 'trinkets and trifles' can be turned into a miracle or developed into a product, 'purely for tourism', as the senior official had witnessed in the case of the remote project to revitalise a ruin in Sesemi.

What is evident in these encounters in Ghana is that value is indeed relative and emergent in actual encounters between things and institutions, rather than an inherent quality. This is similar to the experience gained in the early encounters between Europeans and people living on the West African coast centuries ago. But as Berry notes '[c]onsensus on price does not require consensus on what is being exchanged'.[45] In other words, different ways of valuing objects need not be a problem in a trading situation.

With the arrival of the Protestant Dutch merchants on the coast, new ideas of objects arose, as described in the previous chapter. All objects could potentially be turned into commodities that could be exchanged. In this way the Dutch, and with them most northern European countries, deflated ideas about the mystery of value. Any notion of spirituality as adding mystery to the material world was exhausted, and objects were turned into potential commodities – as Pietz argues, the objects' reality was seen to be proved by 'their silent "translatability" across alien cultures'.[46] If material objects were given other meanings and values, then this was understood as a given culture's credulity and lack of reason.[47] Any other ideas about material objects that went beyond such silent translatability were thought of as being against 'natural reason and rational market activity'.[48] The mystery of value was replaced with arrogance; lack of reason was the only explanation for the unpredictability of value they experienced. Even though this was the beginning of mercantilism and its national protection policies, trade was paradoxically seen as universal, rational, neutral and free; the things exchanged amounted to the same. Centuries later, the businessman and billionaire Bill Gates expressed a similar vision in his aspirations to a 'friction-free capitalism'[49] – a market with no friction in exchange. This frictionless and universal understanding of value (goods and transactions) is challenged by Jane Guyer in her book *Marginal Gains* (2004). Guyer notes that equivalence has been fundamental to the theory of exchange, but she then remarks that ethnography on African monetary exchange 'shows evidence of asymmetry of value, as a permanent and culturally marked feature'.[50] Instead of arising out of and maintaining equilibrium, Guyer argues that value arises out of disjuncture. In order to understand this, one needs to pay attention to the separation between soft and hard currency. Guyer explains how the latter characterises Western money and its tight and 'hard' relations to institutions and laws.[51] Hard currencies are infinitely convertible, and are financially monitored every day. Soft currencies, however, which she argues are characteristic of the Nigerian economy, are not infinitely convertible but restricted to allocated amounts. The Nigerian economy is mainly based on monetisation, with no credit cards, no checks and no automated accounts. At least 60% of the currency issued in Nigeria 'never goes back through the banking system again'.[52] As a result of the West's different currencies, institutions and formal regulations are key instruments in disciplining people's market experiences, whereas in Nigeria market experiences are disciplined through popular conventions.[53]

In a special edition of *African Studies Review*, several scholars who have worked in Africa were invited to comment on Guyer's book *Marginal Gains*. Geschiere, Goheen and Piot follow the thread of the different currencies and write that in economies with 'soft money' people learn to constantly switch between standards. This instability, they argue, inspired by Guyer, is not a sign of weakness in the economies but rather shows 'their ability to bridge enduring disjunctures that allows actors to realise the 'marginal gains' that are crucial to these economies'.[54] Disjunctures are key to understanding processes of valuation and of gains in such systems – as Barber summarises in her comment in the same edition:

> difference and disjuncture, the proliferation of scales of value and methods of reckoning, are not a mere by-product of tribal compartmentalization [...]. Rather, they are something that African merchants deliberately fostered and maintained, because it is in crossing the thresholds between discontinuous scales, and in manipulating alternative, multiple modes of evaluation, that gain lies. This view puts performance center stage.[55]

Disjunctures are to be cultivated rather than erased; it is precisely the lability which is vital in the constitution of value in African economies.[56] This lability is developed rather than seen as an expression of limited and powerless institutions. As Verran puts it, 'What is instituted is an openness that ensures ongoing possibilities for contingency and multiplicity, rather than working toward single, closed standards and norms'.[57] This insight might be very important for understanding more about the values of the Frederiksgave project. As we have heard, the Ghana Museums and Monuments Board (GMMB) played a very unobtrusive role in the reconstruction of the Common Heritage Site. The board members did not have any objections to the way the buildings were reconstructed, and neither did they play an active role in setting up the exhibition. Even though central to the project, the Ghanaian coordinator and archaeologist had only a few comments on the exhibition, and he seemed either forbearing or indifferent towards the stories circulating at the site, shrugging his shoulders when I asked him about the incommensurable histories told. The educational programmes for local guides that were to ensure the transmission of the story developed by the experts were, as we have heard, continually neglected. Of course, the reasons for this difference may be manifold, but instead of understanding it as merely a matter of weak institutions, lack of political will, or neglect or fear of awakening a precarious history, we might also see it as part of an effort not to settle history into one storyline. In other words, to leave room for marginal gains. What looked like passivity to the people from the Danish National Museum were perhaps ambitious ways of cultivating the lability necessary in order to secure gains – a lability which, from the Danes' point of view, had to be eradicated like false idols. The Ghanaian institutions involved in the project might, in fact, play their most important role in securing this openness instead of policing the borders and insisting on hard currency. Therefore, rather than sanctioning the way in which the heritage should be reconstructed, as was the case in the other hot colony of Trankebar in India – where the museum waited several years for approval and a contract from the Indian bureaucracy – in Ghana the ideas from the National Museum were met with positive and rather frictionless statements. The gains for the Ghanaian partners, then, are not achieved through a capacity building that installs sameness and equivalence as a kind of hard, translatable currency. The soft currency of common heritage is more than a side-effect – indeed, the very notion of currencies can be foregrounded as the shared locus of encounter between the different valuations that make up the Frederiksgave site.

A POSTCOLONIAL MOMENT IN HERITAGE WORK

Postcolonial moments are, as we have seen, characterised by containing possibilities of telling differences and sameness in new ways, and of allowing symmetry to be a contingent quality emerging in encounters across divides. Such moments stress that things and their value are not given as such, but appear in so far as we make and shape them; this does not assume the *a priori* existence of entities such as coloniser/colonised as the given starting point. In her book *Science and an African Logic*, Verran argues:

> Postcolonialism here is not a break with colonialism, not a revolution, a history begun when a particular 'us' who are not 'them,' suddenly coalesces as opposition of colonizer. [...] In this narrative frame [the book], colonialism is remade in postcolonial enacting. Postcolonialism is the ambiguous struggling through and with colonial pasts in making different futures.[58]

By struggling through this, I have explored how differences and sameness worked in the Frederiksgave project, and exploded ideas of translatability, valuation and reversal of established hierarchies. My point has been to argue that heritage work might operate productively with the co-presence of multiple currencies, including soft ones. In light of this, the Common Heritage Site, I would argue, cannot be self-identical or given a universal value as a natural culmination of history. As Verran has it, 'Learning to "do" the other's figures is, among other things, good fun'.[59] For all the laughter ringing in this chapter, though, the very serious point of exploring these encounters via postcolonial moments is to show new and other ways to make the world around us, including past events.

PARTIAL HISTORIES AND COMMON KNOWLEDGE

To conclude this book, let me briefly outline the ground covered so far. In order to qualify the Common Heritage Project, I have engaged the Frederiksgave project through four interrelated analytical takes that show how common heritage was *shared, altered, valued* and *generated*. The idea was to explore heritage work on firm and intensely specific ethnographic ground – 'sweating the detail',[60] as Handler and Gable put it, in and through which I show Frederiksgave emerging in particular shapes, dependent on the perspective through which it is seen. Consequently, I have not 'applied' four different theories on heritage, but have made use of ethnography to let the Frederiksgave Common Heritage Project come to life in different ways and interrelate in the pages of this book. A project on collaborative cultural heritage allows for just such experimentation. This is my attempt at developing an anthropology of common ground as a particular kind of postcolonial scholarship. My point here is to suggest that careful attention to details and 'small stories' can provide us with an interesting insight into a vital nerve in the production of both common heritage and ethnographic analysis. Exactly because they are figures that are so meticulously nurtured, details have a strong analytical potential, being well described and thereby explicitly entailing many relations about what they are not. Throughout the book, I have thus relentlessly treated details and small stories as my field site for common heritage. What we see through these is all the common heritage that there can be.

The frictional events, so abundant during fieldwork and appearing in statements, gestures, laughs, disagreements, letters, and other 'details', showed that entities, common heritage included, are produced as figures in relation to other figures and, in this light, the whole book is a study of how subjects and objects emerge awkwardly on common ground. This is the overall anthropological point: that the discipline holds the potential to engage in collective processes of world-making. As we have seen, persons, nations, topography, buildings, histories, to mention but a few of the figures we have met, are thus produced in the ongoing work taking place in the field, as well as on these pages. Generating heritage, then, is not restricted to the work undertaken at the Frederiksgave site, but has equally been my ambition in this text. This is consistent with my anthropological goal of providing a generative analysis, one that adds and composes, rather than subtracts and deconstructs.[61] In the same vein, critique – or maybe even better, *generative* critique – must be understood as field-based suggestions and alternative qualifications of the concerns involved in creating a common ground across differences.

My project shows us nothing but partial histories and a potential for generating common knowledge. While partiality might at first glance appear as impeding commonness, my point is exactly the opposite, namely that generating common knowledge can only begin with partial histories, abandoning any claim to universality that leaves room for only one version. Commonness, in my view, simply implies more than one – but less than many.[62] It demands an engagement in encounters where the outcome is not given in advance, and new figures can emerge. By generating common heritage projects, we are provided with a unique potential to allow for a sameness that does not preclude differences, and are thus enabled to make the most of partiality in knowledge production. Heritage projects have the privilege of engaging with such differences and sameness in active and playful ways, by sometimes leaving topics unsettled and making a virtue of indeterminacy. Any aspiration to understand common heritage as a universal given to be protected and safeguarded for all time may put obstacles in its own path, and leave great potential undeveloped. Part of the magic of heritage, I propose, rests precisely on the sensuousness that explodes the very notion of universality. I like to think of this as posing the question of what heritage might *also* be?

To allow for and nurture engagement with the unpredictability that inevitably pops up in heritage work, and to be aware of its inherent partiality, is to commonly cultivate a postcolonial moment and an analytical humility. This, in my view, is the least we can do.

NOTES

PREFACE

1 Verran 2001: 20.
2 Pyne Addelson 1994; Verran 2001.
3 Talk by Donna Haraway at the California College of the Arts (20 October 2009) https://www.youtube.com/watch?v=3F0XdXfVDXw (accessed 1 March 2010). In her book *Staying with the Trouble* (2016) Haraway quotes Vinciane Despret for a similar point and stresses the obligation to 'start from' the event, not as a matter of loyalty to a cause (Haraway 2016: 131) but 'to learn to do, speak, act *from* them [events], in an act of creation' (Despret 2015: 94).
4 Tsing 2016: 37.

INTRODUCTION: COLLABORATION AND THE FRUITS OF AWKWARD RELATIONS

1 Bredwa-Mensah, Justesen, and Jørgensen 2007: 6.
2 E.g. Bredwa-Mensah, Justesen, and Jørgensen 2007; Kurt-Nielsen et al. 2008.
3 Often a conglomerate of Danes, Germans, Swedes, and Norwegians.
4 Bredwa-Mensah, Justesen, and Jørgensen 2007: 6.
5 An extract from the speech made by the Danish Minister of Culture; see also the Ministry of Culture's official webpage.
6 Sometimes also called the Adinkra symbol.
7 B. Meyer 2010: 10.
8 See e.g. Quarcoo in DeCorse 2001: 71, who uses the symbol as a vignette.
9 Bredwa-Mensah, Justesen, and Jørgensen 2007: 8.
10 Kurt-Nielsen et al. 2008: 58.
11 See e.g.: Kurt-Nielsen et al. 2008: 67; Knippel 2003; but also already Jeppesen aired this sentiment of urgency in 1966: 71–2.
12 Jørgensen in Larsen 2006.
13 Verran 2001: 117–118; Verran 2007: 171ff.
14 Verran 2007: 181.

15 I am not seeking to fill in such existing categories with any so-called data – I refrain from blindly assuming 'gate-keeping concepts', whether custodians of regions or themes (cf. Das 2003: 4; F. Hastrup 2011a: 7).
16 Holbraad 2007: 206–207.
17 Henare, Holbraad, and Wastell (2007).
18 Brichet and Hastrup 2011.
19 See Dilley 1999, K. Hastrup 2004.
20 F. Hastrup suggests that this fieldwork condition of sharing a particular concern and thereby co-creating objects and subjects can be termed a kind of lateral theorisation (Hastrup 2011b).
21 In a later collaborative fieldwork with Frida Hastrup, we have been playing with the metaphor of a snowball to characterise our methodological track. But whereas the snowball never changes its composition and entails a sense of accumulative weight and given direction we prefer to name our methodology 'dustballing' to indicate a flickering character and the unplanned clotting of details across genres that do neither refer back nor accumulate to a meta-point of view (Brichet and Hastrup 2018). A dustball navigates and transforms itself according to the conditions and clues given.
22 Verran 2001: 30.
23 Verran 2009: 173.
24 See also F. Hastrup 2013.
25 Brichet and Hastrup 2011; F. Hastrup 2011b.
26 Tsing 2005: xi.
27 Brichet 2011.
28 The museum was thereby following a trend that has been discussed by anthropologists Mads Daugbjerg and Thomas Fibiger. See the special issue of the journal "History and Anthropology" on Globalised Heritage, edited by Daugbjerg and Fibiger 2011.
29 Tsing 2005: 2.
30 Ibid.
31 Greenough and Tsing 2003: 15.
32 See also Kurt-Nielsen et al. 2008: 55.
33 Altogether, the project was granted approximately $1million.
34 Greenough and Tsing 2003.
35 Ibid: 16.
36 See also Macdonald 2009: 4ff.
37 Strathern 1987: 286ff; 290. I am indebted to the vocabulary and insights presented by Strathern in the article *An Awkward Relationship* (1987).
38 See Littler 2005: 13; Macdonald 2009: 25.
39 For a similar point see F. Hastrup 2011b.

40 UNESCO 1972: Articles 1 and 2.
41 See Byrne [1991] 2008; Smith [2006] 2008; Harrison 2010: 26ff; a similar discussion can be found in the UNESCO report, *Our Creative Diversity* (1996: 36ff); see also Federspiel 1998, 1999; Hylland-Eriksen 2001; Haffstein 2004.
42 Heritage projects thought in relation to communities is a concern treated, for instance, by Waterton and Smith 2010: 8, 11; Watson and Waterton 2010: 1ff; Chirikure et al. 2010: 31ff.
43 Recently, such discussions, with regard to heritage work in Africa, have been adressed in the edited book *Postcolonial Archaeologies in Africa* (Schmidt 2009). See also Smith 2006: 299; de Jong and Rowlands 2010: 22ff; Waterton and Smith 2010: 12.
44 See the two previous notes.

1. CRAFTING THE FIELD OF COMMON HERITAGE

1 The Danish National Museum made a list of relevant literature and posted it on their webpage on the Ghana Initiative. Understood explicitly as relevant for the project planners, this literature thus also became relevant for me to read and discuss with them.
2 Dantzig 1999: vii.
3 Perbi 2007: 23–4.
4 DeCorse 2001: 145ff.
5 Essah 2001.
6 Justesen 2005.
7 Hernæs 2010: xiff.
8 E.g. Kurt-Nielsen et al. 2008: 56; for an earlier but similar argument see Hansen [1967] 2005: 33. This public ignorance has over the last decade been severely challenged. The Danish participation in the slave trade has made it to several newspaper headlines, and has been substantiated and discussed at conferences, museum exhibits and in classrooms.
9 Petersen 1946: 5.
10 A similar argument can be found in Benedict Anderson's canonical *Imagined Communities* (1996), where Anderson suggests that history-telling and writing about the nation can bring its national citizens together (1996: 11ff, 197ff). Richard Handler has argued along the same lines in relation to Quebec's cultural heritage (1985).
11 The volume about the Gold Coast was written by historian Georg Nørregård.
12 Brimnes and Gulløv. 2017.
13 Hansen 2005: 197.

14 Jørgensen and Mikkelsen 2006.
15 Nørregård 1968.
16 Justesen 2005.
17 Bredwa-Mensah 2002.
18 Carstensen 1964 [1842-1850].
19 Awadzi et al. 2005.
20 Forskerforum 2002: 7.
21 Regeringsgrundlag 2001 [Government's platform 2001].
22 Regeringen 2003 [the Government 2003]; Kulturministeriet 2004 [Ministry of Culture 2004].
23 Højgaard 2001.
24 Ibid.
25 Ibid.
26 Grubbe 2002.
27 Trankebar is the Danish name for the Indian town of Tharangambadi in which the former Danish fort mentioned above is located. The town was first and foremost a trading station for ships engaged in the Danish-East Indian trade. Cf. the official webpages of the Ghana-Initiative and the Trankebar-Initiative.
28 Kurt-Nielsen et al. 2008: 58.
29 After my involvement in the project, I arranged a collection of some of the construction materials related to the reconstruction, thinking that such items might be interesting for a potential exhibition on the workings of the Ghana Initiative at the National Museum of Denmark. Later, I made a collection in the village where the reconstruction work was done. This collection work was inspired by and in close dialogue with a collection of 'everyday objects', as the items were called in the correspondence between the Governor and the Director of the Museum, from the area in the 1820s-1840s kept at the National Museum of Denmark.
30 GMMB official webpage.
31 This was backed by a new and growing literature on the subject: e.g. Essah 2001: 47–8; Bruner 2005: 104; Nketia in Perbi 2007: ix; Appiah 2007.
32 UNESCO Slave Route Project, official webpage.
33 This increasing interest has also been discussed by Essah 2001: 47–8; Bruner 2005: 102; Schramm 2010b.
34 Hence the 1972 UNESCO Convention: Articles 1 and 2.
35 An abbreviation for the 'International Council on Monuments and Sites', and a non-governmental international organisation dedicated to the conservation and protection of the worlds' monuments and sites. Like UNESCO the organisation has its headquarters in Paris.
36 ICOMOS, official webpage; ICOMOS 1979.

37 Bruner 2005: 102; Kreamer 2007: 438ff; Schramm 2010b: 76ff.
38 Kreamer 2007: 459.
39 Macdonald 2009: 60ff. Like the contentious Nazi buildings in Nuremberg in Germany, the forts and castles along the Ghanaian coast could at least serve some purpose. In Nuremberg, on the other hand, demolition of the Nazi buildings had been discussed.
40 See e.g. BBC News 2008.
41 Ministry of Tourism, official webpage. With the new government in 2008, 'Diasporan Relations' was again deleted from the ministry's name.
42 Modern Ghana, official webpage, 'Comment' (no named author).
43 For a similar argument see Schramm 2010b: 59ff. See also Nkrumah's own wording: 1961: 44, 125ff, 168, 189; and Appiah 1992: 6ff.
44 Bredwa-Mensah 2003a: 13.
45 Bredwa-Mensah 2003b.
46 See Greenough and Tsing 2003.
47 See Ebron 2000.
48 See for example Tunbridge and Ashworth 1996; Dann and Seaton 2001; Williams 2007; Macdonald 2009.
49 See for example Tunbridge and Ashworth 1996: 7ff; Clifford 1997: 215ff; Macdonald 2009: 10; Harrison 2010: 21; and particularly for Ghana see: Essah 2001: 45; Bruner 2005: 102ff; Schramm 2010a: 72; Ministry of Tourism and Diasporan Relations (of Ghana) official webpage.
50 Dann and Seaton 2001: 25.
51 1996: 129.
52 Tunbridge and Ashworth 1996.
53 Meskell 2002.
54 Lowenthal 2003.
55 Macdonald 2009.
56 Meskell 2002: 558.
57 Logan and Reeves 2009: 3.
58 Meskell 2002: 558.
59 Logan and Reeves 2009: 1.
60 See also Handler and Gable 1997: 79ff.
61 Essah 2001: 47–8; Bruner 2005: 104; Nketia in Perbi 2007: ix; Appiah 2007.
62 Adebayo 2007: 93; Perbi 2007: xv; Schramm 2010b: 32.
63 Bredwa-Mensah quoted in Hellmann 2005a.
64 Hyllestad 2007: 5.
65 Guinea Journals 1849: 701, ad 1837: 447.
66 Macdonald 2009: 3.

2. SHARING HERITAGE THROUGH FRICTION

1   Jensen and Jørgensen 2006: 34.
2   Apart from the Frederiksgave plantation, no further restoration projects have been carried out by the National Museum of Denmark in Ghana. In India, on the other hand, the National Museum of Denmark has renovated Danish-Indian heritage in both Tharangambadi and most recently in Serampore, India (see also the Serampore Initiative, official webpage).
3   The song was written in rhyming Danish but is here translated to English.
4   'Dannebrog' is the name of the Danish flag.
5   Hellmann 2005b.
6   Jensen and Jørgensen 2006: 34.
7   See e.g. Wagner 1981; Handler 1985, 1986a+b; Clifford 1988, 1997; Tsing 1993; Fox and King 2002; Trouillot 2002. Recent discussions about ontology, holism and cosmology have pushed the notion of culture – see e.g. Carrithers et al. 2010; Otto and Bubandt 2010; Abramson and Holbraad 2014.
8   Hence the Danish Museum Act 2006: §5.
9   I borrow the idea of the white coat from Michael Taussig's point about science's need to speak with authority – an authority that is essential since science inevitably lives by transgressing taboos and thereby entails a kind of violence that can be kept at bay and under control by the authority of the white coats (1993: 31–2).
10 Edited by Clifford and Marcus 1986.
11 For a similar point see Verran 2001: 24ff.
12 Knippel 2003.
13 Ibid.
14 The Danish term used was 'dannelse'. This word resonates with the German word '*bildung*' and refers to a general and formative process of self-cultivation based on certain social and/or pedagogical norms. 'Dannelse', therefore, connotes something more than the English 'education' (in Danish 'Uddannelse').
15 Larsen in Kronsted 2002.
16 J. Nielsen 2004.
17 Nietzsche 1994 [1874]: Preface.
18 Larsen in Hellmann 2005b.
19 Jørgensen in Jensen 2010: 80.
20 Ibid: 84.
21 Tsing 2005: 89.
22 Ibid: 91–2.
23 Ibid: 94.
24 Ibid: 89.

25 Ibid.
26 Logan and Reeves 2009: 13.
27 Ibid.
28 Ibid.
29 Hellmann 2005b.
30 As stated in the Danish Museum Act §2 and §23.
31 Venice Charter 1964: opening passage in the Preamble (original emphasis).
32 Athens Charter 1931: §VII.
33 Crinson 2001: 236.
34 Shaw in Crinson 2001: 237.
35 Huxley in Crinson 2001: 237.
36 Verran 2001: 26.
37 Jørgensen and Mikkelsen 2006: 33.
38 Ghana Initiative, official homepage.
39 Kurt-Nielsen et al. 2008: 57.
40 Amoah et al. 2004: 97.
41 Ibid.
42 For a similar point see e.g. Anderson 1996: 170ff; Ingold 2000a: 242.
43 E.g. "Airstrip. Mosque. Crocodile Pond. Cocoa Area. Goldmining. Goldsmithing. Museum, Cave. Northern Architecture. Beach Resort. Castle/Fort" (Amoah et al. 2004: 97).
44 Jørgensen and Mikkelsen 2006: 31.
45 Kurt-Nielsen et al. 2008: 56.
46 Ibid: 67.
47 Pratt 1992: 15.
48 Ibid: 38.
49 Ibid: 39.
50 Dibley 2011.
51 Kurt-Nielsen et al. 2008: 58.
52 Literally meaning "in memory of Frederich" – the name of the Danish king at that time.
53 Brichet 2009: 11ff.
54 DeCorse 2001.
55 Letter of November 14, 2008, from the Wulff family's attorney to the National Museum of Denmark.
56 Here I am inspired by de Laet and Mol's (2000) analysis of how a particular bush-pump in Zimbabwe could be seen as a fluid object, working in multiple ways.
57 Star and Griesemer 1989.
58 See Logan and Reeves 2009.

59 Pratt 1992: 204.
60 Ibid: 202.
61 Winds of change made the museum down-size this pilot project to that of a book with the title "Danskernes huse på Guldkysten 1659-1850", edited by Jørgensen 2015. In English the title would be: The Danes' Houses on the Gold Coast 1659-1850.
62 Tsing 2005: 93.
63 Kurt-Nielsen et al. 2008: 61–62.
64 Christensen 1994: 24ff et al.
65 Kurt-Nielsen et al. 2008: 66.

3. ALTERING HERITAGE THROUGH MIMESIS

1 Quinn and Mills 1998: 83.
2 Thus urged the Director of the Bureau Internationale des Poids et Mesures T.J. Quinn in an open letter concerning the growing importance of metrology and the benefits of participation in the Metre Convention to potential member states in 2003 – though not mentioning stamps.
3 Verran 2001: 95–101.
4 Latour 1999: 58.
5 Ibid: 59.
6 E.g. Trilling 1973; Handler (1986a; 1986b); Gable and Handler (1996) Handler and Gable (1997); Bruner (1994); Jones (2010).
7 Hyllestad 2007: 10–11.
8 Venice Charter 1964: art. 6, 9 and 15.
9 The Nara Document on Authenticity, UNESCO 1994: 11.
10 Ibid: 13.
11 See Jones 2010: 185.
12 Hander and Gable 1997. See also Gable and Handler 1996.
13 Jones 2010.
14 Ibid: xiv.
15 Ibid: xiii.
16 Ibid: xviii.
17 Ibid.
18 Ibid: xix.
19 Ibid: xvi–xvii.
20 Verran 2001, 2002.
21 Taussig 1993: xvi.
22 Verran 2001: 32ff.

23 Strathern 2004: 32ff, 116ff.
24 Turnbull 2003: 55ff.
25 Crowley 1996: 98.
26 Ibid: 100.
27 Verran 2001: 5ff.
28 Daugbjerg 2014: 725.
29 Taussig 1993: 16 (emphasis in original).
30 Ibid.
31 Brichet 2011.
32 G. Meyer 2003; Brichet and Nielsen 2006/07.
33 See Taussig 1993: 47ff.
34 Latour 1999.
35 E.g. Ardener 2007: 173ff.
36 Verran 2001: 30
37 Lévi-Strauss 1966: 23ff.
38 Ibid.
39 Ibid: 23.
40 Ibid: 23ff.
41 Turnbull 2003: 71.
42 Ibid: 75.
43 Hyllestad 2007: 24–5.
44 Tsing 2005: 104.
45 Turnbull 2003: 71.
46 Verran 2001: 102ff.
47 Ibid.
48 Wise 2006: 76.
49 See also Strathern 2004: xvff.
50 Wise 2006: 76.
51 Lévi-Strauss 1966: 24.
52 Ibid.
53 Brichet and Hastrup 2011.
54 Taussig 1993: xviii.
55 Brichet 2011.
56 See Jones 2010.
57 Strathern 2004.
58 Hyllestad 2007: 21.
59 Taussig 1993: 2.
60 Ibid: 31.
61 E.g. Ingold 2000b: 253.

62 Ingold 2000b: 244ff.
63 'Analytical' understood in the etymological sense of breaking up into pieces.
64 Ingold 2000b: 251ff.
65 Ingold 2000b: 244ff
66 Wise 2006: 79.
67 Ibid.

4. VALUING HERITAGE THROUGH THE FETISH

1 Thonning 1803: §11; B. Christensen 1830.
2 B. Christensen 1830, 22 December.
3 Macdonald 2002: 89, 102–3.
4 I am indebted to Birgit Meyers' (2010) analyses of Ghanaian cultural politics in the following.
5 B. Meyer 2010: 10.
6 Pietz 1985: 7, 1987: 37; Guyer 2004: 6; Barber 2007: 112.
7 Pietz 1985: 7.
8 Ibid: 6.
9 Ibid: 10–11.
10 Ibid: 9.
11 Pels 1998: 111.
12 Pietz 1985: note 8.
13 See also Pels 1998: 92.
14 Pietz 1985: 7.
15 DeCorse 2001: 145ff.
16 Ellen 1988: 214.
17 Pietz 1985: 5.
18 Pietz 1987: 24.
19 Ibid: 24–5.
20 See UNESCO official homepage.
21 UNESCO official homepage.
22 Pietz 1987: 25. Flower of copper is also known as chalcanthite.
23 Ibid.
24 Ibid.
25 Much later also a significant theme in STS literature concerned with modern science and the purification of nature and culture in the social production of natural facts. I am grateful to Michaela Spencer for pointing to this parallel.
26 Bredwa-Mensah, Justesen, and Jørgensen 2007: 6.
27 Kurt-Nielsen et al. 2008: 58.

28 The former Danish trading station in southern India, Tharangambadi/Trankebar, is also often referred to as a pocket in time or as too remote a place to be affected by the passage of history (H. Jørgensen 2010).
29 Venice Charter 1964: §9.
30 Kurt-Nielsen et al. 2008: 62–3.
31 In Danish: "historiens vingesus".
32 Kurt-Nielsen et al. 2008: 63.
33 Pliny the Elder 1949 [A.D.77].
34 Pietz 1987: 27.
35 Ibid: 28.
36 Ibid: note 6.
37 Ibid: note 11.
38 Ibid.
39 Poster displayed at the Common Heritage Site.
40 Poster displayed at the Common Heritage Site.
41 See e.g. Bennett 2009: 103.
42 Original title: *Frokost på Christiansborg* (1843) (translation: Lunch at Christiansborg). Available at http://billedarkiv.mfs.dk [accessed 16 July 2018].
43 Pietz 1987: 30.
44 Harden in Pietz 1987: note 14
45 Kurt-Nielsen et al. 2008: 66.
46 Pietz 1987: 30.
47 Ibid: note 6.
48 Ibid: 31ff.
49 Ibid: 29.
50 Ibid: 29ff.
51 Ibid: 34.
52 Ibid: 30ff.
53 Ibid: 35.
54 Ibid: 36.
55 Ibid: 35.
56 Ibid: 37.
57 Ibid: 35.
58 Pietz 1987: 38.
59 Ibid: 35.
60 See Ingold 2000b: 251ff.
61 Pietz 1985: 8.
62 Hegel in Pietz 1985: note 10.
63 Pels: 1998.

64 Ellen 1988: 214.
65 Ibid: note 8.
66 Ibid: 215.
67 Pels 1998: 92–95.
68 Appadurai in Pels 1998: 93.
69 Pels 1998: 94.
70 Ibid: 91.
71 Appadurai 1988; Pels 1998: 98.
72 Pels 1998: 94.
73 Pietz 1987: 38.
74 Pels 1998: 94.
75 Pietz 1985: 7.
76 Ibid; Pels 1998: 92, 97.
77 Pels 1998: 94.
78 Ibid: 98.
79 Ibid.
80 Ibid (original emphasis).
81 Pietz 1985: 14.
82 Ibid: 12.
83 Sartre in Pietz 1985: note 31.
84 Ibid. (original emphasis).
85 Pietz 1985: 9.
86 DeCorse 2001: 145.
87 Pietz 1985: 9.
88 Pietz 1987: 41.
89 Ibid: 39.
90 Pietz 1988: 111.
91 Pietz 1987: 40.
92 Ibid.
93 Ibid: 36.
94 Ibid.
95 Ibid: 41.
96 Pels 1998: 111; Arnold 2006: 6ff.
97 Rømer 2000 [1760]: 93.
98 Ibid: 94.
99 Ibid: 90.
100 Ibid: 91.
101 Pietz 1987: 41, 43.
102 Rømer 2000: 79.

103 Pietz 1985: 7–8.
104 Ibid: 8.
105 Kurt-Nielsen et al. 2008: 66.

5. QUALIFYING HERITAGE THROUGH POSTCOLONIAL MOMENTS

1 Kurt-Nielsen et al. 2008: 63.
2 Verran 2002.
3 Verran 2001: 38.
4 Verran 2002.
5 Verran 2002: 729.
6 Ibid: 730.
7 Verran 2001.
8 Tsing 2005.
9 Holbraad and Petersen refer to this as a 'post-plural perspective' (2009).
10 Verran 2002: 730.
11 Poster in main building at the Frederiksgave site.
12 Poster in main building at the Frederiksgave site.
13 Poster in main building at the Frederiksgave site.
14 Verran 2002: 750.
15 Ibid.
16 Bredwa-Mensah 2002: iii.
17 See also Schramm 2010a: 80.
18 Joseph Project, official homepage.
19 For a similar discussion see also Schramm 2010a: 87ff.
20 See also Appiah 1992: 6ff.
21 For a similar point see also Schramm 2010a: 80.
22 Verran 2002: 729.
23 Ibid: 748ff.
24 Ibid: 750.
25 Yirenkyi 2007.
26 Christiansen 2009.
27 Modern Ghana, official webpage.
28 Macdonald 2009: 60.
29 The ability to own slaves was, according to Danish jurisdiction, made illegal following a slave riot in the West Indies in 1848.
30 Macdonald 2009: 47.
31 Lonely Planet: 2007.

32 Perbi 2007: ix, 11, 196, 205.
33 Odotei in A.F. Larsen 2005.
34 See Anderson 1996.
35 See also Adebayo 2007: 93; Appiah 2007.
36 See also Berry 2007: 64ff.
37 See also Bruner 2005: 109ff.
38 See also Schramm 2010a: 76.
39 Bruner 2005; Mullen 2007; Schramm 2010b.
40 See e.g. Verran 2002: 745–6, 752.
41 Ibid: 730.
42 Ibid.
43 For a similar point see Verran 2001: 38.
44 For a similarly structured disagreement see Fairweather 2005.
45 Berry 2007: 62.
46 Pietz 1987: 36.
47 Ibid.
48 Ibid: 41.
49 G. Nielsen 2015: 45
50 Guyer 2004: 27.
51 Ibid: 3.
52 Ibid.
53 Ibid: 4.
54 Geschiere, Goheen, and Piot 2007: 38.
55 Barber 2007: 112.
56 See Geshiere, Goheen, and Piot 2007: 39, Verran 2007: 170ff.
57 Verran 2007: 172.
58 Verran 2001: 38.
59 Verran 2002: 757.
60 Handler and Gable 1997: 48.
61 See Latour 2010; F. Hastrup 2011b.
62 Mol and Law 2002: 11.

REFERENCES

Abramson A., and M. Holbraad, eds, *Framing Cosmologies: The Anthropology of Worlds*. (Manchester: Manchester University Press, 2014).

Adebayo, A.G., 'Currency Devaluation and Rank: The Yoruba and Akan Experiences', *African Studies Review*, 50.2 (2007): 87–109.

Amoah, E. A., J. A. Cobbinah, G. Y. Dake, and C.K. Ngasso, *Social Studies for Junior Secondary Schools*, 1st vol (Accra, Ghana: Adwinsa Publications Ltd., 2004).

Anderson, B., *Imagined Communities*, 7th edn (New York: Verso, 1996 [1991]).

Appadurai, A., 'Introduction: Commodities and the Politics of Value', in A. Appadurai, ed., *The Social Life of Things: Commodities in Cultural Perspectives* (New York: Cambridge University Press, 1988), pp. 3–63.

Appiah, K. A., *In My Father's House* (New York: Oxford University Press, 1992).

——'A Slow Emancipation', *New York Times*, 18 March 2007.

Ardener, E., 'Comprehending Others', in *The Voices of Prophecy and Other Essays* (New York: Berghahn Books, 2007 [1989]), pp. 159–190.

Arnold, K., *Cabinet for the Curious: Looking Back at Early English Museums* (London: Ashgate, 2006).

Athens Charter, 'Athens Charter for the Restoration of Historic Monuments', <http://www.icomos.org/athens_charter.html> [accessed 1 December 2009], 1931.

Awadzi, T., Y. Bredwa-Mensah, H. Breuning-Madsen, and E. Boateng, 'A Scientific Evaluation of the Agricultural Experiments at Frederiksgave, the Royal Danish Plantation on the Gold Coast, Ghana', *Geografisk Tidsskrift*, 101 (2005): 33–42.

Barber, K., 'When People Cross Thresholds', *African Studies Review*, 50.2 (2007): 111–123.

BBC News, '*Ghana Unveils Presidential Palace*', <http://news.bbc.co.uk/2/hi/africa/7720653.stm> [accessed 29 April 2011], 10 November 2008.

Bennett, T., 'Museum, Field, Colony: Colonial Governmentality and the Circulation of Reference', *Journal of Cultural Economy*, 2.1–2 (2009): 99–113.

Berry, S., 'Marginal Gains, Market Values, and History', *African Studies Review*, 50.2 (2007): 57–70.

Bredwa-Mensah, Y., '*Historical-Archaeological Investigations at the Frederiksgave Plantation, Ghana: A Case Study of Slavery and Plantation Life on a Nineteenth Century Danish Plantation on the Gold Coast* (PhD Thesis, University of Ghana, Legon, 2002).

──'The Common Heritage Project: Developing the Danish Plantation Sites Along the Foothills of the Akuapem Mountains for Cultural Tourism', project description sent to GMMB, unpublished, 2003a.

──'The Common Heritage Project', letter to the Ministry of Tourism, Ghana, unpublished, 15 November 2003b.

Bredwa-Mensah, Y., O. Justesen, and A. Jørgensen, 'Frederiksgave Plantation and Common Heritage Site', <http://www.natmus.dk/sw31724.asp> [Accessed 1 December 2009], 2007.

Brichet, N., 'Bevaring af danske spor i Ghana', unpublished report to the Ethnographic Collection, Danish National Museum, 2009.

──'Awkward Relations and Universal Aspirations: Common Global Heritage in Ghana', *History and Anthropology*, 22.2 (2011): 149–168.

Brichet, N., and G. Nielsen, 'Antropologiske krumspring i et vidensamfund: Om at lave feltarbejde i en agora', *Tidsskrift for Antropologi*, 53 (2006–07): 95–114.

Brichet, N., and F. Hastrup, 'Figurer uden Grund', *Tidsskrift for Antropologi*, 64 (2011): 119–135.

──'Industrious Landscaping: The Making and Managing of Natural Resources at Søby Brown Coal Beds', *Journal of Ethnobiology*, 38.1 (2018): 8–23.

Brimnes, N., P. Olsen, H.C. Gulløv, eds, *Danmark og kolonierne*, 5 vols (Copenhagen: GAD, 2017).

Bruner, E.M., 'Abraham Lincoln as Authentic Reproduction: A Critique of Postmodernism', *American Anthropologist*, 96.2 (1994): 397–415.

──*Culture on Tour: Ethnographies of Travel* (Chicago: University of Chicago Press, 2005).

Brøndsted, J., *Vore gamle tropekolonier* (Copenhagen: Westermann, 1952).

Byrne, D., 'Western Hegemony in Archaeological Heritage Management', in G. Fairclough, R. Harrison, J.H., Jr. Jameson, and J. Scofield, eds, *The Heritage Reader* (Abingdon and New York: Routledge [1991] 2008), pp. 229–34.

Carstensen, E., *Guvernør Edward Carstensens Indberetninger fra Guinea 1842-1850* (Copenhagen: GAD, 1964).

Carrithers, M., M. Candea, K. Sykes, M. Holbraad, 'Ontology is Just Another Word for Culture: Against the Motion', Debate and Discussion (from GDAT 2008), S. Venkatesan, ed., *Critique of Anthropology* 30.2 (2010): 179–185, 185–200.

Chirikure, S., M. Manyanga, W. Ndoro, and G. Pwiti, 'Unfulfilled Promises: Heritage Management and Community Participation at Some of Africa's Cultural Heritage Sites', *International Journal of Heritage Studies*, 16.1–2 (2010): 30–44.

Christensen, B. M., 'Diary Entry for 22.12.1830', Collection of Private Archives, Danish National Archives, 1830.

Christensen, S., *Fakticitetens Ironi: Facetter af kulturrelativismens Idéhistorie* (Aarhus: Aarhus Universitetsforlag, 1994).

Christiansen, M., 'Nyt lys over Danmarks mørke historie – Genopførelsen af det danske slavefort Frederiksgave er et af flere initiativer, som skal bringe Ghana fortrængte fortid i erindring', *Kristeligt Dagblad,* 18 March 2009.

Clifford, J., *The Predicament of Culture: Twentieth-Century Ethnography, Literature and Art* (USA: Harvard University Press, 1988).

——*Routes: Travel and Translation in the Late Twentieth Century* (Cambridge, MA: Harvard University Press, 1997).

Clifford, J., and G. Marcus, eds, *Writing Culture: The Poetics and Politics of Ethnography* (Berkeley: University of California Press, 1986).

Crowley, C. B., *Aristotelian Thomistic Philosophy of Measure and the International System of Units (SI). Correlation of International System of Units With the Philosophy of Aristotle and St. Thomas* (Maryland: University Press of America, 1996).

Crinson, M., 'Nation-Building, Collecting and the Politics of Display: The National Museum, Ghana', *Journal of the History of Collections,* 13.2 (2001): 231–250.

Dann, G., and A. Seaton, 'Slavery, Contested Heritage and Thanatourism', *International Journal of Hospitality and Tourism Administration,* 2.3–4 (2001): 1–29.

Dantzig, A. van, *Forts and Castles of Ghana* (Accra, Ghana: Sedco Publishing Limited, 1999 [1980]).

Das, V., 'Social Sciences and the Publics', in V. Das, ed., *The Oxford India Companion to Sociology and Social Anthropology* (New Delhi: Oxford University Press, 2003), pp. 1–29.

Daugbjerg, M., 'Patchworking the Past: Materiality, Touch and the Assembling of 'Experience' in American Civil War Re-enactment', *International Journal of Heritage Studies,* 20.7–8 (2014): 724–741.

Daugbjerg, M., and T. Fibiger, 'Introduction: Heritage Gone Global: Investigating the Production and Problematics of Globalized Pasts', *History and Anthropology,* 22.2 (2011): 135–147.

DeCorse, C., *An Archaeology of Elmina* (Washington D.C.: Smithsonian Institution Press, 2001).

De Jong, F., and M. Rowlands, eds, *Reclaiming Heritage: Alternative Imaginaries of Memory in West Africa* (Walnut Creek, California: Left Coast Press, 2010 [2007]).

Despret, V., 'Why "I Had Not Read Derrida" Often Too Close, Always Too Far', in L. Mackenzie, and S. Posthumus, eds, *French Thinking About Animals* (East Lansing, MI: Michigan State University Press, 2015), pp. 91–104.

Dibley, B., 'Museums and a Common World: Climate Change, Cosmopolitics, Museum Practice', *Museum and Society,* 9.2 (2011): 154–165.

Dilley, R., 'Introduction: The Problem of Context', in R. Dilley, ed., *The Problem of Context* (New York: Berghahn Books, 1999), pp. 1–46.
Ebron, P., 'Tourists as Pilgrims: Commercial Fashioning of Transatlantic Politics', *American Ethnologist*, 26.4 (2000): 910–932.
Ellen, R., 'Fetishism', *Man*, 23.2 (1988): 213–235.
Essah, P., 'Slavery, Heritage and Tourism in Ghana', *International Journal of Hospitality and Tourism Administration*, 2.3–4 (2001): 31–49.
Fairweather, I., 'The Performance of Heritage in a Reconstructed, Post-Apartheid Museum in Namibia', in M. Bouquet, and N. Porto, eds, *Science, Magic, and Religion: The Ritual Process of Museum Magic* (New York: Berghahn Books, 2005), pp. 161–181.
Fanon, F., *The Wretched of the Earth* (London: Penguin, 2001 [1961]).
Federspiel, K. B., 'Bevidstheden om kulturarven og incitamenter til bevaring', *Nordisk Museologi*, 2 (1998): 3–16.
——'Our Creative Diversity and Contemporary Issues in Conservation', *ICOM 12th Triennial Meeting 1999, Lyon preprint*, vol. I (1999): 166–171.
Forskerforum (author only by initials LPM), 'Fyringer på Nationalmuseet – og ned med kolonierne', *Forskerforum*, 160 (2002): 7.
Fox, R. G., and B. J. King, 'Introduction: Beyond Culture Worry', in R.G. Fox and B. J. King, eds, *Anthropology Beyond Culture* (Oxford: Berg, 2002), pp. 1–19.
Frazer, J.G. The Golden Bough (London: Macmillan, 1963 [1890]).
Gable. E., and R. Handler, 'After Authenticity at an American Heritage Site', *American Anthropologist, New Series*, 98.3 (1996): 568–578.
Ghana Initiative, National Museum of Denmark, <https://natmus.dk/historisk-viden/forskning/forskningsprojekter/ghana-initiativet/om-ghana-initiativet/> [accessed 21 March 2018].
Ghana Museums and Monuments Board, <http://www.ghanamuseums.org/> [accessed 11 May 2011].
Geschiere, P., M. Goheen, and C. Piot, 'Introduction: Marginal Gains Revisited', *African Studies Review*, 50.2 (2007): 37–41.
Greenough, P. and A. L. Tsing, 'Introduction', in P. Greenough and A. L. Tsing, eds, *Nature in the Global South* (Durham and London: Duke University Press, 2003), pp. 1–28.
Grubbe, K., 'Kastellet restaureres', *Berlingske Tidende*, 5 April 2002.
Guyer, J., *Marginal Gains: Monetary Transactions in Atlantic Africa* (Chicago and London: The University of Chicago Press, 2004).
Hafstein, V., 'The Politics of Origins: Collective Creation Revisited', *Journal of American Folklore*, 117.465 (2004): 300–315.
Handler, R., 'On Having a Culture: Nationalism and the Preservation of Quebec's

Patrimoine', in G. W. Jr. Stocking ed., *Objects and Others: Essays on Museums and Material Culture* (University of Wisconsin Press, 1988), pp. 192–217.

——'Authenticity', *Anthropology Today*, 2.1 (1986a): 2–4.

——'Letters' (Handler's reply to Igor Kopytoff's comment on Handler's article 'Authenticity'), *Anthropology Today*, 2.3 (1986b): 24.

Handler R., and E. Gable, *The New History in an Old Museum: Creating the Past at Colonial Williamsburg* (Durham and London: Duke University Press, 1997).

Hansen, T., *Coast of Slaves*, translated from Danish by K. Dako (Accra, Ghana: Sub-Saharan Publishers, 2005)

Haraway, D., 'Talk by Donna Haraway at the California College of the Arts, Graduate Studies Lecture Series. Timken Lecture Hall, San Francisco Campus' (recorded on October 20 2009, published 23 November 2009) <https://www.youtube.com/watch?v=3F0XdXfVDXw> [accessed 1 March 2010].

——*Staying with the Trouble* (Duke University Press, 2016).

Harrison, R., 'What is Heritage?', in R. Harrison, ed., *Understanding the Politics of Heritage* (Manchester: Manchester University Press, 2010), pp. 5–42.

Hastrup, F., *Weathering the World: Recovery in the Wake of the Tsunami in a Tamil Fishing Village* (New York: Berghahn Books, 2011a).

——'Shady Plantations: Theorizing Shelter in Coastal Tamil Nadu', *Anthropological Theory*, 11.4 (2011b): 425–439.

——'Certain Figures: Modelling Among Environmental Experts in Coastal Tamil Nadu', in K. Hastrup and M. Skrydstrup, eds, *Anticipating Nature: Climate Modelling at Different Scales of Knowledge* (London: Routledge, 2013), pp. 45–56.

Hastrup, K., 'Getting it Right: Knowledge and Evidence in Anthropology', *Anthropological Theory*, 4 (2004): 455–472.

Hellmann, H., 'Det er vores fælles historie', *Politiken*, 21 February 2005a.

——'Drømmen om de varme lande', *Politiken*, 21 February 2005b.

Henare, A., M. Holbraad, and S. Wastell, 'Introduction: Thinking Through Things', in A. Henare, M. Holbraad, and S. Wastell, eds, *Thinking Through Things: Theorising Artefacts Ethnographically* (London: Routledge, 2007), pp. 1–31.

Hernæs, P., 'Introduction', in *Closing the Books: Governor Edward Carstensen on Danish Guinea, 1842-1950*, translated from Danish by T. Storsveen (Accra, Ghana: Sub Saharan Publishers, 2010).

Holbraad, M., 'The Power of Powder: Multiplicity and Motion in the Divinatory Cosmology of Cuban Ifá', in A. Henare, M. Holbraad, and S. Wastell, eds, *Thinking Through Things: Theorising Artefacts Ethnographically* (London: Routledge, 2007), pp. 189–225.

Holbraad, M., and M. Pedersen, 'Planet M: The Intense Abstraction of Marilyn Strathern', *Anthropological Theory*, 9.4 (2009): 371–394.

Hylland-Eriksen, T., 'Between Universalism and Relativism: A Critique of the UNESCO Concept of Culture', in J. Cowan, M-B. Dembour, and R.A. Wilson, eds, *Culture and Rights: Anthropological Perspectives* (Cambridge: Cambridge University Press, 2001), pp. 127–148.

Hyllestad, N., 'Frederiksgave, Sesemi, Ghana. Rejseberetninger', unpublished report to the Ethnographic Collections, National Museum of Denmark, 2007.

Højgaard, S., 'Forstander og bygmester vil kalke dansk borg i Indien', *Fyens Stiftstidende*, 24 December 2001.

ICOMOS, <https://www.icomos.org/fr/> [accessed 1 December 2009]

ICOMOS, 'The Forts in Ghana Constitute an Early Evidence of the Joint Activity of the Africans and Europeans, and Deserve Consideration' (review sheet) <http://whc.unesco.org/archive/advisory_body_evaluation/034.pdf> [accessed 29 April 2011), 10 April 1979.

Ingold, T., 'To Journey Along a Way of Life: Maps, Wayfinding and Navigation', in T. Ingold, ed., *Perception of the Environment: Essays in Livelihood, Dwelling and Skill* (London and New York: Routledge, 2000a), pp. 219–242.

—— 'Stop, Look and Listen! Vision, Hearing and Human Movement', in T. Ingold, ed., *Perception of the Environment: Essays in Livelihood, Dwelling and Skill* (London and New York: Routledge, 2000b), pp. 243–288.

Jensen, E., and A. Jørgensen, 'Nationalmuseet i Danmarks tropekolonier', *NYT* (2006): 34–37.

Jensen, T., 'Fortiden er en by i Afrika' (Master's Thesis, University of Copenhagen, Denmark, 2010).

Jeppesen, H., 'Danske plantageanlæg på Guldkysten 1788–1850', *Geografisk Tidsskrift*, 65 (1966): 48–72.

Jones, S., 'Negotiating Authentic Objects and Authentic Selves: Beyond the Deconstruction of Authenticity', *Journal of Material Culture*, 15.2 (2010): 181–203.

Joseph Project, 'Ghana Reaches Out to the Diaspora', <http://www.info-ghana.com/joseph_project.htm> [accessed 1 December 2009].

Justesen, O., ed., *Danish Sources for the History of Ghana 1657-1754*, vols 1 and 2 (Copenhagen: The Royal Danish Academy of Sciences and Letters, 2005).

—— 'Introduction', in *Danish Sources for the History of Ghana 1657-1754*, vol 1 (Copenhagen: The Royal Danish Academy of Sciences and Letters, 2005), pp. v–viii.

Jørgensen, A., ed., *Danskernes huse på Guldkysten 1659-1850* (Copenhagen: Vandkunstens Forlag, 2015).

Jørgensen, A., and H. Mikkelsen, 'Nationalmuseet i Ghana: At genopføre en fælles afrikansk-dansk historie', *Arkæologisk Forum*, 4 (2006): 29–33.

Jørgensen, H., 'Tranquebar – Whose History? Transnational Cultural Heritage in a Former Danish Trading Colony in South India' (PhD Thesis, University of Aarhus, Denmark, 2010).

Knippel, L. O., 'Danske ruiner i Ghana', *Jyllandsposten*, 9 December 2003.

Kreamer Mullen, C., 'Shared Heritage, Contested Terrain: Cultural Negotiation and Ghana's Cape Coast Castle Museum Exhibition "Crossroads of People, Crossroads of Trade"', in I. Karp, C. Kratz, L. Szwaja, and T. Ybarra-Frausto, eds, *Museum Frictions: Public Cultures/Global Transformations* (Durham and London: Duke University Press, 2007[2006]), pp. 435–468.

Kronsted, P., 'Den historiske bevidsthed', *Jyllandsposten*, 30 December 2002.

Kulturministeriet, 'Kulturpolitikkens sigtelinjer', <http://kum.dk/Documents/Publikationer/2004/Kulturpolitikkens%20sigtelinjer/pdf/Kulturpolitikkens_sigtelinjer.pdf> [accessed 11 May 2011], 2004.

Kurt-Nielsen, J., A. Jørgensen, N. Hyllestad, J. Frandsen, and H. Mikkelsen, 'Frederiksgave – Nationalmuseet genopfører slaveplantage i Ghana', in P. K. Madsen and B. Gammeltoft, eds, *Nationalmuseets Arbejdsmark* (Copenhagen: Danish National Museum, 2008), pp. 55–68.

Laet, M., and A. Mol, 'The Zimbabwe Bush Pump: Mechanics of a Fluid Technology', *Social Studies of Science*, 30.2 (2000): 225–263.

Larsen, A. F., 'Den Magnetiske Guldkyst' [in *Slavernes Spor*, no 3, broadcast on DR television, 1 December 2005].

Larsen, B. S., 'En dansk slaveplantage genopstår', *Kristeligt Dagblad*, 23 August 2006.

Larsen, K., *De danske i Guinea* (Copenhagen: Nordiske Forfatteres Forlag, 1918).

Latour, B., 'Circulating Reference', in *Pandora's Hope: Essays on the Reality of Science Studies* (Cambridge, MA: Harvard University Press, 1999), pp. 24–79.

——'An Attempt at a "Compositionist Manifesto"', *New Literary History*, 41 (2010): 471–490.

Lévi-Strauss, C., *The Savage Mind* (London: The Garden City Press Limited, 1966 [1962]).

Littler, J., 'Introduction: British Heritage and the Legacies of "Race"', in J. Littler and R. Naidoo, eds, *The Politics of Heritage: The Legacies of Race* (London: Routledge, 2005), pp. 1–19.

Logan, W., and K. Reeves, 'Introduction', in *Places of Pain and Shame: Dealing with 'Difficult Heritage'* (Abingdon, UK: Routledge, 2009), pp. 1–14.

Lonely Planet, 'Ghana Tourism News: New Museum of Colonial Plantation Life', <http://www.lonelyplanet.com/thorntree/thread.jspa?threadID=1488909> [accessed 17 April 2011], 9 October 2007.

Lowenthal, D., 'Tragic Traces on the Rhodian Shore', *Historic Environment*, 19.2 (2003): 3–7.

Macdonald, S., 'On "Old Things": The Fetishization of Past Everyday Life', in N. Rapport, ed., *British Subjects: An Anthropology of Britain* (Oxford: Berg, 2002), pp. 89–106.

——*Difficult Heritage: Negotiating the Nazi Past in Nuremberg and Beyond* (London and New York: Routledge, 2009).

Meskell, L., 'Negative Heritage and Past Mastering in Archaeology', *Anthropological Quarterly*, 75.3 (2002): 557–574.

Meyer, B., 'Tradition and Colour at its Best': "Tradition" and "Heritage" in Ghanaian Video-Movies', *Journal of African Cultural Studies*, 22.1 (2010): 7–23.

Meyer, G., 'Hvorfor formidling ikke bringer videnskaben ind i samfundet', <http://www.cfje.dk> [accessed 1 December 2009], 2003.

Ministry of Culture (of Denmark), <http://www.kum.dk/sw63952.asp> [accessed 1 April 2008]

Ministry of Tourism Diasporan Relations (of Ghana), <http://www.touringghana.com/mot.asp> [accessed 20 April 2011].

Modern Ghana (no named author), 'Comment' <http://www.modernghana.com/news/98677/1/diaspora-relations.html> [accessed 20 April 2011], 4 May 2006.

Mol, A., and J. Law, 'Complexitites: An introduction', in J. Law and A. Mol, eds, *Complexitites: Social Studies of Knowledge Practices* (Duke University Press, 2002), pp. 1–22.

Museum Act, 'Museumsloven: LBK no. 1505 af 14 December 2006', <https://www.retsinformation.dk> [accessed 1 December 2009], 14 December 2006.

Nielsen, G. B., *Figuration Work: Student Participation, Democracy and University Reform in a Global Knowledge Economy* (New York: Berghahn Books, 2015).

Nielsen, J., 'Kultur-kanon: Interview: "Vi er ved at miste grebet"', *Politiken*, 10 December 2004.

Nietzsche, F., *Historiens nytte* (Copenhagen: Gyldendal, 1994 [1874]).

Nkrumah, K., *I Speak of Freedom: A Statement of African Ideology* (London: William Heinemann Ltd., 1961).

Nørregård, G., 'Guldkysten: De danske etablissementer i Guinea', in J. Brøndsted, ed., *Vore gamle tropekolonier*, vol 8 (Copenhagen: Fremad, 1968).

Otto, T., and N. Bubandt, eds, *Experiments in Holism: Theory and Practice in Contemporary Anthropology* (Hoboken, NJ: Wiley Blackwell, 2010).

Pels, P., 'The Spirit of Matter: On Fetish, Rarity, Fact, and Fancy', in P. Spyer, ed., *Border Fetishism: Material Objects in Unstable Spaces* (New York and London: Routledge, 1998), pp. 91–121.

Perbi, A. A., *A History of Indigenous Slavery in Ghana From the 15th to the 19th Century* (Accra, Ghana: Sub-Saharan Publishers, 2007 [2004]).

Petersen, S., *Danmarks gamle tropekolonier* (Copenhagen: Bianco Lunos bogtrykkeri, 1946).

Pietz, W., 'The Problem of the Fetish', *RES: Anthropology and Aesthetics*, 9 (1985): 5–17.

—— 'The Problem of the Fetish, II: The Origin of the Fetish', *RES: Anthropology and Aesthetics*, 13 (1987): 23–45.

—— 'The Problem of the Fetish, IIIa: Bosman's Guinea and the Enlightenment Theory of Fetishism', *RES: Anthropology and Aesthetics*, 16 (1988): 105–124.

Pliny, G. (the Elder), *Natural History*, The Loeb Classical Library, vol 1 (London: William Heinemann Ltd., 1949 [A.D. 77]).

Pratt, M. L., *Imperial Eyes: Travel Writing and Transculturation* (London and New York: Routledge, 1992).

Pyne Addelson, K., *Moral Passages: Toward a Collectivist Moral Theory* (London and New York: Routledge, 1994).

Regeringsgrundlag, 'Vækst, velfærd – fornyelse', <http://www.stm.dk/publikationer> [accessed 1 December 2009], 2001.

Regeringen, 'Danmark i oplevelsesøkonomien – 5 nye skridt på vejen', <http://www.ebst.dk/file/31519/danmarkikulturogoplevelsesoekonomien.pdf> [accessed 11 May 2011], 2003.

Rowlands, M., and F. de Jong, 'Reconsidering Heritage and Memory', in F. de Jong and M. Rowlands, eds, *Reclaiming Heritage: zAlternative Imaginaries of Memory in West Africa* (Walnut Creek, California: Left Coast Press, 2010 [2007]), pp. 13–29.

Rømer, L. F., *A Reliable Account of the Coast of Guinea (1760)*, translated from Danish by Selena Alexrod Winsnes (Oxford: Oxford University Press, 2000 [1760]).

Quinn, T. J., 'Open Letter Concerning the Growing Importance of Metrology and the Benefits of Participation in the Meter Convention, Notably the CIPM MRA', <http://www.bipm.org/utils/en/pdf/importance.pdf> [accessed 31 March 2011], August 2003.

Quinn T. J., and I. M. Mills, 'Le Système international d'unités: The International System of Units', in *Bureau international des poids et mesures, Pavillon de Breteuil F-92312* (Sèvres Cedex, France: Organisation Intergouvernementale de la Convention du Mètre, 1998), pp. 83–121.

Schmidt, P., 'What is Postcolonial about Archaeologies in Africa?', in P. Schmidt, ed., *Postcolonial Archaeologies in Africa* (Santa Fe, USA: School for Advanced Research Press, 2009), pp. 1–20.

Schramm, K., 'Slave Route Projects: Tracing the Heritage of Slavery in Ghana', in F. de Jong and M. Rowlands, eds., *Reclaiming Heritage: Alternative Imaginaries of Memory in West Africa* (Walnut Creek, CA: Left Coast Press, 2010a [2007]), pp. 71–98.

―――*African Homecoming: Pan-African Ideology and Contested Heritage* (Walnut Creek, CA: Left Coast Press, 2010b).

Serampore Initiative, National Museum of Denmark, <https://natmus.dk/historisk-viden/forskning/forskningsprojekter/serampore-initiativet/aktuelle-projekter/ [accessed 21 March 2018].

Smith, L., *Uses of Heritage* (Abingdon, UK: Routledge, 2008 [2006]).

Star, S.L., and J. R. Griesemer, 'Institutional Ecology, "Translations" and Boundary Objects: Amateurs and Professionals in Berkeley's Museum of Vertebrate Zoology, 1907-39', *Social Studies of Science*, 19 (1989): 387–420.

Strathern, M., 'An Awkward Relationship: The Case of Feminism and Anthropology', *Signs: Journal of Women in Culture and Society*, 12.2 (1987): 276–292.

―――*Partial Connections* (Walnut Creek, CA: AltaMira Press, 2004).

Taussig, M., *Mimesis and Alterity: A Particular History of the Senses* (New York and London: Routledge, 1993).

Thonning, P., 'Indberetning om det danske Territorium i Guinea fornemmelig med Hensyn til nærværende Kultur af indiske Kolonial Producter eller Beqven for samme. Til Det Kongelige Vestindiske-guinesiske Rente og General told Kammer', in *National Archives: Dep. For udenlandske Anlig (302), Gruppeordn sager 1756-1848, Guinea, Litra G, 1775-1847, boks 872*, 1803.

Trankebar Initiative, National Museum of Denmark, <https://natmus.dk/historisk-viden/forskning/forskningsprojekter/tranquebar-initiativet/om-tranquebar-initiativet/> [accessed 21 March 2018].

Trilling, L., *Sincerity and Authenticity* (Cambridge, Massachusetts: Harvard University Press, 1973 [1971]).

Trouillot, M. R., 'Adieu, Culture: A New Duty Arises', in R.G. Fox and B. J. King, eds, *Anthropology Beyond Culture* (Oxford: Berg, 2002), pp. 37–60.

Tsing, A. L., *In the Realm of the Diamond Queen* (Princeton: Princeton University Press, 1993).

―――*Friction: An Ethnography of Global Connections*, 1st edn (Princeton: Princeton University Press, 2005).

―――*The Mushroom at the End of the World: On the Possibility of Life in Capitalist Ruins* (Princeton: Princeton University Press, 2016).

Tunbridge, J. E., and G. J. Ashworth, *Dissonant Heritage: The Management of the Past as a Resource in Conflict* (England: John Wiley and Sons. Inc., 1996).

Turnbull, D., *Masons, Tricksters and Cartographers* (London and New York: Routledge, 2003).

UNESCO, 'Convention Concerning the Protection of the World Cultural and Natural Heritage, 1972, <http://whc.unesco.org/archive/convention-en.pdf> [accessed 1 December 2009].

UNESCO, 'Our Creative Diversity, 1996, <http://unesdoc.unesco.org/images/0010/001055/105586e.pdf> [accessed 1 December 2009].

UNESCO, 'Convention for Safeguarding of the Intangible Cultural Heritage', 2003, <http://unesdoc.unesco.org/images/0013/001325/132540e.pdf> [accessed 1 December 2009].

UNESCO, 'The Nara Document on Authenticity', 1994, <http://www.international.icomos.org/naradoc_eng.htm> [accessed: 1 December 2009].

UNESCO, <http://whc.unesco.org [Accessed: April 2011]

UNESCO, 'Slave Route Project', <http://portal.unesco.org/culture/en/ev.php-URL_ID=25659andURL_DO=DO_TOPICandURL_SECTION=201.html> [accessed 30 April 2011].

Venice Charter, 'International Charter for the Conservation and Restoration of Monuments and Sites', 1964, <http://www.icomos.org/venice_charter.html> [accessed 1 December 2009].

Verran, H., *Science and an African Logic* (Chicago: The University of Chicago Press, 2001).

——'A Postcolonial Moment in Science Studies: Alternative Firing Regimes of Environmental Scientists and Aboriginal Landowners', *Social Studies of Science*, 32.5–6 (2002): 729–762.

——'The Telling Challenge of Africa's Economies', *African Studies Review*, 50.2 (2007): 163–182.

——'On Assemblage: Indigenous Knowledge and Digital Media (2003–06), and HMS Investigator (1800-1805)', *Journal of Cultural Economy*, 2.1–2 (2009): 169–182.

Wagner, R., *The Invention of Culture* (Chicago: University of Chicago Press, 1981 [1975]).

Waterton, E., and L. Smith, 'The Recognition and Misrecognition of Community Heritage', *International Journal of Heritage Studies*, 16.1–2 (2010): 4–15.

Watson, S., and E. Waterton, 'Heritage and Community Engagement', *International Journal of Heritage Studies*, 16.1–2 (2010): 1–3.

Williams, P., *Memorial Museums: The Global Rush to Commemorate Atrocities* (Oxford: Berg, 2007).

Wise, N., 'Making Visible', *Iris*, 97 (2006): 75–82.

Wulff. J., *Da Guinea var dansk – Breve og dagbogsoptegnelser fra Guldkysten 1836-1842* (Copenhagen: Nyt Nordisk Forlag, Krohns Bogtrykkeri, 1917 [1836-1842]).

Yirenkyi, G., 'The Story Behind the Sesemi Museum', *Ghanaian Times*, 13 November 2007.

MATTERING PRESS TITLES

An Anthropology of Common Ground
Awkward Encounters in Heritage Work
NATHALIA BRICHET

Ghost-Managed Medicine
Big Pharma's Invisible Hands
SERGIO SISMONDO

Inventing the Social
EDITED BY NOORTJE MARRES, MICHAEL GUGGENHEIM, ALEX WILKIE

Energy Babble
ANDY BOUCHER, BILL GAVER, TOBIE KERRIDGE, MIKE MICHAEL,
LILIANA OVALLE, MATTHEW PLUMMER-FERNANDEZ AND ALEX WILKIE

The Ethnographic Case
EDITED BY EMILY YATES-DOERR AND CHRISTINE LABUSKI

On Curiosity
The Art of Market Seduction
FRANCK COCHOY

Practising Comparison
Logics, Relations, Collaborations
EDITED BY JOE DEVILLE, MICHAEL GUGGENHEIM AND ZUZANA HRDLIČKOVÁ

Modes of Knowing
Resources from the Baroque
EDITED BY JOHN LAW AND EVELYN RUPPERT

Imagining Classrooms
Stories of Children, Teaching and Ethnography
VICKI MACKNIGHT

www.ingramcontent.com/pod-product-compliance
Ingram Content Group UK Ltd.
Pitfield, Milton Keynes, MK11 3LW, UK
UKHW041427100125
4058UKWH00032B/359

9 780995 527799